STUDIES IN RAILWAY EXPANSION
AND THE
CAPITAL MARKET IN ENGLAND
1825–1873

Studies in
Railway Expansion
and the
Capital Market in England
1825-1873

SEYMOUR BROADBRIDGE

FRANK CASS & CO. LTD.
1970

First published in 1970 by
FRANK CASS AND COMPANY LIMITED

Copyright © 1969 Seymour Broadbridge

SBN 7146 1287 1

Printed in Great Britain by
Billing & Sons Limited, Guildford and London

Contents

Part I

THE DEVELOPMENT AND OPERATION OF THE LANCASHIRE & YORKSHIRE RAILWAY NETWORK

Part II

THE EARLY RAILWAY CAPITAL MARKET

LIST OF TABLES IN TEXT

LIST OF TABLES IN APPENDIX

LIST OF MAPS

Acknowledgements

THIS work is a much-revised version of a thesis which was approved for the degree of Ph.D. in the University of London, and the first debt I wish to record is to the University for awarding me a Post-graduate Studentship tenable at the London School of Economics in the years 1952–54. My gratitude is due also to H. L. Beales and Professor W. Ashworth (both of whom supervised my research when they were Readers in Economic History in London University); to F. C. Mather (Southampton University); to Harold Pollins (Ruskin College); to John Elliott (Admiralty) for his work on the maps; to M. D. Greville, for permission to use his 'Genealogical Table of the Railways of Lancashire'; to officials of the House of Lords Record Office and House of Lords Library; to officials of the British Railways Board; to the Editors of *The Economic History Review*, for permission to reprint material used in my article 'The Early Capital Market', Second Series, Vol. VIII, No. 2, 1955; and to my mother and my wife.

It is a very pleasant duty to single out the Archivist and his staff at the British Transport Historical Records Office at Royal Oak, London, for special acknowledgement. Although they were extremely busy coping with a huge influx of records, I was allowed to benefit from their wide knowledge of railway history, and from their great kindness and tolerance. These virtues were also displayed by their colleagues at Euston Station, where I was admitted to the strong-rooms to disturb minute-books which looked as though they had rested peacefully for a century. It follows that their kind provision of washing and dining facilities was equally important.

None of the above-mentioned people is, however, in any way responsible for the views expressed in this book.

SEYMOUR BROADBRIDGE

Sheffield, April 1967

Introduction

THIS book is a study of mid-nineteenth-century railway finances. It also provides, incidentally, an outline of the early history of the Lancashire & Yorkshire Railway, which was one of the twelve largest companies in the country before the Amalgamation Act of 1921. The company's position in the industrial centre of Britain made it an important part of the railway network, but it has not been favoured by railway historians; there is no history of the Lancashire & Yorkshire which may be put alongside Tomlinson's study of the North Eastern, nor MacDermot's of the Great Western, nor even Stretton's of the Midland. This study is not, however, to be compared with the standard histories of the great railway companies of the nineteenth century. The emphasis is on finance, and no attempt is made to cover the history of the Lancashire & Yorkshire from its origins in the 1825 scheme for a line between Manchester and Leeds to the amalgamation of the Company with the London & North Western preparatory to the formation of the L.M.S. in 1921. Chapter 1 of Part I describes the development of the Company's network and is intended to provide a background to the study of the railway's finances. It shows how the territorial expansion of the Company took place. Without this background the rest of the book would be more difficult to understand.

Chapter 1 has been divided into three sections to emphasise the significance of the years 1841, 1850 and 1873 in the history of the Lancashire & Yorkshire. The main line of the Manchester & Leeds, which was the nucleus of the Lancashire & Yorkshire, was completed in 1841. 1850 was the year which marked the end of the expansive era of the 1840s: with minor exceptions, most of the projects of that decade were finished by then. 1873 saw the first down-swing in the dividend after the boom of the early 1870s, a decline which was to be a persistent trend. These dates have not been made the rigid limits of the three sections; in places they overlap, where the development of the networks of particular companies has been traced, in an attempt to avoid the confusion that arises when construction is separated from incorporation, and in an attempt to deal more effectively with the congestion of the 1840s. Section I, therefore, includes an account of the other constituent companies of the Lancashire & Yorkshire which were sanctioned in the 1830s.

The narrative of these lines takes us into the 1840s. Section II encompasses the transformation of the Manchester & Leeds into the Lancashire & Yorkshire, which was the result of the boom of 1844 and 1845. For the sake of clarity, it carries the story of some of the projects of those years beyond 1850.

Chapter 2 is an analysis of the financial results of operating the Manchester & Leeds and its successor, and is based upon a series of statistical tables presented in the Appendix. These are tables of traffic receipts and traffic expenses, of gross receipts and outgoings on revenue account, of net traffic receipts and net revenue, of dividends and interest, and of capital. The difficulties involved in any attempt to understand and use nineteenth century railway accounts are described in a short introduction to the chapter. The character and actions of railway directorates were freely impugned in the years of our period, and it follows that the published accounts were suspect to many. We shall see that some at least of the criticisms and accusations were, in the years 1846 to 1849, only too well justified. At times the various accounts, presented biannually to the proprietors, are almost incomprehensible, and since reclassification of items was necessary, the Appendix contains extensive notes on the compilation of the tables.

The plans to use loan capital as one of the bases of the equity-holder's prosperity foundered in the years 1844 and 1845. At the same time the not extravagant hopes of the period 1836 to 1843, hopes for an expanding traffic and prosperity on the Manchester & Leeds proper, became submerged in the mania. The Company had itself to blame for some of the misfortunes after 1845, but it was proper for its directors to point to mitigating circumstances—even some of the militant shareholders recognised this in 1850, and, in any case, the shareholders themselves were at fault. In the Hudson age they were enthusiastic about absorptions and amalgamations; enthusiastic about aggrandisement in general, and their attitude would have made it difficult for the directors to call a halt, even if they had wanted to.

The low level of dividends from 1848 is easily explained: both capital and facilities had expanded too rapidly; receipts were diluted. By 1850, when business was definitely reviving, the railways had become so over-capitalised that they still out-stripped the economy. The over-capitalisation of the Lancashire & Yorkshire lasted until the mid-1850s, and although by 1857 the growth of both the local and the national economy had produced more traffic than the Company could cope with, it is still necessary to draw attention to the effects of the mania on the capital *structure* of the railways, and to ask how far the accusations of extravagance and mistaken financial policies are justified. Some light will be thrown on the relative fortunes of the various kinds of capital stock between 1842 and 1873. Although the Company had no intention of giving extensive permanent preferences in the 1840s, and although the story of the preference shares of the Lancashire & Yorkshire is very complicated, there is no doubt that ordinary stock suffered. It is only the higher level of dividends after 1860 that makes the ordinary shareholder's return at all comparable with that of preferred stocks, and these grew so rapidly in the 1860s that when the operating results deteriorated after 1873, the equity-holder's relative position weakened once again. Even the promise of 1860 was rather spoilt by the American Civil War. The setback was comparatively brief, and until 1873 there was almost unbroken prosperity, but by then the bad times of the later 1870s and 1880s were on the horizon. In each year between 1870 and 1873 Company officials expressed their hope that the disturbing rise in expenses was at an end. But they were wrong; the increase in working expenses outstripped the increase in gross traffic receipts by £133,000 in 1873, and the boom was over.

Part II is a study of the railway capital market. It is directly linked to Part I because much of the material used relates to the group of companies which amalgamated in the Lancashire & Yorkshire in 1847, but it also ranges over the wider aspects of the early capital market. Chapter 3 describes the methods of raising, and the sources of loan capital, and is based principally on the *Reports and Accounts*, which were published biannually, and the Proceedings of the Finance Committees of the Manchester & Leeds and Lancashire & Yorkshire Railways. The Proceedings of the Board of Directors are also used. Immediately the major obstacle to writing a coherent, comprehensive account of the financial dealings of the Company becomes clear. The Manchester & Leeds was by no means the first in the railway field, but railway accounting, and methods of keeping minute-books, were in their infancy. Practice in recording even the same item changed, and there are many gaps.

T. S. Ashton once wrote that blue-books provided detail of the pathology, rather than the physiology, of social life, and he suggested that business records would help to provide a more balanced picture of economic and social history.[1] Unfortunately, the Finance Committee minutes also provide a great deal of its pathology, often at the expense of its physiology, and they certainly do not present a complete record of the Company's finances. Their content depended

---

[1] T. S. Ashton, *Iron and Steel in the Industrial Revolution*, Preface to the First Edition (1924).

very much upon which particular financial problem, or aspect of its finances, was uppermost in the Committee's mind. In spite of this, there is information which, when used with the *Reports and Accounts*, throws some light on both the methods of raising temporary capital that were employed by the Company, and the sources that were tapped.

The first section of Chapter 3 distinguishes three methods of raising loan capital, and of these, only one proved to be of really lasting significance, although all were important at one time or another. The most important method throughout the period 1837 to 1873 was that of raising money on mortgage debentures. This money is called temporary because it could be withdrawn at the end of the stated life of the mortgage, but in effect much of it remained permanently with the Company, and one of the financial characteristics of the later 1860s was the large-scale conversion of this loan debt into 4 per cent Debenture Stock, that is, into permanent stock. The end of the period witnessed a significant development in another method of raising temporary finance. In the 1860s, and particularly in the early 1870s, there is a very pronounced tendency for shareholders to pay up the full amount of shares, in advance of calls, probably because dividends were so high, and they hoped to encourage the Company to make calls quickly. Thus the second method of raising temporary money, that of accepting money in advance, was important at the very beginning and at the end of our period. The remaining method, the raising of money on promissory notes, or on bonds, was important from an early date, but was affected by legislation in 1844, which restricted the legal life of bonds. Until the later 1840s, however, this method was used to a considerable extent by the Company.

The second section of Chapter 3 deals with the sources of temporary capital. This bears little resemblance to the Chapter on share capital, because the information available is of a different kind, and we are, therefore, restricted to a description of the kinds of sources which were drawn upon. Both banks and insurance companies were important and, in addition, banks proved to be vital creditors at dividend time. The Company put its business in the hands of several banks in Lancashire and Yorkshire for two main reasons. First, so that advances might be obtained more easily, and secondly, as evidence of its keenness to bring business to the towns it served. It is also shown that the Company and several of the banks were linked through the presence on the railway board of partners or directors of these banks. The treatment of the next group—individual creditors—is not easy, because the information about them consists largely of a mass of names which, in contrast to the subscription contracts and Parliamentary Papers used in Chapter 4, were seldom accompanied by any indication of occupation, status or address. This is doubly unfortunate because individual creditors were the most important source of loans, but it is possible to deal with this source only in general terms, apart from shareholders and directors of the Company, who are more easily distinguished. The remaining sources which were all much less important, are briefly outlined, and then, in the final section some general remarks are made about the size of loans, their duration, and the rate of interest they carried. As far as the rate of interest is concerned, the most striking characteristic is its stability over the whole period, within the range $3\frac{1}{2}$ to 5 per cent; but there was a pronounced tendency towards a secular decline between 1850 and 1870. Over the whole period there does not appear to be any consistent correlation between the length of loans and the rates they carried. Whether or not a loan would receive a larger rate if it were invested for a longer period would depend as much upon the Company's current attitude towards the loan debt as against stock, as upon any other factor. There was great inconsistency in this matter.

Chapter 4 investigates the sources from which a group of companies in Lancashire and the West Riding derived their permanent share capital. Its two sections discuss the geographical sources and the functional sources of share capital in the years 1835 to 1845. Chapter 5, which seeks to show how far the results of the study contained in Chapters 4 fit into the traditional account of the relevant aspects of railway finance in this period, is also a contribution to the reconsideration of the early railway capital market.

Any analysis of share capital sources is limited by the amount and quality of the material available, and this particular study of share capital sources has been further limited to the period before the great mania of 1845: none of the contracts used was a product of that furore of speculation. Since the Lancashire & Yorkshire failed to build a number of lines which were projected in 1845 and sanctioned in 1846 and 1847, and since there can be no doubt that it was the schemes of 1845 which provided, in the wildly speculative atmosphere of that year, the greatest scope for the 'men of straw', 1845 seemed a convenient dividing date. While it is not implied that any contracts should be dismissed out of hand—one of the objects of these chapters is to argue that contracts may be valuable evidence—the absence of lists of shareholders, for the Lancashire & Yorkshire, as distinct from subscribers, makes the task of testing the validity of the contracts an extremely difficult operation. Much of the material upon which we must depend for the sources of share capital is unacceptable at its face value, if only because of the harsh things that have been said about subscription contracts. This means that detailed tests of validity have to be made. If there were shareholders' registers and transfer books this would be a simple, if arduous task. There are none for the Lancashire & Yorkshire and so other means have to be devised. Because of this, any presentation of results in an unduly abbreviated form would be misleading as there are many qualifications to be stated. But it is believed that the generalisations on the early railway capital market made by, for instance, G. H. Evans,[2] can only be tested by the kind of study contained in these chapters.

The major conclusions of this part of the book are as follows: firstly, concerning the various constituent companies of the Lancashire & Yorkshire, it was found that the overwhelming proportion of the capital promised to the companies came from what might be termed 'locally interested' counties—Lancashire, Yorkshire and Cheshire. For reasons given, the contracts may be used and accepted as substantially accurate evidence of railway share capital sources. Where it can be established that subscribers remained shareholders, it is found that the majority of these were the 'interested' people. Of the subscribers, merchants and manufacturers contributed the greater proportion of the capital promised to the companies. So far as merchants are concerned, this is by no means a new conclusion. Manufacturers, on the other hand, have not received anything like the attention they appear to merit as suppliers of railway companies' capital. In some of the lists they were decidedly important, and this has suggested some reflections on industrial surpluses and 'ploughing back'.

Much has been said on the participation of clerks, clergymen, widows, spinsters and others in railway finance. The percentage contributions of these classes of people to the lists that have been analysed make it clear that, for the Lancashire & Yorkshire at least, they were unimportant as sources of subscriptions, let alone actual share capital. There is, moreover, no evidence that they participated in the promising of capital to any greater extent, relative to other groups, in periods of boom as opposed to periods of comparative depression or normal business.

A second group of conclusions are those which have been suggested by both the material relating directly to the constituent companies of the Lancashire & Yorkshire, and to railways in general. In Chapter 5 it is argued that the traditional view of pre-1840s railways—that they were 'locally' financed—is an inaccurate one.

[2] G. H. Evans, *British Corporation Finance, 1775–1850* (1936), *passim*.

The high proportions of initial capital subscribed to our companies by residents of Lancashire, and, to a lesser extent, Yorkshire, are to be regarded not as confirmation of the traditional account of early railway financing, but as confirmation of the paramount influence of Lancashire and its bordering areas in the early railway capital market. The activities of the 'Liverpool party' have been emphasised, but their incompatibility with the 'local finance' concept does not seem to have been recognised. Some participation of Lancashire business men in railway financing on a national scale need not have been incompatible with a predominance of local financiers in their particular lines, but the evidence suggests that the Lancashire interest in railways extended to a major interest in most of the important companies of the 1830s, if not in later concerns. The importance of Lancashire in the financing of companies nearer home was, therefore, a natural outcome of the situation in the early railway capital market, not, as Evans believed, of 'remoteness from capital centres' which brought about 'local finance' in transport undertakings.

Part I

The Development and Operation of the Lancashire & Yorkshire Railway Network

CHAPTER 1

Origins and Development
1825 to 1873

I

THE MANCHESTER & LEEDS RAILWAY, 1825 TO 1841

THE Manchester & Leeds—which changed its name to the Lancashire & Yorkshire Railway in 1847—was originally conceived as an important link in the chain of railway communication between Liverpool and Hull.[1] It was one of three companies projected in the first railway boom of 1824–25 to connect the two ports: the Liverpool & Manchester, the Manchester & Leeds, and the Leeds & Hull railways. Of the three, only the Liverpool & Manchester was successfully incorporated. The committee of the Manchester & Leeds, which was formed in 1824, decided to postpone its measure after the boom had broken, while the Leeds & Hull was destined to be split into two companies, the Leeds & Selby, and the Hull & Selby.[2] The Selby lines were sanctioned in 1830 and 1836 respectively and, since the Manchester & Leeds was also finally sanctioned in 1836, it was over a decade after the original attempts in the mid-twenties that the complete scheme of east–west communication between Liverpool and Hull was finally authorised. There was constant emphasis on the Manchester & Leeds as an integral part of an east–west link, but another strong motive was the desire to achieve better transport facilities between Manchester and Leeds themselves.

---

[1] See, for example, W. W. Tomlinson, *The North Eastern Railway: its Rise and Development* (1914), p. 98; W. T. Jackman, *The Development of Transportation in Modern England* (1916), pp. 565–66; and H. G. Lewin, *Early British Railways* (1925), p. 45.

[2] As an interesting sidelight on the attitude towards the railways as late as 1829, it may be remarked that the reason given for the shortening of the original Leeds & Hull project to the Leeds & Selby scheme was the objection that the competition of the free tidal river from Hull to Selby would be too great: cf. G. G. Macturk, *A History of the Hull Railways* (1879), p. 17. Considering this, and the position of the Leeds & Selby in the east–west scheme, Clapham's judgement on the line is misleading: 'In September 1834, the Leeds and Selby followed—a twenty-mile line with no very apparent objective.' Cf. *An Economic History of Modern Britain* (1930), I, p. 383.

Edwin Butterworth, an enthusiastic contemporary pamphleteer, maintained that:[3]

> 'The effecting of a rapid communication betwixt the metropolis of the chief cotton manufacture, Manchester, and the chief seat of the woollen trade, Leeds, was the principal object which was sought to be attained by the formation of the Manchester & Leeds Railway.'

That these motives were strong enough to stimulate railway promotion without aid of boom conditions—although the successful opening of the Liverpool & Manchester was probably an incentive—is shown by the second attempt at incorporation in 1830. On 18 October, at a meeting held in Manchester, it was decided to introduce a bill for a railway from Manchester to Leeds. The company was to have a capital of £800,000 in shares of £100. To secure a broad representation of the interests local to the line, a board of 29 directors was appointed: 10 were residents of Manchester, 8 of Leeds, 4 of Liverpool, 3 of Halifax, 2 of Bradford and 1 of Todmorden. The engineers appointed to survey the projected line were Stephenson and James Walker.[4] The bill was introduced by Lord Morpeth in March 1831, but there was considerable opposition and as Parliament was dissolved in the April the second attempt failed.[5]

Yet another attempt in the same year was unsuccessful, after the Company's bill was rejected in committee stage, and after a reconsideration by the Commons.[6] The project was then shelved until September 1835, when the first real national boom in railway promotion was under way. A new subscription contract was drawn up and signed, principally by the 1830 subscribers, who were given the chance of resuming their original shares, plus an additional number which could be taken up in proportion to the first holdings.[7] The minutes of the Board of Directors of the projected Manchester & Leeds Railway Company are recorded from 23 November 1835, when the first meeting opened with Samuel Brooks (who had

---

[3] E. Butterworth, *A Descriptive History of the Manchester and Leeds Railway* (1854), p. 2. (Typescript copy, British Transport Historical Records Office.)

[4] Walker was the engineer for the Leeds & Selby, and he was also consulted by the Liverpool & Manchester in 1829: cf. G. S. Veitch, *The Struggle for the Liverpool and Manchester Railway* (1930), p. 58.

[5] The bill was for the line from Manchester to Sowerby Bridge only.

[6] For accounts of these attempts at incorporation, see *A Companion to the Manchester and Leeds Railway* (1841), also Butterworth, *op. cit.*

[7] Proceedings of the Old Company, *in* Proceedings of the Directors of the Projected Manchester & Leeds Railway Company, 11 April 1836. The Old Company was wound up at this meeting.

presided over the meeting of 18 October 1830) in the chair. The directors present were: John Smith, Thomas Fielden, William Haynes, Henry Houldsworth, Thomas Broadbent, James Wood, Robert Gill and Henry Forth. Of these, Wood was appointed chairman, Gill, Haynes and Smith a sub-committee of Finance, and Brooks, Gill, Fielden and Houldsworth a sub-committee of Management.[8] Wood, Gill, and J. S. Brackenbury, the Company's solicitor, were the Company's representatives in London during the Parliamentary proceedings over the new bill.

It is obvious from the Proceedings of the Directors, and from the *Report* of the House of Lords Committee, which considered the bill, that the effective support for it far outweighed the effective opposition, although its opponents could not safely be ignored. The Manchester & Leeds Board made determined efforts at conciliation by sending out deputations in response to the objections that were coming in from interested parties. One such deputation was sent to a meeting of the Rochdale Canal proprietors at Middleton for an 'amicable settlement of the differences between the Companies'.[9] This was a wise policy, because it reduced the number of petitions against the bill when it came before the Lords Committee. Thus, while it was reported that the Calder & Hebble Navigation Company had petitioned against the bill in February 1836, in April it was stated that most of this company's differences with the Manchester & Leeds had been settled.[10] Negotiations with the Rochdale Canal Company, which had helped to wreck the 1831 bill,[11] had also been fruitful.

The outcome of the negotiations with the Aire & Calder Navigation Company, which had stated itself to be antagonistic from the start, and which maintained its opposition throughout the Parliamentary proceedings, was less successful. The first mention of its attitude occurs in the Proceedings of the Directors on 18 January 1836, when a letter from Mr. Leather, Jnr., of the Aire & Calder, was read, 'announcing [its] decided hostility'. In April, the Secretary of the Manchester & Leeds stated that the opposition of the canal company was such that a settlement out of Parliament was unlikely.[12] After the bill had received the Royal Assent, the directors reported that while the Calder & Hebble and Rochdale Canals had

[8] Proceedings of Directors, 23 November 1835. They were all residents of Manchester, and were all merchants, with the exception of Brooks (a banker), and Houldsworth (a spinner).
[9] *Ibid.*, 28 December 1835.
[10] *Ibid.*, 11 April 1836.
[11] Jackman *op. cit.*, p. 566.
[12] Proceedings of the Directors, 11 April 1836.

persevered in only minor points, the opposition of the Aire & Calder 'remained unabated from first to last, the most decided and unaccommodating that they could offer'.[13]

Not only were there the canal companies to be taken into consideration, but also individual property holders, a Gas Company, with the directors of which a conference was held on the points in dispute, and the projected Huddersfield & Leeds Railway Company.[14] The final result of this activity is contained in the report of the Lords Committee. The only petitions enumerated against the bill were those of:[15]

'. . . the Committee of Directors of the Undertakers of the Navigation of the Rivers Aire & Calder, and also the Petition of the Merchants, Traders and other Inhabitants of Leeds, whose Names are thereunto subscribed, . . . the Petition of Richard Sutcliffe of Mytholm Royd . . . against such Parts of the said Bill as affect his Interests . . . .'

Petitions in favour of the bill came from Todmorden, Leeds, Hebden Bridge, Mytholm Royd, Halifax (from which there were two), Bradford, Manchester, Liverpool, Wakefield and Huddersfield.[16] It is not, of course, at all certain that the Manchester & Leeds bill would have failed if efforts had not been made to reduce opposition before the bill went to committee. It is possible, however, that if all those with objections had gone to Parliament, the delays would have been far greater and the expense even higher, quite apart from the possibility of defeat. The Lords Committee decided for the bill, and gave good reasons for its decision; but whether or not a railway bill passed through Parliament was not wholly a question of intrinsic merit.

The route sanctioned by the Committee was from Manchester to Altofts, near Methley, via Littleborough, Todmorden, Hebden Bridge, Dewsbury, Wakefield and Normanton. (Map facing p. 216.) When all factors had been taken into consideration, it was found that this line, rather more than 60 miles in length, including the section from Altofts to Leeds, would best meet the deficiency of 'The present Means of Conveyance by Land and Water'; and that it had been satisfactorily established that revenue was likely to be

---

[13] *Reports & Accounts of the Manchester & Leeds Railway Company*, 8 September 1836.
[14] Proceedings of the Directors, 25 January 1836, 30 January 1836, 4 February 1836, and 14 April 1836.
[15] British Parliamentary Papers, 1836 (House of Lords Paper, 147) XII, *Report of the Lords Committee on the Manchester and Leeds Railway Bill*, p. 39.
[16] *Ibid.*, p. 39.

sufficient to meet annual charges, and still allow a profit to the 'Projectors'.[17] The bill received the Royal Assent on 4 July 1836. Ordinary capital of £1,300,000 in shares of £100, and borrowing powers to the extent of £433,000 were authorised. The clause sanctioning the capital issue stated that £1,042,100 had already been promised, but stipulated that the whole of the £1,300,000 was to be subscribed before any of the powers for the compulsory purchase of land were to be used.[18] These powers were to cease if the land had not been contracted for within two years, and if the railway was not completed within seven years then all powers except those relating to any part built were to lapse.[19]

The 200 pages of the Act contain many clauses designed to protect the interests of the various individuals and corporate bodies which would be affected by the railway. The rights of the Calder & Hebble Canal were dealt with in Clauses 20 to 31; those of the Rochdale Canal in 9 to 19; clause 31 enacted that compensation was to be given to the Aire & Calder for rendering certain of its plans impracticable. Other sections provided for the rights of the Commissioners of the Manchester Police, of the Manchester Gas Works, of the Manchester and Salford Water Company, the Warden and Fellows of Christ College, Manchester, and so on. All this was not, of course, unusual in a railway Act before 1845, but it does help to explain the difficulty many companies found in knowing just what they could, and could not do.

Like many other companies, the Manchester & Leeds soon found it necessary to alter the route which had been sanctioned after so much laborious negotiation. In 1837 another Act allowed deviations and alterations to be made in the line.[20] One of the main objectives was 'to form a more intimate connection with . . . Rochdale', because of 'the great amount of traffic' with Manchester.[21] The new Act did not alter the capital powers, and the alterations sanctioned did not in

---

[17] As far as the Altofts–Leeds part was concerned, the situation was complicated by the presence of three more bills before Parliament, all of which proposed to carry lines into Leeds from near Methley. The Manchester and Leeds Act (6 & 7 W. IV, c. 111) sanctioned a line into Leeds. But clause 209 stipulated that in view of the identical routes of the Manchester & Leeds and the North Midland companies from Altofts to Leeds, and because only one line was necessary, the North Midland was to make it. Clause 291 gave the Manchester & Leeds power to build this line, which was to be 10 miles long, if the North Midland had not seriously commenced construction within 18 months of the passing of the Act. The latter company did, in fact, build it.

[18] 6 & 7 W. IV, c. 111, s. 168.

[19] *Ibid.*, ss. 165 and 166.

[20] 7 W. IV, c. 24, s. 2.

[21] *Reports & Accounts: Report of the Special General Meeting of the Proprietors*, 9 November 1836.

any substantial way affect the route, but they did delay the beginning of construction; it was not until August 1837 that work was begun on the line. By September 1837 four contracts had been let for a total of 11¼ miles, and it was stated at the meeting of the proprietors in that month that the contractors were under heavy penalties to complete the works by May 1839.[22] By March 1838 works on 24 miles had been let for a total of £500,000. These contracts included the Summit Tunnel, near Littleborough, which was the most difficult part of the line. By March 1839 the entire works were contracted for, with the total expense estimated at £1,933,799.[23]

The forecast in the directors' report for the meeting of September 1838, that the section of the line from Oldham Road in Manchester to Littleborough would be opened by May 1839, was not far wrong. Exactly three years after the first Act received the Assent, that is, on 4 July 1839, the Manchester–Littleborough stretch was opened.[24] Rochdale was thus provided with railway facilities, but it should be remembered that lines were opened without stations: it was not until March 1840 that this part of the line, which was only 13½ miles long, was ready for general goods carrying.[25] In October 1840 the 27 miles of road between Hebden Bridge and Normanton were opened, and the entire line was completed in March 1841, when the engineering difficulties presented by the Summit Tunnel, which was 2,869 yards long, were finally overcome. The 8-mile stretch from Hebden Bridge to Todmorden had already been opened in January 1841.[26]

By March 1841 the Company had obtained another Act, and was petitioning Parliament for yet further capital powers. The Act of 1839, besides authorising an additional share capital of £650,000 and additional borrowing powers to the extent of £216,000, sanctioned branches to Oldham and Halifax, an extension from Oldham Road in Manchester to Hunt's Bank in Manchester (where the Manchester & Leeds was to link up with the Liverpool & Manchester), and gave other powers.[27] The Act of 1841 is an interesting item in the history of the Company since it authorised the Manchester & Leeds first preference issue of £487,500, as well as further borrowing

---

[22] *Reports & Accounts*, 14 September 1837. The directors could not resist pointing out that the (Rochdale?) canal had stopped, owing to lack of water, and that land carriage had had to be substituted at an increased cost of 50 per cent.

[23] *Ibid.*, 18 March 1839.

[24] Map facing p. 216. H. G. Lewin in the *text* (his map is correct) of his *Early British Railways*, p. 73, confuses the opening date with the beginning of construction.

[25] *Reports & Accounts*, 12 March 1840.

[26] *Ibid.*, 1839–41.

[27] 2 & 3 Vict., c. 55, ss. 2, 114, and 118.

powers of up to £162,500.[28] By 1841, therefore, the Manchester & Leeds had completed its main line, from Manchester to Normanton, was constructing various branches, and had increased its authorised share capital from £1,300,000 to £2,437,500. It was also empowered to borrow a total of £811,500.

The Company had not experienced any really serious difficulties during the four and three-quarter years between its incorporation and the completion of its main line. There had, of course, at an early stage been trouble over land purchase, and the sanguine attitude of the directors was not entirely justified. In March 1839 they reported to the proprietors that land purchases were practically complete; that the Parliamentary estimate of £200,000 should not be exceeded by more than £50,000; and that this was a good result, in view of the 'vexatious and unrelenting opposition'.[29] But a year later they were sadly pointing out that their earlier forecast had seemed reasonable because negotiations for purchase were so advanced. 'In consequence', however, 'of many cases of difficulty and dispute which afterwards arose, and of additional purchases rendered requisite by local circumstances during the progress of the works, which could not possibly have been foreseen', they now estimated that the cost of the land would be nearer £300,000.[30]

Against this must be considered the well-known fact that practically all railway estimates were exceeded. The Summit Tunnel alone cost £108,000 more than the estimate; the original contractor had abandoned the contract at an early date, and had paid a penalty of £3,000. When the contracts for the tunnel were let, the aggregate yardage expected was 4,567; the actual length of tunneling completed was 5,432 yards (in course of construction three additional tunnels were found to be necessary). The original estimate was £38 per yard; the actual average cost was £80 per yard.[31] Altogether, the total excess of expenditure on works, establishment, and rolling stock was well over £500,000, and of this only £96,000 was allocated to land expenses.[32] There is no doubt that there was extortion from railway companies by landowners,[33] and there were many attempts to get exorbitant sums from the Manchester & Leeds, but on the whole its experience confirms Harold Pollins' view that the part

[28] 4 Vict., c. 25, ss. 2 and 8. Clause 3 authorised the issue 'in such Manner, for such Prices' as a meeting of the Proprietors ordered.
[29] *Reports & Accounts*, 18 March 1839.
[30] *Ibid.*, 3 March 1841.
[31] *Ibid.*, 3 March 1841.
[32] *Ibid.*, 16 September 1841.
[33] Even so, the examples given are often not wholly accurate. Cf. H. Pollins, 'A Note on Railway Constructional Costs, 1825 to 1850', *Economica*, November 1952.

played by excessive land purchase prices in the capital costs of railways has been over-emphasised.[34] Although the Manchester & Leeds found it 'absolutely necessary . . . to give notices for juries to many landowners, to assess the value of their respective properties . . .', this action alone was sufficient in all but seven cases in the period up to September 1838. On the seven occasions on which the landowners had forced the Company to court, the total demanded was £146,448, the total awarded was only £44,628.[35]

The Manchester & Leeds was also fortunate in its shareholders, for throughout the construction of the main line it never needed to take legal action to enforce the payments of calls on shares. Indeed, on several occasions the directors complimented the proprietors on the punctuality with which they paid their instalments, even in the depressed years from 1837 to 1842. In March 1842 it was proudly announced that not a single call had been unpaid.[36] Subsequently there were some arrears, but instalments were paid without any serious coercion by the Company, and a considerable amount was even paid in advance. This illustrates the comparatively secure atmosphere in which the directors acted, and compared very favourably with the experience of the Eastern Counties Railway, for example.[37] This was obviously an important factor in the crucial period of construction: it meant that the Company did not have to turn to special inducements in order to secure funds. Thus in 1839—a year in which the issue of preference shares by other companies greatly increased—the second capital Act of the Company sanctioned ordinary half-shares. In 1841, as we have already observed, preference shares were issued, but even here, as we shall see, difficulty in raising ordinary share capital was certainly not the only reason for the issue.

The Lancashire & Yorkshire railway was the outcome of the amalgamating policy of the Manchester & Leeds, which was incorporated in 1836. But it was in 1831 that the first part of the Lancashire & Yorkshire was sanctioned, when the Manchester, Bolton & Bury Canal Navigation Company obtained an Act to build a railway from Bolton to Manchester. The capital authorised was £204,000, which could be raised either upon mortgage, or by creating shares.[38] This must be one of the first, and one of the few, examples

---

[34] *Ibid., passim.*
[35] *Reports & Accounts*, 17 September 1838.
[36] *Ibid.*, 17 March 1842.
[37] More will be said on the subject of calls in Part II.
[38] 1 & 2 W. IV, c. 60, ss. 13, 17 and 19.

of a canal company being enterprising enough to convert into a railway. The date, 1831, indicates that the move was prompted by the successful opening of the Liverpool & Manchester in 1830. The Company was authorised to fill, stop up, or drain as much of the canal as was required except for the Bolton to Bury section, which was to be maintained.[39] There were subsequent alterations to the route, and the Manchester, Bolton & Bury did not, in fact, build the line in or on the canal, but alongside it. Between 1831 and 1838, when it was opened, there were three additional authorisations of capital, which brought the total capital powers up to £650,000, of which £454,000 were share capital and £196,000 were borrowing powers.[40] By 1845, when the bill to merge the Manchester & Leeds and the Manchester, Bolton & Bury was presented to Parliament, the amalgamation movement was in full swing. The bill was objected to on Standing Orders,[41] and was postponed until the next session, when it was passed. A product of one mania—the canal mania of the early 1790s[42]—the Company lost its independence during an even greater one.[43]

Several other railways which were sanctioned in the 1830s were later to be associated with the Manchester & Leeds and Lancashire & Yorkshire. These were the Wigan Branch, the Preston & Wigan, the Preston & Wyre, the Preston & Longridge, and the Bolton & Preston, which were sanctioned in 1830, 1831, 1835, 1836 and 1837 respectively. The Preston & Wyre Railway, Harbour, and Dock Company was leased to the Lancashire & Yorkshire and the London & North Western Railways in 1849 after a complicated history involving thirteen Acts of Parliament. Its line from Preston to Fleetwood was opened in July 1840, and the two branches to Lytham and Blackpool operated from 1846. The Preston & Longridge, whose line was also completed in 1840, was absorbed in 1856 by the Fleetwood, Preston & West Riding Junction,[44] which, in turn, was

---

[39] *Ibid.*, ss. 50 and 52.
[40] The Acts passed after the incorporating Act are enumerated in 9 & 10 Vict., c. 378: 2 & 3 W. IV, c. 69; 5 & 6 W. IV, c. 30; and 1 & 2 Vict., c. 25. Samuel Laing set the capital cost of this 10-mile line at a prodigious £777,000—see B.P.P. 1844 (318) XI, *Fifth Report of the Select Committee on Railways*, Appendix 2, p. 4.
[41] *Reports & Accounts of the Manchester & Leeds Railway Company*, 3 September 1845.
[42] The canal was incorporated by 31 Geo. III, c. 68.
[43] 9 & 10 Vict., c. 378, *An Act to incorporate the Manchester, Bolton, and Bury Canal and Navigation and Railway with the Manchester and Leeds Railway Company*.
[44] The F.P. & W.R. Jc. had been given power to lease or purchase the P. & L. by its Act of Incorporation: 9 & 10 Vict., c. 246, s. 47.

taken over by the Lancashire & Yorkshire and the London & North Western in 1867.[45]

The only connection which the Wigan Branch and the Preston & Wigan had with the Lancashire & Yorkshire was that a part of their line, between Euxton Junction and Preston, was to be controlled jointly by the Manchester & Leeds and the Grand Junction Railways under an Act of 1846.[46] The two Wigan lines had already amalgamated in 1834 to form the North Union Railway:[47] a logical combination since the Preston & Wigan was merely an extension of the Wigan Branch. But, according to Lewin, and also to Cleveland-Stevens, it is notable since it marked the first recorded amalgamation with Parliamentary sanction.[48] The North Union was to absorb the Bolton & Preston before it was split up between the Manchester & Leeds and the Grand Junction Railways, and it is with the Bolton & Preston part of the North Union that we are concerned. The Bolton & Preston, like the Preston & Wyre and the Preston & Longridge, was a product of the boom of the middle 1830s, but it was sanctioned after the boom had broken, in 1837.[49] It had extremely strong local support, including that of Manchester, since it would, together with the Manchester & Bolton, provide a shorter route between Manchester and Bolton than the route already provided by the Liverpool & Manchester and the North Union Railways. The main support for the Company came from Bolton, Manchester, Liverpool and Warrington in that order.[50]

It was quite obvious that the Bolton & Preston would be a serious competitor of the North Union, and when the new line from Bolton to Euxton Junction was opened in 1843 a 'ruinous' rate war followed (almost all railway competition was 'ruinous' to the companies concerned). The Bolton & Preston was at a disadvantage since it did not have independent access to Preston; it had to be content with running powers over the 5½-mile stretch of the North Union line from Euxton Junction to Preston, and this naturally gave the latter company plenty of opportunity for obstruction.[51] It is

[45] *Reports & Accounts*, 14 August 1867.

[46] C. E. R. Sherrington, *A Hundred Years of Inland Transport* (1934), pp. 182–83, says that the North Union was vested in the Lancashire & Yorkshire and the London & North Western Railways in 1864. This is most probably a misprint for 1846, but he complicates the matter further since neither the Manchester & Leeds nor the Grand Junction had yet changed its name.

[47] 4 W. IV, c. 25, *An Act for uniting the Wigan Branch Railway Company and the Preston and Wigan Railway Company*.

[48] Lewin, *Early British Railways*, p. 27; E. Cleveland-Stevens, *English Railways: Their Development and Their Relation to the State* (1915), p. 18.

[49] 1 Vict., c. 121.

[50] See below, Chapter 4, pp. 126–27, 133.

[51] Clause 4 of 1 Vict., c. 121, prohibited the Bolton & Preston from building the

not necessary to go into the details of this competition—an adequate account will be found in Lewin's *Early British Railways*[52]—which led to the amalgamation of 1844.[53] It is worth recording, however, that the process of excessive rate reduction, followed by consolidation and reversion to the original rates, and a negation of the objects of the first supporters of the Bolton & Preston, was typical of the history of railway competition and combination as recognised by Parliamentary enquiries from Cardwell's Committee to the Departmental Committee on Railway Agreements and Amalgamations which reported in 1911.[54]

The assets of the old Bolton & Preston were vested in the Manchester & Leeds in 1846, under the agreement with the Grand Junction by which the latter undertook to pay 60/94ths of an annuity of £66,063 in return for the control of the main line of the North Union from the Liverpool & Manchester through Wigan to Euxton Junction, and the former the remainder of the annuity in return for the Bolton & Preston section of the North Union.[55] The Bolton & Preston line from Bolton to Euxton Junction, 14¾ miles long, had been opened in 1843.[56] The line from Euxton Junction to Preston was to be controlled and worked jointly by the Manchester & Leeds and the Grand Junction. This was the first of many such agreements made by the Manchester Company.

Chorley–Preston section of the line until three years had elapsed: the company was to use the North Union line, when this was completed. This provision was later modified by 1 & 2 Vict., c. 56, ss. 4 and 17, which allowed the Bolton & Preston to extend from Chorley to Euxton Junction, to link up with the North Union.

[52] pp. 143–45. Also 50, 55, 103, 153, and 175, for further details of the Bolton & Preston.

[53] 7 Vict., c. 2, *An Act to effectuate the Sale by the Bolton and Preston Railway Company of their Railway . . . to the North Union Railway Company.*

[54] 1911 Cd. 5631; XXIX, Pt. 11, *Report of the Departmental Committee on Railway Agreements and Amalgamations*, pp. 5–7.

[55] 9 & 10 Vict., c. 231, *An Act for vesting in the Grand Junction Railway Company and the Manchester and Leeds Railway Company the North Union Railway, all the Works . . .* For these details see ss. 22, 23 and 30.

[56] There had been difficulties during construction and the Bolton & Preston had had to obtain two further Acts, the second of which authorised a preference issue: 5 Vict., Sess. 2, c. 15, the preamble of which stated that the company had been unable to raise the full amount of authorised capital. Clause 2 sanctioned an issue of capital which amounted to the difference between the amount originally authorised and the amount actually raised.

II

THE LANCASHIRE & YORKSHIRE RAILWAY, 1841 TO 1850

IN 1841 the Manchester & Leeds had only just opened its main line and was still a comparatively small company. By 1850 it had transformed itself into the Lancashire & Yorkshire, one of the giants of the railway world and, with a few minor exceptions, the projects of the 1840s, or rather, those which had been proceeded with, had been completed.[57] 1850 saw the end of a period of immense expansion, although it did not, of course, mark the end of the growth of the Lancashire & Yorkshire network.

The depression of 1839 to 1843 had not destroyed the faith of the Manchester & Leeds directorate in the prospects of their company. Even though the first year's complete working of the main line, which had been opened throughout in March 1841, ended in a year of acute depression and of Plug Plot and Chartist violence, the Board was still optimistic:[58]

> 'the Directors cannot but feel gratified at the prospect of remuneration, which is held out to this Company and ascertained by the sure test of experience.'

They reported that passenger mileage had already exceeded the Parliamentary estimate of 1836 by upwards of 60 per cent, a result which they attributed to their unique provision of really extensive third-class facilities. The Manchester & Leeds had, from the first, decided that the best policy in an area such as the textile districts was to encourage the short-distance traveller; in other words, to provide accommodation for the poorer classes at low fares. The Company was thus able to pay a dividend for the second half of 1842, a period which was said to be the worst half-year for business, and for railway receipts in general. In spite of the bad condition of trade and industry, the Manchester & Leeds traffic receipts had increased slightly, business from new sources was coming in steadily, and there were high hopes for the future.[59]

The reason why the burst in railway promotion began to get under way in 1843, has long been a subject for debate. The continued success of the Liverpool & Manchester, and other companies, which were paying upwards of 10 per cent, the amount of capital seeking

---

[57] To preserve continuity the account has, for certain companies such as the East Lancashire Railway, been taken well into the 1850s, or even later. But 1850 is a distinct dividing date.

[58] *Reports & Accounts*, 17 March 1842.

[59] *Ibid.*, 2 March 1843.

investment more remunerative than Consols, and the low rate of interest, are all factors which have received emphasis. When added to the revival of confidence, and the emergence of trade and industry from the depression in 1843, they make up the conditions for a new wave of railway promotion. As early as September 1843 the directors of the Manchester & Leeds expressed a growing desire to expand. It is true that since 1839 they had been occupied with building the main line, besides a few branches, and the junction with the Liverpool & Manchester at Hunt's Bank (in Manchester), which had been sanctioned in 1839. But the Oldham branch had been opened on 31 March 1842, and it is doubtful whether the other projects, in spite of the many difficulties particularly involved in the Hunt's Bank extension,[60] would have deterred further enterprise if conditions had been favourable for it. R. C. O. Matthews has written that it seems improbable[61]

> 'that the relative absence of new railway projects between 1838 and 1843 was mainly the result of general business stagnation. Even if the state of business had been better than it was after 1837, it would still have been a matter of common prudence for promoters to wait before starting anything fresh until they could see what the railway map of the country would look like when the lines so far projected had been completed.'

Mr. Matthews agrees, however, that the 'timing of . . ., the mania, on the other hand, was very much affected by the state of trade, and particularly by the state of confidence',[62] and it is more likely that poor business conditions and existing commitments were the reasons for the lack of promotion between 1838 and 1843. The promoters of railway enterprise whose activities resulted in wild schemes were not noted for their contemplation of the railway map of Britain. The railway promotions of 1844 which, when sanctioned in 1845, involved almost £60 million of shares and loan capital, should have been enough to call a halt to promotion, but the authorisations of 1846 amounted to more than double that figure. What was a matter of common prudence for the Boards of companies, such as the Manchester & Leeds, was the attitude of the merchants and manu-

---

[60] The Liverpool & Manchester, which had also secured an Act to build its part of the connecting line, had been very dilatory in taking steps to carry out its share of the project. The extension of the Manchester & Leeds line was opened in January 1844, and through traffic between Liverpool and Hull became possible in the May of the same year.
[61] R. C. O. Matthews, *A Study in Trade-Cycle History: Economic Fluctuations in Great Britain, 1833–1842* (1954), pp. 112–13.
[62] *Ibid.*, p. 112.

facturers, the classes who supplied by far the greater proportion of capital. While the Manchester & Leeds directors were fond of praising the shareholders for the promptitude with which they paid calls, it was thought necessary in 1841 to reassure them that calls would be kept down to a minimum.[63]

Whatever the reasons for the revival of activity in the years after 1842, we find the directors stating, in their report for September 1843, that since the various main works had been completed and the connection with the Liverpool & Manchester was in sight, attention was being given to the possibility of opening branch lines to 'populous towns and districts'. Surveys had already been made between Cooper Bridge and Huddersfield, and others were in progress for branches to Ashton, Bury and Bradford.

The directors' statement provides an excellent illustration of the attitude which led companies to regard areas as being their 'territory', and which led to the numerous Parliamentary battles of the 1840s and of later years:[64]

> 'In the opinion of your Directors the permanent interests of the Company will be essentially promoted by proceeding at the earliest period with every branch which the nature of the country admits, and the importance of the district warrants. They believe that the most certain source of income will always be found in the local traffic, which, as trade and population increase, must grow in proportion, and that any addition to this branch of business will not only contribute to the facilities for extending the more distant traffic, but *increase the ability in case of competition to retain it.*'

At this early date, self-protection by means of expansion was already in mind. The expansion of companies, and the building of branches, has often been explained as reaction to competitive flotations; here we have a statement of intended extension to the limit, before any serious provocation could be claimed. But this is not to say that anything like the mania was intended. It was also at this time that the Manchester & Leeds began to come to agreements with canal companies, in order to increase the rates which had been cut as a result of competition.

---

[63] *Reports & Accounts*, 16 September 1841. The meeting approved the issue of preference shares.

[64] *Ibid.*, 6 September 1843. (My italics.) In his discussion of the activity (or lack of it) of the Manchester & Leeds in the West Riding in 1844–45, Lewin, in *The Railway Mania*, p. 40, states that the policy of the Board 'was not one of extension'. This statement contrasts with the confident declaration of the directors themselves.

It was in 1843, therefore, that the Manchester & Leeds embarked upon the policy which was to become so familiar a feature of railway development in the 1840s. The continued improvement in the condition of trade was reflected in the traffic receipts, and the financial results of the second half of the year yielded a dividend at the rate of 7 per cent per annum. It is not surprising, therefore, that no fewer than six applications to Parliament were mentioned in the *Report* for 14 March 1844, plus an agreement with the Hull & Selby, for which Parliamentary sanction was to be sought. This agreement provided that the business of the two companies should be under joint management from 31 December 1843. All capital required from that date, and all revenue remaining after charges had been met (with the exception of interest charges on capital borrowed) were to be divided between the Hull & Selby and the Manchester & Leeds in the proportions $16\frac{1}{4}$ per cent and $83\frac{3}{4}$ per cent respectively. The agreement proved abortive but was the preliminary to much negotiation between the two companies.

Of the six applications mentioned, only two, which were successful, need consideration. The first is a curiosity, because it sanctioned a branch already built. In April 1841, the Manchester & Leeds opened a short branch to Heywood, one-and-a-half-miles long, without any legal powers. In view of the preamble to the Act of 1844 it seems probable that some difficulty had arisen over land.[65] At all events, the Heywood Branch Act regularised the situation by giving the Company power to purchase land with the consent of owners and occupiers, and authorised a capital issue of £2,100 to meet the expense.[66]

The second measure was a more substantial one: the Ashton, Stalybridge & Liverpool Junction Act of 1844 sanctioned a line from the main line of the Manchester & Leeds at Newton (Manchester) to Ashton and Stalybridge. The new company was sponsored by the Manchester & Leeds, which was authorised to lease or to purchase what was, in effect, merely a branch railway.[67] The preamble to the Ashton, Stalybridge & Liverpool Junction Railway Act of 1845, which amended the previous Act and authorised a branch to Ardwick (Manchester), announced that the Company had been

---

[65] 7 Vict., c. 16: 'And whereas it is expedient . . . [to enable] the said Company to purchase and hold the Land upon which the said Railway has been so formed . . .'

[66] *Ibid.*, ss. 2 and 3. This sum was subscribed by two persons.

[67] 7 & 8 Vict., c. 82, *An Act for making a Railway from the Manchester and Leeds Railway to . . . Ashton-under-Lyne and Stalybridge*. Clause 342 states: 'the Railway by this Act authorized . . . will be a Branch' of the Manchester & Leeds.

C

transferred to and vested in the Manchester & Leeds.[68] The line from Miles Platting to Ashton was opened on 15 April 1846, and Ashton and Stalybridge were connected on 5 October of the same year.[69] The Ardwick branch was opened in November or December 1848.[70]

During 1844 there was considerable railway activity affecting the Manchester & Leeds. The chain of railway communication between Liverpool and Hull was completed, through the joint efforts of the Manchester & Leeds and the Liverpool & Manchester. The Manchester & Leeds branch line into Halifax was also opened. In addition, a number of the constituent companies of the Lancashire & Yorkshire were floated, and two companies which were to become part of the East Lancashire Railway network were sanctioned,[71] namely the Manchester, Bury & Rossendale, and the Blackburn & Preston companies. The former was designed to provide the Rossendale district with better railway facilities than those proposed by the Manchester & Leeds, whose plans were limited to linking Bury with their main line by extending the Heywood branch. The dissatisfaction of the business interests of Bury and the Rossendale area was intense and they gave very strong financial support to the Manchester, Bury & Rossendale.[72] The same high degree of financial support from Bury was repeated when the subscription contract of the Blackburn, Burnley, Accrington & Colne Extension Railway was drawn up early in 1845: this Company was merely an extension of the Manchester, Bury & Rossendale. The relatively strong backing from Manchester probably reflects the more direct communication proposed between Manchester and Bury, and this support was repeated for the Blackburn, Burnley, Accrington & Colne.[73] The Manchester, Bury & Rossendale's line was to be from a junction with the Manchester, Bolton & Bury at Clifton through Bury, terminating in Lower Booths, in the Rossendale Valley.[74] The project did not suffer from the competition of the Manchester & Leeds' proposal to build its Heywood extension to Bury. The

[68] 8 & 9 Vict., c. 109.
[69] *Reports & Accounts*, 9 September 1846, and Lewin, *Railway Mania*, p. 245.
[70] Both Lewin, *Railway Mania*, p. 391, and M. D. Greville, *Genealogical Table of the Railways of Lancashire* (August 1952, unpublished), give the date as 18 December 1848. The Manchester & Leeds *Reports and Accounts* (7 March 1849) and the Company *Engineer's Report* (1 March 1849) give 20 November 1848.
These lines may be seen on the map facing p. 216.
[71] The Lancashire & Yorkshire and the East Lancashire amalgamated in 1859.
[72] See the *Manchester, Bury and Rossendale Subscription Contract* (House of Lords Record Office). Also G. H. Tupling, *The Economic History of Rossendale* (1927), p. 225.
[73] See below, Chapter 4, pp. 122–36.
[74] 7 & 8 Vict., c. 60, s. 236.

Company's scheme was judged to be a competing line and was rejected in favour of the Rossendale bill.[75]

The Blackburn & Preston, also sanctioned in 1844, was to build a line from Blackburn through Pleasington and Walton-le-Dale to a junction with the North Union Railway at Farington.[76] The absorption of this Company by the Manchester, Bury & Rossendale was presaged both by its second Act, obtained in 1845, which authorised a junction with the proposed Blackburn, Burnley, Accrington & Colne,[77] and by the latter's Act of Incorporation, which included a clause to the effect that it would be advantageous if the Manchester, Bury & Rossendale were to construct the lines, which were to extend from a junction with the Rossendale company in Tottington Higher End, diverge at Habergham Eaves, and link up the towns mentioned in the title. The Act also contained clauses giving the company power to lease or to sell to the M.B. & R.[78] In the same year, 1845, the M.B. & R. changed its name to the East Lancashire Railway,[79] and a year later it absorbed the Blackburn & Preston.[80]

The Manchester, Bury & Rossendale had, therefore, grown in just two years from a company authorised to build a 14-mile line to one which had powers to build about 50 miles of railway,[81] and the complexity of its development is particularly striking. Its amalgamating career was marked by yet another absorption in 1846, when the Liverpool, Ormskirk & Preston's Act provided for its sale or lease to the East Lancashire.[82] The L.O. & P's main line was to be from a junction with the projected Liverpool & Bury Railway at Walton-on-the-Hill through Ormskirk to a junction with the Blackburn & Preston; various branches were also sanctioned. The East Lancashire obtained further Acts which authorised alterations, deviations and branches, as well as extensions such as that into Preston, which was sanctioned by an Act passed in 1847. There were, in addition, a number of lines built in conjunction with the Lancashire & Yorkshire. But it is sufficient here to outline briefly the dates on which the East Lancashire's lines were opened. We have already seen that the Blackburn & Preston was opened in June 1846, two

---

[75] The Bury branch was, however, sanctioned in 1846.
[76] 7 Vict., c. 34, s. 226.
[77] 8 & 9 Vict., c. 103, s. 3.
[78] 8 & 9 Vict., c. 35, ss. 15, 38 and 39. One of the lines was to go to Blackburn, the other to Burnley and Colne.
[79] 8 & 9 Vict., c. 101, s. 6.
[80] 9 & 10 Vict., C.302, *An Act to unite and consolidate the Blackburn and Preston Railway Company with the East Lancashire Railway Company.*
[81] This figure includes the 9½-mile stretch of the Blackburn & Preston, opened in June 1846.
[82] 9 & 10 Vict., c. 381, ss. 49–50.

months before it was absorbed by the East Lancashire. In September, the original Manchester, Bury & Rossendale line from Clifton Junction to Rawtenstall was opened, but the bulk of the network was completed in 1848 and 1849—the peak years of railway mileage opened during the 1840s. In March 1848 the extension from Rawtenstall to Newchurch was completed; in June, Blackburn to Accrington; in August, Accrington to Stubbins; in September, Accrington to Burnley; in February 1849, Burnley to Colne; and in April 1849, the Liverpool, Ormskirk & Preston line from Walton Junction to Lostock Hall. The rest of the lines were opened as follows: the Preston extension in September 1850; Newchurch to Bacup in October 1852; and Ormskirk to Rainford in March 1858.[83]

By this time, 1858, the East Lancashire was in close working agreement with the Lancashire & Yorkshire, and amalgamation took place in the following year. The two companies had been on far from amicable terms in the mid-1840s but it soon became obvious that it was to the advantage of both to come to terms, and amalgamation had been discussed since the early 1850s.

We now turn to the companies which were projected in 1844 and incorporated in 1845. It is argued below, in the discussion on the sources of share capital, that these companies may be regarded as pre-mania flotations, since they were all in the midst of their Parliamentary process by the time the real promotion mania got under way in April 1845. It is often not appreciated that incorporation took place months after flotation, assuming a successful first application to Parliament, and this has produced misleading comments on the course of the mania, especially when it comes to designating 1846 as the peak year of railway activity.[84] The number of companies which obtained their Acts in the session of 1845, and which later amalgamated with the Manchester & Leeds or Lancashire & Yorkshire Railways, is impressive, and so for the Manchester & Leeds it is 1844 and not 1845 which must be marked out as the most important year of the 1840s so far as the *promotion* of its network is concerned.

There were five of these companies: the Blackburn, Burnley, Accrington & Colne, which has already been dealt with; the Blackburn, Darwen & Bolton; the Liverpool & Bury; the Huddersfield & Sheffield Junction; and the Wakefield, Pontefract & Goole.[85] The

[83] See Lewin, *Railway Mania*, *passim*, and Greville, *Railways of Lancashire*, *passim*.

[84] See A. D. Gayer, W. W. Rostow, and A. Schwartz, *The Growth and Fluctuation of the British Economy, 1790–1850* (1953), Vol. 1, p. 437: 'the next year produced a deluge of railway activity that dwarfed even that of 1845 . . .'

[85] For the moment we are not considering those schemes of 1844–45 which came to grief, but which were revived later.

Blackburn, Darwen & Bolton's 14-mile line was from Blackburn to Bolton via Darwen and Turton, and joined the Manchester, Bolton & Bury in Great Lever.[86] In 1847 it amalgamated with the Blackburn, Clitheroe & North-Western Junction Railway as the Bolton, Blackburn, Clitheroe & West Yorkshire Railway,[87] which in turn was absorbed by the East Lancashire and Lancashire & Yorkshire Railways in 1857. The West Yorkshire opened lines from Blackburn to Sough in August 1847; Sough to Bolton in June 1848; and Blackburn to Chatburn in June 1850.[88] The Liverpool & Bury, the third of the constituent companies incorporated in 1845, was sponsored by the Manchester & Leeds in order to break the monopoly of the Liverpool & Manchester. Two main lines, as well as two branches, were projected: from the Borough Gaol in Liverpool through Wigan to near Bolton, where this line was to meet the Bolton & Preston; and from Bury to the Manchester, Bolton & Bury Railway, which it would join near Bolton. The branch railways were to serve various collieries.[89] The idea of providing a competitive alternative to the Liverpool & Manchester was not a lasting one. It was reported in March 1852 that the Lancashire & Yorkshire and the London & North-Western Railways had agreed to divide the passenger traffic between Liverpool and Manchester, and the intermediate towns of Bolton and Wigan; one of the objects of the agreement was 'the abolition of duplicate trains. . . .'[90] This arrangement was made fairly soon after the Liverpool & Bury lines had been opened in November 1848,[91] and after the Lancashire & Yorkshire, in conjunction with the East Lancashire, had extended the line to Tithebarn-street (the Exchange) in Liverpool in May 1850.[92] The building of the Liverpool & Bury's lines had therefore involved close working with the East Lancashire as well as the London & North-Western, and was a factor contributing to the eventual amalgamation of the E.L. and L. & Y.

The two remaining companies of the Lancashire & Yorkshire

---

[86] 8 & 9 Vict., c. 44, s. 15.
[87] The North-western Junction's Act of 1846 had authorised the Company to lease or to sell to the Blackburn, Darwen & Bolton: Cf. 9 & 10 Vict., c. 265, s. 39.
[88] Cf. Greville, *Lancashire Railways*, and Lewin, *Railway Mania*. This Company had entered into an agreement with the Lancashire & Yorkshire as early as 1850. See *Reports & Accounts of the Lancashire & Yorkshire Railway*, 6 March 1850, for a resolution approving the terms of the proposed agreement for both the working and the ultimate amalgamation of the companies.
[89] 8 & 9 Vict., c. 166, s. 15 and Preamble. The Company was absorbed by the Manchester & Leeds in 1846: 9 & 10 Vict., c. 282.
[90] *Reports & Accounts of the Lancashire & Yorkshire*, 3 March 1852.
[91] *Ibid.*, 7 March 1849, i.e., opened throughout for passengers.
[92] *Ibid.*, 4 September 1850.

sanctioned in 1845 were both Yorkshire companies: the Huddersfield & Sheffield Junction, and the Wakefield, Pontefract & Goole. At a general meeting of the Manchester & Leeds in September 1845, the directors were authorised to enter into agreements with a number of companies, one of which was the Huddersfield & Sheffield Junction,[93] although there was no indication in previous reports that the Manchester & Leeds was interested in this railway. The latter's Act, which sanctioned a line from Huddersfield to Penistone, where it was to form a junction with the Sheffield, Ashton-under-Lyne & Manchester Railway, empowered it to sell or to lease to one or more of four companies: the Manchester & Leeds, the Sheffield & Manchester, the Manchester & Birmingham, and the Midland.[94] In fact, it amalgamated with the Manchester & Leeds by an Act of 1846.[95] Its main line of $13\frac{1}{2}$ miles from Huddersfield to Penistone was opened in July 1850, together with the Holmfirth branch.[96]

The Wakefield, Pontefract & Goole, the result of the desire of the Manchester & Leeds to obtain its own complete and independent east coast—west coast communication, was to be the final link in the chain (the other links being the Liverpool & Bury, the Heywood extension,[97] and the Manchester & Leeds) and was to start from a junction with the Manchester & Leeds in Wakefield, pass through Pontefract, and end in the docks at Goole.[98] It Act authorised a capital of £365,000. The Manchester & Leeds was empowered to subscribe half of this,[99] to appoint five of the directors, and to lease or buy the new concern.[100] Another Act was obtained in 1846 which sanctioned further branches, and the Manchester & Leeds quickly went ahead with construction. The main line was opened to the public in April 1848, while the Askern branch, which was just over 10 miles in length, was opened two months later. By means of this branch the Lancashire & Yorkshire joined the Great Northern at Shaftholme Junction, near Doncaster.[101] Yet another branch, from Pontefract to Methley to a junction with the Midland, was ready in October 1849. The Methley branch was, according to the directors

---

[93] *Ibid.*, 3 September 1845. There were five West Riding companies mentioned in this resolution.
[94] 8 & 9 Vict., c. 39, s. 35.
[95] 9 & 10 Vict., c. 277.
[96] *Reports & Accounts of the Lancashire & Yorkshire*, 4 September 1850.
[97] Authorised along with other branches, by 8 & 9 Vict., c. 54, and opened in May 1848.
[98] 8 & 9 Vict., c. 172, s. 30.
[99] This provision is important for the correct analysis of capital sources: See below, p. 141 footnote 87.
[100] 8 & 9 Vict., c. 172, ss. 6, 21, 42, and 43.
[101] *Reports & Accounts of the Lancashire & Yorkshire*, 6 September 1848.

of the Manchester & Leeds, designed to connect Leeds directly with Goole, and they had agreed at an early date with the Wakefield, Pontefract & Goole Board to build the line.[102]

While the object of the Methley branch was being explained by the Manchester directors, it was announced that powers were to be sought to extend it to Askern. This proposal was the outcome of a general desire to improve the Manchester & Leeds' connections with the south, through Lincolnshire. Thus the Wakefield, Pontefract & Goole was to serve two objects; completing the east–west line unified under the control of the Manchester & Leeds, and providing direct links between Leeds and the south. Already, in September 1844, the Boston, Lincoln & Wakefield Railway was to be given 'cordial support', since it would, by providing a direct connection between Lincoln and Wakefield, increase the traffic of the Manchester & Leeds proper.[103] Then, in September 1845, came the proposal to link up with the London & York (Great Northern) by means of the Askern branch. The two branches from the Wakefield, Pontefract & Goole to Methley and Askern, together with the simultaneous opening of the Great Northern line between Retford and Doncaster, and the completion of the Knottingley branch of the York & North Midland, would mean that[104]

> 'the most direct route between Lincolnshire and Leeds, Bradford, Wakefield, and York, will include twenty miles of the Wakefield, Pontefract & Goole Railway, and will bring that undertaking into fuller operation. . . .'

The continuing concern of the Lancashire & Yorkshire to maintain its traffic in the area bounded by the towns of York, Wakefield and Doncaster, is seen in the many complicated agreements with the Great Northern and North Eastern companies whose schemes the Lancashire & Yorkshire was continually opposing, not only for the reason just stated, but also because of the desire to keep the connection with London and the south. In fact, this desire led to one of the most grandiose schemes thought up by the Company, although the immediate cause of it was the authorisation of the North-Eastern's lines between Doncaster and Wakefield (1862), and from Doncaster to York (1864). The L. & Y's response to this threat came in February 1865, with the revelation of an agreement with the Great Eastern Railway. In conception it ranks second only to the efforts to

[102] *Ibid.*, 6 March 1850, for the opening of the line; *ibid.*, 3 September 1845, for its purpose.
[103] *Ibid.*, 5 September 1844.
[104] *Ibid.*, 5 September 1849.

amalgamate with the London & North-Western in the early 1870s, and it is convenient to consider it here, although it lies outside the limits of this section.

The statement about the agreement with the Great Eastern expressed concern about the North Eastern lines and went on to say:[105]

'. . . [the] Directors were much gratified at having a proposition made to them by the Great Eastern Railway Company for the construction of a Line of Railway, on joint account from Long Stanton—a place about six miles north of Cambridge— through Peterborough and Lincoln, to join your Railway at Askern, passing through a rich agricultural country singularly well adapted for the construction of a first-class Trunk Line, cheap in execution, and of excellent gradients. The result of negotiations between the two Boards has been the deposit of Bills, by which it is proposed to construct the Trunk Line referred to, about 113 miles in length with a Branch . . . to the port of Goole, thus completely uniting your system of Railways, upwards of 400 miles in length, with the Great Eastern system (of 660 miles). . . . The total mileage of the new Lines, . . . is 132 miles.'

The agreement included running powers for the Lancashire & Yorkshire over the entire Great Eastern system and was the culmination of twenty years of effort, from 1844 to 1864, to gain a direct connection with all-important London. It shows a remarkable development from a comparatively small local network in 1844 to a great provincial company with metropolitan aspirations only twenty years later. It may also be seen as the product of the last railway mania, and the failure of the scheme was probably fortunate for the shareholders of the Lancashire & Yorkshire.

This account of only one part of the activities of the Lancashire & Yorkshire in our period illustrates not only the wastage of time and money on futile schemes, but also the forces which were for ever driving railway boards to expand—not only to cover what they regarded as their legitimate territory, but to combine with other networks. It was not only the failure of the positive schemes, which led to a great deal of wasted capital, but also the continual negotiation and Parliamentary opposition caused by the companies' conception of the threat to their interests. Positive schemes and opposition were, of course, not mutually exclusive policies—in the 1840s this was obvious—but after 1850 they often appeared to be.

[105] *Ibid.*, 15 February 1865.

The second of the two functions which the Wakefield, Pontefract & Goole was to serve was the completion of the Liverpool–Humber link up. It was not until 1846 that the connection was secured even on paper, and it was in the same year that amalgamations created so much public concern and led to Parliamentary enquiry. The answers of D. O'Brien and Captain Coddington before the Select Committee on Amalgamations of 1846 give a summary of the schemes contemplated by the Manchester & Leeds, and a good statement of the Company's policy. The aim of the Manchester & Leeds, they claimed, was to get communication from Liverpool to Hull into the hands of one company. They also pointed to the other basic motive of the Board, the attempt to keep all intermediate towns between the two ports in the Manchester & Leeds orbit by connecting them with the main line.[106] These men had only to look at the statements of the directors themselves to arrive at this conclusion. In the boom year of 1845 the Board reported:[107]

> 'It may be sufficient in the meantime to say, that it appears to your Directors to be both the interest and the duty of the Company to provide *adequately* for the convenience of the vast population in the districts both in Lancashire and Yorkshire contiguous to the main line wherever the latter can be made instrument to that end, and that they will endeavour to secure to the public all the advantages of unity of management and arrangement throughout the complicated net-work of railways which the local position of the population requires. . . .'

A year later, when most of the legislation securing these aims had been passed, the directors said that the main line could be regarded as extending from Liverpool and Preston in the west, to Goole and Hull in the east; while connecting lines would pass through all the important commercial and industrial towns of Lancashire and Yorkshire. The population of these towns was, they estimated, about 3 to 4 millions.[108]

The additions to the network promoted in 1845 and sanctioned in 1846 were by no means insignificant. One of the most important of them, however, the West Riding Union, was not prosecuted with anything like the same vigour with which other, and possibly inferior, additions were built. In fact, a large part of the West Riding Union, which was the outcome of an enormous amount of nego-

---

[106] B.P.P. 1846 (275) XIII, *Second Report of the S.C. on Railways and Canals Amalgamation, Minutes of Evidence*, QQ. 128 and 129.
[107] *Reports & Accounts*, 3 September 1845. Again, this contrasts with H. G. Lewin's view of the policy of the Board, see below, pp. 27–28.
[108] *Ibid.*, 9 September 1846.

tiation and Parliamentary battling, was abandoned, and it is noteworthy that other commitments arising out of the boom of 1845 were found to be very burdensome, in contrast to the *authorisations* of 1845. The distinction between the authorisations and the flotations of 1845 is of some importance and is emphasised in Part II.

Ignoring two companies whose applications failed, three new projects obtained incorporation in 1846. These were the West Riding Union Railways, a company with the very ponderous title of the Sheffield, Rotherham, Barnsley, Wakefield, Huddersfield & Goole Railway, and the Liverpool, Ormskirk & Preston. The L.O. & P. has been included in the account given of the East Lancashire Railway, by which it was absorbed, and needs no further consideration here.

The West Riding Union emerged only after a very complicated process of negotiation with groups of West Riding business people. Its Act authorised a large capital of £2 million in shares, and borrowing powers of over £600,000.[109] The Manchester & Leeds was empowered to subscribe just over £604,000,[110] and it absorbed the new company almost immediately. Eight lines connecting a multitude of places, including Huddersfield, Halifax, Bradford, Cleckheaton, Dewsbury and Leeds, were to be built, and would have provided the Manchester & Leeds with an even more comprehensive network in the West Riding had it taken advantage of all its powers under the Act. A total of 45½ miles had been authorised, but the mere fact of incorporation in 1846 was a drawback. In September 1846 the Company reported that work was well under way on the railways sanctioned in 1845 under the auspices of the Manchester & Leeds, the Liverpool & Bury, the Wakefield, Pontefract & Goole, and the Huddersfield & Sheffield Junction. It was expected that one or more of them would be finished by the end of 1847.[111] So there was plenty to occupy the Board's attention. In addition there were many other schemes of consolidation under consideration: the Manchester & Leeds was no exception to Lewin's statement that the number of projects sanctioned in 1847 was surprisingly large in view of the commitments of the two previous years.[112]

At first there was no indication that there was likely to be trouble over the West Riding Union. According to the Board's statement of March 1847 a considerable amount of land had been purchased for

[109] 9 & 10 Vict., c. 390, ss. 4 and 7.
[110] *Ibid.*, s. 30.
[111] *Reports & Accounts*, 9 September 1846.
[112] H. G. Lewin, *Railway Mania*, p. 283. Although there were, in the authorisations of 1847, many revivals of earlier schemes.

the lines, and the accompanying report of the engineer, John Hawkshaw, said that the Halifax, Cleckheaton, and Bradford contracts had already been let. The apparent optimism before the crash is illustrated by the directors' decision to accept calls in advance at the permanent rate of 5 per cent per annum, 'to a limited amount', and by their reference to the fact that 'Trustees and many other parties seeking Railway investments give a preference in their purchases *to shares paid up in full.* . . .'[113] The tone of these comments conflicts with the growing difficulty of non-payment of calls, a difficulty ignored by the directors in this *Report.* As early as October 1846 the Finance Committee of the Manchester & Leeds resolved that the shares of those Huddersfield & Sheffield Junction holders who had defaulted were to be forfeited,[114] and reference was later made to defaulters on Manchester & Leeds shares.[115] In January 1847 the arrears of calls were already totalling over £200,000, and in April they were over £250,000.[116]

By September 1847 it was obvious that conditions had changed: it was proposed 'to regulate the course of expenditure from time to time strictly in reference to the conditions of the Money Market'; and, therefore, to concentrate on particular and integral parts of the network.[117] Since construction of the lines sanctioned in 1845 was far advanced, the axe could only fall on the 1846 and 1847 projects. Naturally there were other considerations: for instance, the increasingly amicable relations between the Great Northern and the Manchester & Leeds may explain why work on the Sheffield & Barnsley line went ahead, while the West Riding Union lines were neglected. But opposition to the Company's policy increased and in September 1851 the shareholders decided to resist attempts to enforce the construction of the W.R.U. lines from Bowling to Leeds, and from Salterhebble to Huddersfield, and to apply for permission to abandon the unconstructed lines.[118] The attempt to force the Company was unsuccessful, and only 18 of the 45½ miles were actually constructed. They were opened in July 1848, May 1850, August 1850, and January 1852.[119]

Lewin believed that the failure to construct these lines was

---

[113] *Reports & Accounts*, 10 March 1847.
[114] Proceedings of the Finance Committee of the Manchester & Leeds, 16 October 1846. Nevertheless, many calls were paid in advance throughout 1847.
[115] *Ibid.*, 28 October 1846.
[116] *Ibid.*, 20 January 1847 and 7 April 1847.
[117] *Reports & Accounts*, 1 September 1847.
[118] *Ibid.*, 3 September 1851.
[119] *Ibid.*, 6 September 1848; 4 September 1850; 3 March 1852 for the opening of these lines, which may be seen on the maps facing p. 216

probably due to the influence of the London & North-Western, which did not want the Company to have independent access to Leeds;[120] and he attributed the failure to build the other lines to the Manchester element on the Board, remarking that it justified the view held in many quarters that this element was keener on developing the system in Lancashire than in Yorkshire.[121] This was also the view of Thomas Normington, who blamed excessive centralisation of management in Manchester for what he thought was the inefficiency of the Lancashire & Yorkshire.[122] Against this may be argued, in the first place, that the West Riding Union was only one company whose lines the L. & Y. failed to build; two Lancashire companies suffered the same fate. The Oldham Alliance Railways, sanctioned in 1847, were completely abandoned and were revived only in part after many years had elapsed, and the Manchester & Southport, also sanctioned in 1847, was the subject of a dispute similar to that which raged over the West Riding Union. Secondly, to repeat a point made before, the lines which were abandoned were those which were sanctioned in 1846 and 1847, after many lines had been commenced in 1845 and 1846. By March 1848 the length of railways under construction amounted to 127 miles.[123] Finally, the anxiety continually expressed in the *Reports* of the Lancashire & Yorkshire Board over the activities of such companies as the Great Northern and the North-Eastern, and the scheme to link up with the Great Eastern, do not indicate a lack of interest in the Yorkshire section of the network.

The Yorkshire project which did get more positive attention was the Sheffield & Barnsley, sanctioned in the same year as the West Riding Union. This was, in any case, a much smaller scheme: the total mileage was only 26, including branches, and the part for which the Lancashire & Yorkshire was to become responsible was only 9 miles long. The Sheffield & Barnsley Act provided that the Manchester & Leeds might lease or purchase the portion of the system north of Barnsley station,[124] and nominate half of the first Board of Directors.[125] The route taken was from Barnsley to

---

[120] H. G. Lewin, *Railway Mania*, pp. 409–10.
[121] *Ibid.*, p. 269.
[122] Thomas Normington, *The Lancashire and Yorkshire Railway* (1898), *passim*. It is evident from what Normington wrote that he believed himself to have been shabbily treated by the Company, in whose employ he was for many years. It is, therefore, probably unwise to place too much reliance upon his statements.
[123] *Reports & Accounts*, 1 March 1848.
[124] 9 & 10 Vict., c. 354, ss. 47 and 48.
[125] *Ibid.*, s. 20. They were all Manchester & Leeds directors.

Horbury Junction, near Wakefield, and the line was partially opened in January 1850.[126]

There were several abortive or near-abortive projects in 1846 which may be disposed of quickly. For instance, the proposal to amalgamate the Manchester & Leeds with the Leeds & Bradford was shelved, and although the Liverpool, Manchester & Newcastle Junction was successfully incorporated, the Manchester & Leeds, which was supposed to provide several of its directors and to subscribe £200,000 of its capital,[127] regarded it with scant respect. Later on the Lancashire & Yorkshire was so enthusiastic about this project that in spite of the rejection of the bill to abandon it the shareholders were assured that the ultimate prosecution of the line was so remote as not to be worth worrying about.[128] More important than ephemeral schemes were the problems of the Hull & Selby and of access into Hull. As early as 1843 the Manchester & Leeds had agreed with the Hull & Selby to work the companies under joint management, but the scheme had fallen through.[129] It was revived in 1845, and an Act obtained in 1846 authorised the Hull & Selby to lease or sell to either or both of the York & North Midland and the Manchester & Leeds.[130] Yet in 1850, the Lancashire & Yorkshire was disclaiming any responsibility for the Hull line, and the directors declared that they were 'protected, by existing agreements, from any such liability' when they were called upon by the Y. & N.M. to take joint possession of and responsibility for working the line.[131] It is more than likely that the Lancashire & Yorkshire considered that its right to run trains into Hull, and to use the facilities there, was sufficient, especially if it incurred no liability in the process. But the Company's policy towards communication with Hull was very confused, involving yet further agreement with the York & North Midland in 1852, abandonment of the Hull & Selby to the North Eastern in 1855, and an attempt to obtain an Act linking it with the Hull & Selby in 1862; not surprisingly the attempt failed.

When the smoke had cleared after the 1846 session, it was found that the Manchester & Leeds, if it exercised all its powers, would control 343 miles of railway, both projected and completed. Of this only 79¾ miles represented the growth of the original Manchester &

---

[126] *Reports & Accounts*, 6 March 1850. The line was not open for full public use until July 1850.
[127] 9 & 10 Vict., c. 90, s. 9.
[128] *Reports & Accounts*, 6 September 1848.
[129] See above, p. 17.
[130] 9 & 10 Vict., c. 241. In September 1846 the shareholders of the Manchester & Leeds endorsed this proposal.
[131] *Reports & Accounts*, 6 March 1850.

Leeds. All the rest had been obtained through amalgamation and lease.[132] The Company was either to shelve, or to lose control over some of it, but by far the greater proportion represented real expansion. 1847 brought extra commitments when three more companies, two of which were sponsored by the Manchester & Leeds, gained incorporation. It is true that the Oldham Alliance[133] yielded nothing concrete at all, but the main line of the Manchester & Southport which was, like the West Riding Union, the cause of legal action against the Lancashire & Yorkshire, for failure to build, was eventually completed. It was to go to Southport via Wigan from Pendleton, near Manchester, and there were to be 11 branches.[134] The Manchester & Leeds could subscribe up to £575,000 (the total capital was £775,000), and was well represented on the Board.[135] At first the M. & S. appeared to be receiving better treatment than the Oldham Alliance, because Hawkshaw, the Lancashire & Yorkshire's engineer, reported in February 1848 that 3 miles of the Southport line were being worked upon.[136] In fact, those 3 miles were in Wigan, and were part of the Liverpool & Bury as well as of the Manchester & Southport.[137] It is clear from the directors' *Reports* that there was no intention of building the other lines. After the opening of the three miles in Wigan in November 1848 there is no reference to the Company until September 1851, when the proprietors of the Lancashire & Yorkshire resolved to ask the directors of the Manchester & Southport to resist the efforts that were being made to compel construction of the rest of the line.[138] However, the L. & Y. had to withdraw its abandonment bill and in 1852 decided, 'reluctantly', in the face of a previous determination not to incur any further capital outlay on new works, on preliminary proceedings for the purchase of land for the line between Wigan and Southport.[139] The amalgamation of the two companies was reported in March 1855,[140] and the line from Wigan to Southport was opened in the following month. With belated good grace the Board said that the line had been constructed at a moderate cost and would therefore be a valuable asset.[141]

The Liverpool, Crosby & Southport, the third of the 1847 railways, was the last of the 1840s. Its main line was opened from Waterloo to Southport in July 1848, and two shorter lines were completed in 1850 and 1851.[142] The L.C. & S. was operated by the Lancashire &

---

[132] *Ibid.*, 9 September 1846.
[134] 10 & 11 Vict., c. 221, s. 15.
[136] In *Reports & Accounts*, 1 March 1848.
[138] *Reports & Accounts*, 3 September 1851.
[140] *Ibid.*, 7 March 1855.
[142] M. D. Greville, *Lancashire Railways*.

[133] 10 & 11 Vict., c. 232.
[135] *Ibid.*, ss. 4, 12 and 31.
[137] *Ibid.*, 6 September 1848.
[139] *Ibid.*, 1 September 1852.
[141] *Ibid.*, 5 September 1855.

Yorkshire from 1851,[143] and the two companies formally merged in 1855.

In this section the account of the development of the Lancashire & Yorkshire in the period 1841 to 1850 has at times been taken well into the 1850s and 1860s, but it is clear that 1850 marked the end of an era. The 1840s marked the most important decade in the history of many networks because the majority of their constituent companies were incorporated and absorbed, and in addition a large amount of construction was completed between 1843 and 1850. The tale of the 'aftermath' is familiar: in common with many other railways, the Lancashire & Yorkshire had financial troubles, disputes with shareholders, and legal difficulties. It was guilty of malpractices, but, again like most other large companies, it built the majority of the lines which had been sanctioned during this remarkable decade.

III

THE LANCASHIRE & YORKSHIRE RAILWAY, 1850 TO 1873

By 1850 the second distinct phase in the development of the Lancashire & Yorkshire Railway had ended. There was still the West Riding Union line from Halifax to Sowerby Bridge to be completed, and the Company was to be forced to build the main line from Manchester to Southport. But these are minor matters; what is important is that generally speaking the commitments of the 1840s had been met. The growth of the Company may easily be illustrated: from a paid-up capital of about £2¾ million at the end of 1841, to over £11½ million at the end of 1850; from 50 miles of line to a total of 268 miles worked. The receipts from 216 miles belonged exclusively to the Lancashire & Yorkshire. A large proportion of this mileage had, of course, been projected by independent or semi-independent companies; only a fairly small part was authorised for the Manchester & Leeds itself. Many of the companies were, from the start, destined for absorption by the Manchester & Leeds, although this was often for fear that traffic might be subtracted from existing lines rather than as a result of positive action by the Company. This is true in spite of the repeated promises the Manchester & Leeds made to provide railway facilities for as many towns as was practicable.

That the Company came to regret the acquisition of some of its lines is evident from statements made after the boom had broken, and the consequences of the policy of preserving 'territorial in-

[143] *Reports & Accounts*, 5 March 1851.

tegrity'[144] had become apparent. Regret was expressed, for instance, over the Huddersfield & Sheffield Junction when the directors tried to answer criticisms of their expansion policy in the 1840s. From general remarks made in September 1850 we can see that their policy might have been different if the Manchester & Leeds had not been confronted with so many competitive schemes in 1844, 1845, and 1846:[145]

'. . . That the chief additions to the original undertaking are Lines *not projected* by your Directors, but originating with independent Companies, and completed or in progress at the period of amalgamation—Lines for the most part effecting objects in accordance with the general design of the Manchester & Leeds Company and occupying positions more or less injurious or otherwise to the permanent interests of the Company, according as they might become combined with one or other of the numerous systems of Railways occupying the great Manufacturing district.'

It is possible, therefore, that while the Manchester & Leeds might eventually have got around to lines such as those of the West Riding Union, it was pressure to come to terms, to project, and to absorb which led to the excessive expansion of the 1840s. The Board insisted that it was too early, especially in view of the depressed conditions of the time, to assess the true results of their policy; and they emphasised that, even in the case of the Huddersfield & Sheffield Junction, they felt justified in resisting the invasion of their district.

In spite of this, they still had to face the fact that the dividend declared was at the rate of only 2 per cent per annum for the half year ending 30 June 1850. The decline in dividends was common to all companies, but this did not make it any easier to bear, and the Board attempted to placate the shareholders by remarks praising the population of the Lancashire area—none was more enterprising, etc. They were also of the opinion that the decline in dividend had reached its lowest point; from now on the only movement must be upwards. They were, in fact, wrong, for the next two declarations remained at 2 per cent. It was not until March 1852 that an increase was announced, and the unprofitable trend continued for some time, with the dividend standing at only 3½ per cent for the first half of 1854.[146] But from 1855 there was a fairly steady improvement as a

---

[144] Or territorial monopoly: cf. W. E. Simnett, *Railway Amalgamation in Great Britain* (1923).
[145] *Reports & Accounts*, 4 September 1850. (Directors' italics.)
[146] *Ibid.*, 6 September 1854.

result of better traffic returns, and the trend continued, apart from the early years of the American Civil War, until 1873.

Most of the Lancashire & Yorkshire's growth after 1850 was merely a result of amalgamation with companies which were not only in existence but had already built their lines. There was still a considerable amount of Parliamentary activity to protect the Company's interests, an activity which was, to a much greater extent than that of the 1840s, purely negative. A good example of this is the opposition to a company proposing to build those lines of the West Riding Union which the Lancashire & Yorkshire had abandoned by Act of Parliament. On the positive side, the network was increased by just over 200 miles between 1850 and 1873.[147] Of this, about 170 miles were contributed by the various companies which were absorbed after 1850. These companies were the East Lancashire, the Bolton, Blackburn, Clitheroe & West Yorkshire Railway (the 'Blackburn'), the Liverpool, Crosby & Southport, the Manchester & Southport, the Lancashire Union, and the Fleetwood, Preston & West Riding Junction. Apart from a small number of these 170 miles which were built jointly by the Lancashire & Yorkshire and the East Lancashire, the building activity of the Company between 1850 and 1873 was relatively small.[148]

As in other periods, the building of lines was dictated partly by protective motives, partly by local pressure, and partly by a policy of providing extended facilities. Very often schemes were successfully opposed in Parliament, without the Company introducing any rival scheme of its own. From the *Reports* of the directors they appear to have been very successful in avoiding encroachment by companies such as the Great Northern, and even by the concerns which were working in agreement with the Lancashire & Yorkshire, such as the East Lancashire and the London & North-Western. The East Lancashire tried on more than one occasion to obtain powers that would affect the L. & Y. and E.L. joint lines and stations in Liverpool; and in 1851 alone, two such attempts were rejected by Parliament.[149] Sometimes, as with the Great Northern's bill of 1851, which proposed the building of stations at Wakefield and Knottingley, an

---

[147] For all the lines opened between 1850 and 1873, see map facing p. 216.
[148] The estimates of the mileages, and the view of the building activity of the Company in this period, are derived from the following: the Lancashire & Yorkshire *Reports & Accounts*, H. G. Lewin, *Railway Mania*, M. D. Greville, *Lancashire Railways*, and information contained in the *Report of the J.S.C. on Railway Companies Amalgamation*, B.P.P., 1872 (364), XIII, Pt. 11, pp. 9 and 19. This last source, especially, must be consulted with great care, as there are several inaccuracies.
[149] *Reports & Accounts*, 5 March 1851 and 3 September 1851.

D

agreement seemed the best way of resolving the difficulty.[150] But there was hardly a company in Yorkshire and Lancashire with which the Company did not clash at one time or another, and this meant a constant drain on the Company's financial resources. In spite of this, the directors were very much given to making this kind of statement:[151]

> 'The friendly relations . . . with other [there was a dispute with the G.N.] neighbouring Companies, including the London and North-Western, Midland, and Manchester, Sheffield, and Lincolnshire Companies, have been fully maintained.'

At another date the Company omitted for obstreperous behaviour might well be the London & North-Western.

The first signs of a revival of positive activity came in 1852, when it was reported that an application was being made to Parliament for powers to provide additional station accommodation at Liverpool and Rochdale.[152] This revival remained on a very small scale for some time, and was confined to schemes such as the Liverpool Dock Branch, which was considered 'imperatively necessary'.[153] The scheme was certainly worth while, for it gave the Lancashire & Yorkshire direct access to the Liverpool Docks, and its importance may be gauged from the speed with which it was built. The Act authorising the branch from Kirkdale, as well as certain connecting lines in Liverpool, received the Royal Assent in June 1854;[154] work began the following month, and the branch was opened for traffic in March 1855.[155] All this time, from 1850 to 1855, traffic receipts had been unsatisfactory, especially passenger receipts, which caused anxiety until well into 1855, although goods traffic revived earlier. There is no doubt that the poor financial results caused the marked disinclination to undertake any further commitments, other than those considered absolutely necessary. Construction was limited to the Liverpool branch, the Manchester & Southport line, which had been forced on the Lancashire & Yorkshire, and small projects like station extension and the doubling of track on the Sheffield & Barnsley branch. These works were all finished in 1855, and the next few years were occupied solely with agreements, proposed amalgamations (with the East Lancashire and the 'Blackburn') and nego-

---

[150] *Ibid.*, 3 September 1851.
[151] *Ibid.*, 3 March 1852.
[152] *Ibid., loc. cit.* The Act obtained, 15 & 16 Vict., c. 132, also authorised certain abandonments.
[153] *Ibid.*, 1 March 1854.
[154] 17 Vict., c. 58.
[155] *Reports & Accounts*, 5 September 1855.

tiations with canals. This was in spite of improved commercial and financial conditions; it was even said in 1857:[156]

> 'The increase in the Traffic, which has occasionally exceeded the Company's power to move it, has necessitated the provision of increased accommodation in the Shape of Engines, Carriages, and Wagons.'

When the Company did decide to branch out again, it chose an inauspicious time. The project is interesting because it illustrates the point made earlier that, given time, the Lancashire & Yorkshire would have come to schemes which were all forced on it in a couple of years. The Oldham to Rochdale, and Royton, branches, formed part of the Oldham Alliance Railways, which had been sanctioned in 1847 and subsequently abandoned. They were revived in September 1857, when it was announced that surveys were to be made preparatory to an application to Parliament. The lines envisaged were about 7 miles in length,[157] but traffic fell off sharply in November and December 1857 as a result of the 'serious depression in Commercial affairs', and the 'state of the Money Market' made it inexpedient to apply to Parliament.[158] It was not until the Company was forced to take action, once again as a protective measure, that the bill was reintroduced in 1859.[159] It was passed and the branches were opened in December 1863: a striking contrast to the speed with which the Liverpool Dock branch was prosecuted.[160]

The Lancashire & Yorkshire found a considerable number of projects threatening it in the sessions of 1858, 1859 and 1860 which, the Board pointed out, put up its 'working expenses'. These projects, combined with good financial results in 1860—dividend reached 6 per cent for the first time since the 1840s—induced it to embark on the first serious phase of expansion for many years. In spite of the compulsion felt by the directors (they 'considered it their duty' to introduce the schemes), the shareholders forced them to withdraw one bill and to eliminate part of another. One of the bills was rejected by Parliament in favour of a competing London & North-Western scheme, while four others were passed. Three of the Acts authorised branches and extensions, the fourth was merely a money bill.[161] After 1860, in spite of the seriously adverse effects of the early

---

[156] *Ibid.*, 4 March 1857. In this year the one exception to these remarks, the Middleton branch, which was sanctioned in 1854, was opened. This branch was a revival of earlier, lapsed powers.

[157] *Ibid.*, 2 September 1857.   [158] *Ibid.*, 17 February 1858.

[159] *Ibid.*, 16 February 1859.

[160] The contracts were not let until the early months of 1862.

[161] *Reports & Accounts*, 13 February 1861.

years of the American Civil War, the Lancashire & Yorkshire was more or less continuously engaged in promoting schemes, opposing projects, and coming to agreements. Practically all the additions of the 1850–73 period that were actually built by the Company were opened in the 1860s.

A feature of many of the branches and other works sanctioned in the 1860s was the dilatoriness with which they were carried out. C. E. R. Sherrington once wrote:[162]

> 'The later 'sixties had witnessed the opening of many new branches by the enterprising Mancunian concern, each tapping some new industrial centre, . . .'

This is true up to a point. It is clear from the following list that most of the openings were in 1869 and 1870, but some of the branches authorised in 1865 were still not finished in 1873, especially those of the Halifax area, and Sherrington's phraseology is rather misleading. The Halifax district of Ovenden–Heckmondwike–Stainland–Meltham–Ripponden–Luddenden received particular legislative attention in the 1860s, but many of the branches authorised for the area took a remarkably long time to build. One of the explanations of this is the existence of many competing schemes; the Lancashire & Yorkshire applied for powers as a protective measure and, once they were obtained, proceeded at a very leisurely pace with the works. The Lancashire & Yorkshire was not, according to its directors, an aggressive company. It only wanted to live in peace with its neighbours, and if they would have the good taste to avoid projects unpalatable to the Lancashire & Yorkshire, then the Company would show similar good feeling:[163]

> 'Your Directors having carefully abstained from engaging in any new Lines prejudicial to the interests of neighbouring Companies, had hoped that they should have been saved any serious contest in Parliament . . . (But) the London and North-western and Midland Railway Companies have again deposited a Bill authorising the making of an entirely new and costly Railway between Huddersfield and Halifax.'

No doubt this kind of trouble figured among the motives of the directors of the Company when they came to the decision that their railway would serve its area better if it merged with the London & North-Western. The attempts at amalgamation, agreed upon by the proprietors of both companies in October 1871, became famous.

[162] C. E. R. Sherrington, *Hundred Years of Inland Transport*, p. 182.
[163] *Reports & Accounts*, 13 February 1867.

LINES OPENED BETWEEN 1860 AND 1873[164]

Lancashire	Opening
Blackpool to Lytham	April 1863
Salford and Victoria stations connection	1865
Bootle branch	August 1867
Horwich to Hindley	September 1868
Horwich branch	February 1870
Rochdale to Facit	November 1870
Boar's Head to Adlington } Chorley to Cherry Tree }	November 1869
Shawforth branch	December 1870

Yorkshire	Opening
Methley railway	1865
Dewsbury branch	August 1866 to February 1867
Huddersfield to Meltham	February 1869 to August 1869
Heckmondwike branch	February 1869 to August 1869
New Hull Dock	July 1869

They were part of a rush of mergers which were proposed in the early 1870s and which resulted in the appointment of the Joint Select Committee on Railway Companies Amalgamation in 1872. In spite of the suspension of the Amalgamation Bill of 1872, and its reintroduction and rejection in 1873, the Company's directors were still confident of its success when it was reported that a further attempt would be made in 1875.

The significance of 1873 in the history of the Lancashire & Yorkshire does not lie solely in the failure of the amalgamation proposals: more important was the definite change in the financial situation. It was in 1873 that dividends started falling after some years of steady increase, topped by the boom in traffic and profits in 1871 and 1872. There were few complaints about the steep increase in working expenses when traffic receipts and dividends were rising at a fast rate, but when receipts ceased to rise quickly it was found that working expenses did not move as sympathetically as they had between 1870 and 1872. There was little realisation that the decline in the dividend was going to last for many years. From $9\frac{1}{8}$ per cent, for the second half of 1872, it fell to 3 per cent for the first half of 1886, and not once in the 1880s did it reach 6 per cent. The Great Victorian Prosperity was well and truly over.

[164] This list has been compiled from the *Reports & Accounts of the Lancashire & Yorkshire Railway* and, for the Lancashire lines, with the help of M. D. Greville, *Lancashire Railways*. There is some discrepancy between Greville and the *Reports*. Often the different dates given for the same line refer to openings for either goods or passenger traffic.

CHAPTER 2

Traffic and Profits
1842 to 1873

I

THE ACCOUNTS

MANY nineteenth-century writers argued not merely that railway accounts were badly drawn up, incomplete and incomprehensible—as if that were not enough—but that they were rendered so deliberately by scheming boards of directors who wanted to hoodwink their proprietors. Charges were made that dividends were paid out of capital, that expenses which should have gone into revenue account were placed instead in capital account; that there was, in fact, fraud on a colossal scale, and that where there was not deliberate fraud there was mismanagement to an extent that was almost criminal.

Arthur Smith's views of the directorate of the Manchester & Leeds and Lancashire & Yorkshire are quoted in Chapter 5. He also charged *every* company with misapplication of capital receipts.[1] Smith tended to be rather violent, and it is unlikely that the chicanery was as all-embracing as he insisted. But there are many more sober pamphleteers of the period 1840 to 1870 who state the fact of misapplication without the imputations of evil intent. Writing in 1867 Joseph Lee Thomas said, more in sorrow than in anger:[2]

'My own impression is that an impartial and complete investigation of Railway accounts, would show that dividends have been paid which could not have been, had all the items strictly chargeable against revenue been so debited; the average working expenses of Railways would not, I fear, ... be found to be much less than 60 per cent of the receipts.'

A civil engineer complained, seven years earlier, that 'The accounts are, ... so extended and complex that few have either the time or the

---

[1] *The Bubble of the Age; or the Fallacy of Railway Investment, Railway Accounts, and Railway Dividends* (1848), p. 7.
[2] *A Letter on the Present Position of Railways* (1867), p. 14.

qualifications for unravelling their mysteries. . . .'[3] Complex they are, but extended in the right direction they are not. The mode of keeping accounts changed time and time again until a standardised form was prescribed by the Regulation of Railways Act of 1868. Items suddenly appear, and just as suddenly disappear; separate figures for items are given one year, and composite figures the next; and so on. No wonder that Thomas Wrigley should write in 1867:[4]

> 'It is one of the worst features of the Railway system that we can place no reliance upon any statement, whether of acts or figures, issued by a Railway Board . . . there is unfortunately no room to doubt that . . . the Directors have paid dividends out of Capital.'

Wrigley demanded the abolition of directors' control over the capital account. Examples of these criticisms could be multiplied, but sufficient has been said to show that there appears to be almost as much justification for discarding railway accounts as for ignoring subscription contracts as reliable evidence of the sources of share capital. In both cases, however, this view is mistaken.

The various changes in the methods of keeping accounts, and the resulting problems, will be dealt with in due course.[5] For the moment, it is as well to state the major difficulty involved in trying to determine the financial success or failure or rectitude of the Company. It soon becomes apparent, on examining the accounts, that all does indeed turn on the question of allocation of expenses between revenue and capital accounts, and it is here that the published accounts are inadequate. It is not possible to tell from them whether a certain amount charged in the capital account for permanent way, for example, should be smaller, greater or, indeed, there at all. New permanent way, built under the terms of a new Act, is a legitimate capital charge; renewal of permanent way should be a revenue charge; and, remembering the charges of chicanery, should there have been any expenditure on permanent way at all?

Again, nineteenth-century writers were alive to this problem, and more than one pamphleteer attempted to classify expenses as chargeable to either revenue or to capital acccunt. At best, opinions were not identical, and at worst were flatly contradictory. Dionysius

---

[3] *Plan for Lessening the Taxation . . . by the Purchase and Improved Administration of the Railways . . .* (1860), p. 17.
[4] *Railway Reform. A Plan for the Effectual Separation of Capital from Revenue* (1868), p. 10.
[5] Recommended to the reader is H. Pollins' 'Aspects of Railway Accounting Before 1868', which is in Littleton & Yamey (eds.), *Studies in the History of Accounting* (1956), pp. 332–55.

Lardner maintained that it would never be possible to close the capital account, as many urged, because a natural increase in traffic rendered it imperative to expand, for instance, rolling stock and permanent way. This should not be done out of revenue, as that would be unjust to the person who bought shares only to sell them.[6] This solicitude for the speculator was unusual: most contemporaries were more concerned with the proverbial widows and orphans who relied on the income from such investments, and Lardner himself made the customary reference to them. In contrast to Lardner, Jeffrey Whitehead, by his own account 'Of the Stock Exchange', argued that such works could not 'as a rule be fairly debited to capital account'.[7] Whitehead believed that capital spent on new lines, subscriptions to other companies (but these were merely a necessary evil), rolling stock for new lines, and Parliamentary expenses on new lines, should be charged to capital account. In addition to obvious items connected with the working of the railways, most additions and alterations to, and renewal of, lines and stations, and Parliamentary expenses excepting those necessitated by new lines, should be charged to revenue account.[8]

It is worth mentioning that these accounts were audited. Not until 1845 was there any legislation compelling audit, and even then companies already in existence were exempted. But the Manchester & Leeds employed auditors from the start—in 1836. From the outset, also, these auditors' names appeared on the published accounts below their statement certifying the correctness of the accounts. The methods of auditing mid-nineteenth-century railway accounts, and hence the audits themselves have, along with most other railway practices, been severely criticised. On the audits Lardner said:[9]

> 'It is well known that on the presentation of each half-year's report, auditors are appointed by the meeting of shareholders, to examine and check the balance-sheet. The witnesses produced before the House of Lords (in 1849), consisting of public accountants, eminent railway directors, and others, distinguished by special knowledge on such subjects, were unanimous in declaring this system of audit to be destitute of all efficiency.'

On the same page of his book Lardner quotes a witness, Mr. King, who had been secretary to two companies, as saying that the audit

[6] *Railway Economy* (1850), p. 118.
[7] Jeffrey Whitehead, *Railway Finance* (1867), p. 4.
[8] *Ibid., loc. cit.*
[9] Lardner, *op. cit.*, p. 510.

was 'a complete farce' to which he could not 'attach the slightest value or importance'. Whitehead wanted an independent Government audit.[10] The demand for such an audit was general, but Samuel Salt believed that the answer to the railways' problems was not 'the so-much-vaunted Government audit, *however desirable and necessary a good and efficient audit may be*',[11] but 'judicious' instead of 'puerile and improper management'.[12]

All this seems very depressing, and it is impossible to know whether these criticisms applied to all companies,[13] but at some time or another they had to face realities. Even the most ill-conducted company at some time had to pay low dividends, or no dividends at all, and it is most unlikely that the trends discernible over the years are inaccurate. There is evidence that at least occasionally the auditors of the Lancashire & Yorkshire took their job seriously. They wrote to the directors on 8 November 1850 drawing attention to several— though not very large—items which, they thought, should have been charged to revenue and not to capital account. Samuel Swarbrick, of the Accountant's Office, gave a detailed reply and examination of these items, but (and this is ominous proof that the railway companies did indeed juggle with the accounts even at that late date) he told the Finance Committee that the Company's margin for dividends and interest was small, and cautioned the Board against charging all the items to revenue. In the event, it was ordered that some of the items were to be charged to revenue, some to capital account.[14]

In July 1853 the auditors again wrote to the Company 'Calling attention to a list of items . . . which they suppose to have been omitted from the last Half Year's accounts'. The Secretary was to furnish particulars to the auditors and to express the hope that they would be considered satisfactory.[15] The date of the first communication—1850—is significant, because this was the era of rebellious shareholders' meetings and demands for independent audit.[16] The 1853 incident shows that the auditors' efforts did continue after the clamour had quietened down. Later in our period the Board was

[10] Whitehead, *op. cit.*, p. 9.
[11] Samuel Salt, *Railway and Commercial Information* (1850), p. ix.
[12] *Ibid.*, p. vi.
[13] According to Harold Pollins, 'many railway companies gave their auditors much more power than was laid down by the legislation of 1845'. Cf. H. Pollins, 'Railway Auditing—A Report of 1867', *Accounting Research*, Vol. 8, No. 1, January 1857.
[14] Proceedings of the Finance Committee, 18 November 1850.
[15] *Ibid.*, 6 July 1853.
[16] See *Reports & Accounts*, 4 September 1850, for a long statement by the Board in which defence against recent charges and justification of recent actions was attempted.

occasionally subjected to hostile letters, or enquiries about accounting practices. They always answered that they had *never* paid dividends out of capital receipts, that they had *never* exceeded their legal borrowing powers, and so on. Certainly they claimed too much, although some sympathy can be felt for the directors of the Manchester & Leeds. Their company was to serve an area with very good traffic potential and was in a much more favourable position than, for instance, the railways of East Anglia. The mania brought about tremendous problems; some of these problems are well known: the competing projects, the competing finished lines, the dilution of traffic, the financial crises, and the arrears of calls. In the letter of 1850 already quoted, the auditors pointed out that 'the state of arrears on calls necessarily creates very great intricacy in the Interest and Dividend Accounts'. Quite apart from the pressure of crises, the immense increase in share transactions, resulting from the great extension of share capital, must have created serious problems of administration as well as of accounting. In 1847 a resolution was put before the Finance Committee recommending increases in the salaries of clerks 'in consequence of the very great increase in the labours and responsibilities of the Transfer Office'.[17]

In addition, just as an undeveloped country is hampered today in its attempts to expand by a lack of good administrators, so did the railway companies of a country pioneering the new method of transport lack experienced employees. The concentration of railway development into comparatively short periods, during which the demand for railway equipment, materials and personnel of all sorts was very great, must have aggravated the problem. To make matters worse, railway clerks were inclined to abscond with cash and there were also many examples in the early years of dismissals of clerks, on the grounds of inaccuracy and carelessness, from the Secretary's Office and other departments. Sometimes it was said that an employee did his best, but was not good enough. More often there seemed to be no extenuating circumstances. If nothing else, the Manchester & Leeds could claim fame for having had the dubious honour of employing Patrick Branwell Brontë as a booking clerk in 1840 and 1841. A drunkard and, at least later in life, a drug addict, he did not last long.[18] It is not surprising that accounts varied and

---

[17] Proceedings of the Finance Committee, 4 August 1847.
[18] See *ibid.*, 9 October 1840 to 7 January 1842, for payment of Brontë's salary. He was, apparently, dismissed in January 1842 from Luddenden Foot station 'for carelessness and neglect of duty'. Cf. M. Lane, *The Brontë Story* (1953), and Mrs. Gaskell's famous *Life*, for further details of Brontë's ill-fated railway career, which had been announced so light-heartedly by Charlotte in 1840: 'A distant relation of mine, one Patrick Branwell, has set off to seek his fortune

were inaccurate, quite apart from any deliberate falsification. In April 1841 an assistant book-keeper was dismissed and another appointed;[19] in August the same year the new book-keeper was sacked.[20] These vicissitudes were still being recorded in the Finance Committee minutes in 1853.[21]

Knowledge of these difficulties may temper some of the criticisms of the railway companies, but it does not banish the problems created for the historian of railway finances by the many inconsistencies and by the expedients resorted to. These problems are fully covered in the Appendix, which presents a series of tables with explanatory notes. The tables contain statistics of receipts and expenditure, of capital structure, dividends and interest, which form the basis of the following analysis of the financial results of operating the Lancashire & Yorkshire Railway network.

II

TRAFFIC AND PROFITS

The Manchester & Leeds was projected in 1825 at the beginning of one of the greatest periods of economic expansion Britain has ever experienced. The first great boom associated with the railways, that of the mid-1820s, collapsed before the Company had been incorporated, but success came at the height of the second great mania of the nineteenth century in 1836. The line from Manchester to Normanton, near Leeds, was opened during an economic depression that was especially severe in Lancashire, which experienced all the upheavals of the turbulent 1840s: a decade of Chartist troubles, Plug Plot riot, growing prosperity, speculative mania, collapse of company flotation, and of financial crisis. Yet this same decade was noted for very rapid economic development at home, and for the virtual completion of the basic railway network of the country.

In this decade the Lancashire & Yorkshire emerged as a major company. The Manchester & Leeds did what most other railway companies did: it projected, it defended, it amalgamated. It started doing these things when business conditions were most favourable, when confidence was good, when funds were abundant. It con-

---

in the wild, wandering, adventurous, romantic knight-errant-like capacity of clerk on the Leeds and Manchester Railroad. Leeds and Manchester—where are they? Cities in the wilderness, like Tadmor, alias Palmyra—are they not?'
[19] Proceedings of the Finance Committee, 16 April 1841.
[20] *Ibid.*, 6 August 1841.
[21] *Ibid.*, 7 December 1853.

tinued, like so many other companies, to project, defend and amalgamate when all these conditions were disappearing. In 1847 it had become so big, on paper at any rate, that its Board decided that the time had come to adopt the sort of grandiloquent title that several other companies were taking. The new company, the Lancashire & Yorkshire, prosecuted with varying degrees of enthusiasm most of the schemes which had been sanctioned for its constituent companies in the years 1844 to 1847. Thus, in some of the worst years of its history, the Company found itself becoming one of the dozen largest railway companies in the country.

In 1850, just before 'The Great Victorian Boom' began, the Company's directors took stock. Their current building programme was now completed, after three or four most unpleasant years during which there had been local and national, railway and independent, enquiries into the whole railway set-up and the malpractices of boards of Directors in particular. Trade and industry had not suffered after 1845 as they had suffered in the years between 1840 and 1842. Conditions for the railways were, however, vastly different in 1850 from conditions in 1842: one of the worst years of the nineteenth century. In the year when Peel and Gladstone, in response to terrible economic conditions, embarked on a free trade policy that was to split their party, the Manchester & Leeds paid a 5 per cent dividend. In 1850, economically a much better year, the Lancashire & Yorkshire could manage only 2 per cent. Too many lines, at too great a cost, had been built; there was too much capital to be serviced by lines, the receipts of which were diluted by competition. It took the Company a long time to pull itself out of this depressed condition.

For the country, the 1850s was a decade of expansion at home and abroad, but the railways continued to struggle in the midst of these booming conditions. Not until the second half of 1856 did the net revenue of the Company afford a 5 per cent dividend, and in none of the years of this decade was there sufficient profit to pay 5 per cent over the whole twelve months. The Company shared in the boom of 1855 to 1857, but suffered a sharp reverse in 1858.

It appeared that the 1850s were well left behind when, during the second half of 1860, a 6 per cent dividend was paid for the first time since 1848. The American Civil War intervened, however, to ruin for a time the promise of the new decade. Lancashire's staple was cut off, and the Company suffered, along with most other businesses in Lancashire, which was affected far more than the country at large; it was, in 1862, almost 1842 again. For Britain the mid-1860's marked yet another period of rapid expansion, and even before the end of the Civil War the Lancashire & Yorkshire was sharing in the prosperity sweeping the country. There were still plenty of complaints about the slowness of much of Lancashire's business to recover, but, with the exception of 1869, the years from 1864 to the end of our period were prosperous for the Company. The expansion of 1870 to 1873 brought record dividends to the Lancashire & Yorkshire, although, as we shall see, there were in 1873 signs of a much less prosperous future. Already the increase in working expenses was outstripping the increase in gross traffic receipts. Net traffic receipts and net revenue actually declined in 1873 and the decline continued in 1874. 1873 was indeed a turning point; never again were the railways to enjoy prosperity such as they had experienced in 1872.

On the whole, the Company's operating results were a fairly sensitive economic indicator. There is one obvious qualification: the late 1840s and early 1850s were dominated by tremendous expansion in railway facilities which had temporarily outstripped the capacity of the economy to use them. The return on capital is not, therefore, a very good indicator, but the movement of the trade cycle can be seen in the movement of traffic receipts. By early 1857 the economy had caught up with the Lancashire & Yorkshire and the Company was having difficulty in coping with the increase in traffic. 1857 was the peak year of a trade cycle.

Although the Company took rather longer than the country as a whole to pull out of the effects of the American Civil War, its financial experience fairly closely follows the trade cycle pattern set out by Rostow: 'the setback of 1861–2 is to be regarded rather as an interruption in a major cycle expansion than as a minor cycle contraction. . . .'[22] The movement of gross traffic receipts of the Lancashire & Yorkshire between 1860 and 1866 conforms exactly to this pattern: peak in 1860, trough in 1862, rapid recovery to 1866. Conformity to the cycle is not always so close; it would be surprising if it were. Although the Lancashire & Yorkshire network was in the heart of the industrial system of the country, and its traffic figures therefore usually quickly reflected the ups and downs of the trade cycle, a nineteenth-century railway company's receipts could not, of course, be a perfect reflector of fluctuations in economic conditions. Its mileage and receipts might increase by amalgamation, and even a mileage increase as a result of economic expansion could distort the pattern of railway receipts, bearing in mind the time it takes to build a railway line. By the time of completion, general economic conditions might be worsening (in the nineteenth century they usually

[22] W. W. Rostow, *British Economy of the Nineteenth Century* (1948), p. 33.

were), but the new mileage would result in an increase in traffic receipts. Fares and charges might change and further distort the pattern of traffic receipts. These questions should be raised, but it is impossible to answer some of them. It is also impossible to isolate and analyse, for example, the results of working the original Manchester & Leeds line over the whole period, for the traffic figures do not exist. And even if they did one could never know how far these results were influenced by the feeding of its traffic from branch and other lines.

The method of dealing with the results is as follows: since the basis of the results is naturally the traffic receipts and the working expenses, these have been related in a narrative and compared with paid-up capital. Next, because the revenue account was not confined solely to traffic receipts and working expenses, and because it is of use to separate the loan capital and the interest paid on it, gross receipts and gross expenditure on revenue account are compared with one another, and also with capital paid up on all stock other than loan stock. This second analysis yields the net revenue applicable to dividends on ordinary and on guaranteed and preference stock. The next stage is to turn from the net revenue figures to the dividend and interest payments made by the Company from the balances which it had at its disposal. The difference between the net revenue figures and these balances is outlined in the Appendix. In brief, the former measure the annual results of operation, the latter also embrace surpluses carried forward, and depreciation allowances, which have been included in independent estimates of gross expenditure on revenue account, and therefore excluded from the net revenue figures.

The payments actually made as dividends and interest are linked with an analysis of the capital structure, and finally, further remarks are made on the vexed question of the payment of dividends out of capital, together with a comparison of expenditure and receipts on capital account, in order to ascertain how much scope the Company had for paying dividends out of capital.

Traffic Receipts and Working Expenses

Gross Traffic Receipts, Working Expenses and Net Traffic Receipts are given in Table 1 on p. 48. There are some fairly distinct trends in these figures. Most noticeable, and most interesting, are the movements in the ratio of working expenses to gross traffic receipts, which increased steadily between 1842 and 1850 from the low figure of

24 per cent to 40 per cent in 1849 and 1850. It is, perhaps, surprising that the percentage did not rise more in this period. The increase in the general level of prices in late 1846 and during 1847 was, however, apparently dominated by the rise in agricultural prices, and the tremendous expansion of railway building operations did not have the inflationary effect which might have been expected. Prices did rise rapidly, however, up to 1845, and the wages of the more skilled railway staff were enhanced by the great demand for drivers, engineers, firemen, and clerks. In March 1850 the directors of the Lancashire & Yorkshire put forward the following explanation of the increased percentage of working expenses:

> 'Your Directors feel it necessary to remark, in reference to the proportion of the working expenses of the half-year to its receipts, that the opening of new lines involved an immediate fixed charge for the requisite staff and working of trains, whilst the receipts from such lines for a considerable period must be necessarily small, and hence arises an increase in the percentage of working expenses' which would continue for some time after the beginning of operation.

Gross traffic receipts were also affected by the severe competition from other railways and from canals, and this again meant an increase in the relative burden of working expenses.

According to the Company, it was not the first time that such competition had affected receipts. Similar conditions had existed at the end of 1842 and early in 1843. A more detailed consideration of the various factors affecting the movement of receipts and working expenses is to follow; for the moment we are only concerned with the broad movement of working expenses. The Company was successful in its attempts to reduce these expenses in the 1850s, and they only once reached the proportion of 1849–50, and that was in the depressed year of 1858. In 1850, the building of lines was more or less finished for some time, and an added help was the increased level of rates which were authorised by Parliament in the same year. But prices were rising, especially in 1854, when the Company stated that there had been an extraordinary rise in the prices of labour and materials of all kinds employed in the manufacturing and repair shops. There was, therefore, to be no return to the low percentages of 1842–47.

It is not necessary to find price and wage inflation to explain every increase in the proportion of working expenses. Apart from the factor already mentioned, that of the staffing of a line at its opening, working expenses were often more prone to rise quickly when

TABLE 1

GROSS TRAFFIC RECEIPTS, WORKING EXPENSES,
AND NET TRAFFIC RECEIPTS, 1842 TO 1873

Year	Gross Traffic Receipts £000's	Working Expenses Amount £000's	Working Expenses % of G.T.R. %	Net Traffic Receipts Amount £000's	Net Traffic Receipts % of G.T.R. %
1842	227	55	24	172	76
1843	242	66	27	176	73
1844	289	77	27	212	73
1845	334	96	29	238	71
1846	338	106	31	232	69
1847	357	125	35	232	65
1848	443	159	36	284	64
1849	553	224	40	329	60
1850	740	300	40	440	60
1851	831	307	37	524	63
1852	885	341	38	544	62
1853	966	378	39	588	61
1854	1,014	391	38	623	62
1855	1,064	400	37	664	63
1856	1,178	436	37	742	63
1857	1,229	458	37	771	63
1858	1,224	492	40	732	60
1859	1,753	663	38	1,090	62
1860	1,954	740	38	1,214	62
1861	1,932	785	41	1,147	59
1862	1,719	701	41	1,018	59
1863	1,832	720	39	1,112	61
1864	2,024	775	38	1,249	62
1865	2,142	833	39	1,309	61
1866	2,386	920	38	1,466	62
1867	2,487	997	40	1,490	60
1868	2,563	1,106	43	1,457	57
1869	2,549	1,083	42	1,466	58
1870	2,653	1,153	43	1,500	57
1871	2,907	1,272	44	1,635	56
1872	3,164	1,437	45	1,727	55
1873	3,318	1,724	52	1,594	48

receipts were increasing than they were to fall when receipts were falling, as may be seen during the years 1861–63, 1868 and 1873. In order to see this more clearly, it is necessary to examine annual rates of change in Table 2 on p. 49. The explanation of these figures will include what there is to say on the problems of increased mileage,

TABLE 2

ANNUAL FLUCTUATIONS IN GROSS TRAFFIC RECEIPTS,
WORKING EXPENSES, AND NET TRAFFIC RECEIPTS,
1842 TO 1873

| | Annual Change in Gross T. R's | | Annual Change in Working Expenses | | Annual Change in Net T. R's | |
| | Amount | | Amount | | Amount | |
Year	£000's	%	£000's	%	£000's	%
1842	—	—	—	—	—	—
1843	15	7	11	20	4	2
1844	47	19	11	17	36	20
1845	45	15	19	25	26	12
1846	4	1	10	10	- 6	- 2
1847	19	6	19	18	0	0
1848	86	24	34	27	52	22
1849	110	25	65	41	45	16
1850	187	34	76	34	111	34
1851	91	12	7	2	84	19
1852	54	6	34	11	20	4
1853	81	9	37	11	44	8
1854	48	5	13	3	35	6
1855	50	5	9	2	41	6
1856	114	11	36	9	78	12
1857	51	4	22	5	29	4
1858	- 5	0	34	7	- 39	- 5
1859	539	43	171	35	358	49
1860	201	11	77	12	124	11
1861	- 22	- 1	45	6	- 67	- 5
1862	-213	-12	-84	-12	-129	-11
1863	113	6	19	3	94	9
1864	192	10	55	8	137	12
1865	118	6	58	7	60	5
1866	244	11	87	10	157	12
1867	101	4	77	8	24	2
1868	76	3	109	11	- 33	- 2
1869	- 14	0	-23	- 2	9	1
1870	104	4	70	6	34	2
1871	254	9	119	10	135	9
1872	257	9	165	13	92	6
1873	154	5	287	20	-133	- 8

amalgamations, and variations in rates and fares. There can be no
correction of the annual traffic receipts to allow for changes in
railway tariffs. Given the actual charges, and there were, of course,
thousands of these, it might be possible to compile series of 'real'

E

traffic receipts and working expenses, although the British Railways Board does not have the Company's rate books. The *Reports & Accounts* contain references to the rates and fares charged by the Lancashire & Yorkshire, but not a single figure is given, either of individual rates, or of general levels. Comparison of physical traffic returns with money income would be an imperfect guide and it has consequently not been attempted. To know the maximum rates and fares authorised by Parliament is again of little help, because the railway companies seem rarely to have charged the maxima; certainly the Manchester & Leeds and Lancashire & Yorkshire did not during the early 1840s. The directors' report of March 1842 stated that the Manchester & Leeds was adopting a policy of low fares and rates in order to induce large numbers of people to use its facilities. At a very early date the Company provided third-class facilities which were apparently better than those provided by most companies. This policy, it was insisted, was sound, because of the local nature of much of the Company's traffic: short hauls between the many towns of Lancashire and Yorkshire, short trips by the local populace of artisans, business people, and so forth. In 1846 it was said, in one of several references to the low rates and fares charged by the Company, that the policy of 'low fixed rates, irrespective of distance' was based on the penny postage idea.

The Board did not acknowledge in 1842 that the bad state of trade and industry had influenced its decision to adopt the 'low rate—many trips' system, but it is quite possible that the depression was of some importance. Between 1836 and 1842 the shareholders had patiently waited for some return on their capital. Unlike some other railway companies, the Company did not pay interest on calls, and unfortunately for them the line was opened during a depression. In 1843, when recovery had begun, gross traffic receipts increased by 7 per cent over 1842, but working expenses shot up by 20 per cent. In the first quarter of the year there had actually been a deficiency, and over the whole year net traffic receipts rose by only 2 per cent. Involved as it was in short-distance traffic, the Company, unlike other lines, such as the London & Birmingham, depended very much upon large passenger and tonnage figures, as distinct from passenger/miles and ton/miles. The competition suffered, particularly from December 1842, at the hands of the canal companies, was therefore all the more serious. The recovery in business was to a large extent offset by the 'excessive reduction in rates' caused by this competition. In addition to the canal companies, the Company had to keep an eye on the road-coach traffic, which proved to be an effective source of competition in the area.

Out of an increase in gross traffic receipts of £13,231 in the last six months of 1843, £11,533 came from the increase in goods traffic. Most railways expected to gain much of their revenue from goods traffic, and most were surprised to find that after a short while passenger receipts increased in importance. In 1844 gross traffic receipts rose rather faster than working expenses, and this was apparently due to the continued success of the developing passenger traffic, with the 1843 positions of goods and passenger receipts almost reversed. In the first half of 1845 the positions were yet again reversed, and of a total increase in receipts of, in round figures, £24,000, about £18,000 were derived from goods traffic. After the trade cycle had passed its peak, the increase, and later the maintenance of receipts, depended more on passenger traffic. The steep rise in working expenses was caused by the rise in prices and the difficulty the Company had in coping with the increased traffic: it was found that there were not enough wagons and carriages, which presumably meant shorter and more frequent trains. The Company also pushed up the proportion of working expenses by 'an important reduction', early in 1845, 'on the Passenger fares and in the rates on certain classes of Merchandise, . . .'

1846 was a depressed year, and there were many influences working against the prosperity of the Company. There was a decline of 2 per cent in net traffic receipts, compared with 1845, and these receipts, expressed as a percentage of paid-up capital, fell from 7 per cent to 5 per cent. In the first half of the year goods traffic receipts declined but were just compensated for by an increase in receipts from the passenger traffic. Receipts had also suffered from the inactive state of the corn trade and from a reduction in the shipment of twist and manufactured goods in some of the spring months. Yet another adverse factor was the imposition by Parliament of new, reduced maximum fares and rates. While the opening of the Ashton branch in the second half of the year had helped to mitigate some of these adverse effects, the competition from the new Sheffield & Manchester, and Leeds & Bradford, lines had stimulated them.

All in all, 1846 was a gloomy year, nationally and locally, and it was a portent. By mid-1847 the Lancashire & Yorkshire was working 121 miles of line, compared with the 50 or so of three years earlier, but financially 1847 was a worse year than 1846, as reference to Table 3, p. 53, will show. In spite of the greatly increased mileage, gross traffic receipts rose by only £19,000 over 1846, and the whole of this was absorbed by increased working expenses. The public, the directors maintained, was enjoying the improved accommodation provided for £50,000 less per annum than before—all at the Company's expense. This was the product of the Government's inter-vention to reduce fares and rates in 1846, in the last six months of which the Company had carried 233,515 more passengers and yet had received £3,125 less than in the last half of 1845. The effects were even worse in 1847, but the major factor was, of course, the poor state of the economy from the spring of 1846 onwards. For the Company, trade appeared to be, no doubt exaggeratedly, in a state of 'unexampled stagnation' in 1848; yet the Board seemed satisfied as income had not diminished. Gross traffic receipts had risen and were to increase by £86,000, or 24 per cent for the whole year, but, since by September 1848 the mileage worked by the Company had increased to 173, some increase in receipts was surely warranted. Further stagnation would have brought near bankruptcy.

Another reason why the Board had no cause to congratulate itself unduly was that after 1845 it had taken on certain white elephants. Since the January of that year, it had contracted agreements with the Manchester & Bolton, the North Union, and the Preston & Wyre railway companies, and had so far lost something in the region of £67,000 as a result. 'Defence of territorial integrity' etc., would no doubt be the arguments used to justify these agreements, but one is entitled to wonder just how far, given efficient working by the Company, failure to have taken over these small companies would have injured the Manchester & Leeds.

In 1847, 1848 and 1849 the increase in gross traffic receipts was almost entirely due to the operation of new lines and branches. Furthermore, in each of these years the rate of increase in working expenses exceeded that in gross traffic receipts, although at first sight annual increases in net traffic receipts of 22, 16, and 34 per cent, in 1848, 1849 and 1850 respectively, appear quite creditable.[23] What this represented in terms of a return on all the capital expended may be seen from Table 3. The decline in the fortunes of the Company in 1846 is clearly shown by the decrease in return on capital from 6·9 to 4·7 per cent, and from the end of 1846 until the end of 1849 net traffic receipts yielded only 3 per cent per annum on the fast-growing capital. The over-expansion of capital is evident from the figures for 1850 and 1851, which were years of increasing prosperity; the rate of return was an improvement on the three preceding years but was still low.

From 1846 until 1849 economic conditions were poor, and the expansion of capital and dilution of receipts worsened an already unfavourable situation. In these years, the Board stated, the number of passengers and the amount of freight conveyed on the Manchester

[23] See above, Table 2, p. 49.

TABLE 3

NET TRAFFIC RECEIPTS AND TOTAL PAID-UP
CAPITAL, 1842 TO 1873

Year	A Total Paid-up Capital £000's	B Net Traffic Receipts £000's	B as % of A
1842	2,963	172	5·8
1843	3,100	176	5·7
1844	3,205	212	6·6
1845	3,430	238	6·9
1846	4,948	232	4·7
1847	7,554	232	3·1
1848	9,272	284	3·1
1849	10,644	329	3·1
1850	11,625	440	3·8
1851	11,770	524	4·4
1852	11,768	544	4·6
1853	12,050	588	4·9
1854	12,273	623	5·1
1855	12,692	664	5·2
1856	12,820	742	5·8
1857	13,546	771	5·7
1858	13,689	732	5·3
1859	18,246	1,090	6·0
1860	18,816	1,214	6·0
1861	19,158	1,147	6·0
1862	19,459	1,018	5·2
1863	19,663	1,112	5·6
1864	20,052	1,249	6·2
1865	20,384	1,309	6·4
1866	22,087	1,466	6·6
1867	22,452	1,490	6·6
1868	22,747	1,457	6·4
1869	23,044	1,466	6·4
1870	23,288	1,500	6·5
1871	23,902	1,635	6·8
1872	24,254	1,727	7·1
1873	25,333	1,594	6·3

& Leeds *proper* had been nearly stationary, and the directors were well aware of the unfortunate financial effects of a stationary income at a time when capital was rapidly growing. These effects continued, however, even in 1850 and 1851, when gross traffic receipts went up by £278,000, an increase which was due in part to expansion of mileage but also to improving economic conditions. In early 1850 competition from railway and canal companies was still strong, but the age of agreement was near. The directors were now hopeful that the proportion of working expenses could be decreased. Firstly, Parliament had authorised an increase in rates; secondly, the Company had made arrangements with neighbouring companies to end 'the ruinous competition' of the last twelve months, and thirdly, the effects of opening so many lines at once should gradually lessen.

By the end of 1850 the Company was working 268 miles of line, and the receipts on 225 of these went exclusively to the Lancashire & Yorkshire. In this year both gross traffic receipts and working expenses increased by 34 per cent and net traffic receipts went up proportionately. The holder of ordinary stock must have wished that all capital had received the same rate of return. But at this time the Company was paying out bonus dividends on £20 Preference Fifths[24] as well as meeting a heavy interest burden (on loans contracted at a time of high interest rates), and the ordinary shareholder received not 4 per cent, but 2 per cent. Still, there was improvement, and this continued into 1851. For the first time since 1844 gross traffic receipts showed a greater rate of increase than working expenses (12 to 2 per cent) and net traffic receipts went up by 19 per cent.

For the rest of the 1850s the efforts to keep working expenses down were partially successful. In four of the eight years, gross traffic receipts increased faster than the expenses. Now the rate of return of net traffic receipts on paid-up capital was between $4\frac{1}{2}$ and 6 per cent in each year, and traffic gradually caught up with the facilities provided. With the exception of 1858, which was a depressed year, dividends on ordinary stock were more than 4 per cent between 1855 and 1859 inclusive. 1856 was the best year of the 1850s for the Company (early 1857 saw the peak of a trade cycle), when gross traffic receipts increased by £114,000, working expenses by only £36,000, and the dividend was $4\frac{3}{4}$ per cent. In fact, traffic was now overtaking facilities. In March 1857 the Board stated:[25]

> 'The increase in the Traffic, which occasionally has exceeded the Company's power to move it, has necessitated the provision of increased accommodation in the Shape of Engines, Carriages, and Wagons.'

But already conditions were changing, and while 1857 as a whole yielded a $4\frac{5}{8}$ per cent dividend, this is an average of 5 per cent in the first half, and $4\frac{1}{4}$ per cent in the second half. Working expenses went up faster than gross traffic receipts, and continued to rise while the

[24] See Appendix, pp. 189–90.   [25] *Reports & Accounts*, 4 March 1857.

receipts were falling by £5,000 in 1858. They were once again displaying their familiar characteristic of continuing to rise when traffic receipts were more or less stationary. The result was a decline of 5 per cent in net traffic receipts and a dividend of 3⅞, in 1858. 'Unfortunate Competition' was once again to the fore: naturally, when receipts were declining the existence of any neighbouring company must have seemed doubly unfortunate. Since the mileage on which the Company earned income was now 257, it was bound to be in competition with a considerable number of networks. Rates were reduced, and the Lancashire & Yorkshire was again experiencing the unfortunate truth that it is much more difficult to cut services than it is to expand them. Moreover, as we shall see, the Company was reluctant in 1861 to sack workers merely because business conditions were temporarily depressed, and this may have been influencing the ratio of working expenses in earlier years.

From 1859 until early 1861 trade was increasingly prosperous. The amalgamation of the Lancashire & Yorkshire and East Lancashire companies in mid-1859 (the accounts were amalgamated from the beginning of the year) brought a favourable increase in receipts relative to working expenses, and 1860 was also a good year. In 1859 it was found that the cost of coal, coke and firewood had been reduced by nearly £8000. In 1860, Parliamentary proceedings and extensive repairs and improvements of working stock resulted in working expenses increasing at a rate only slightly faster than that of gross traffic receipts. As so often happened, another of the Board's 'unfortunate occurrences' intervened to spoil the situation. This time it was the American Civil War which brought financial troubles. Early in 1861 the very severe weather had already retarded an otherwise satisfactory increase in receipts, and had increased working expenses. No sooner was this over than Civil War broke out in the United States. Efforts to reduce working expenses were, the Board said, 'impeded by the want of cordiality, well known to exist, among Railway Companies'.[26] Presumably the directors meant that companies endeavoured to attract traffic by cutting rates and fares. The combined Lancashire & Yorkshire and East Lancashire companies now owned and operated over 360 miles of network in an area which was served also by leading companies such as the London & North-Western and the Midland. Its difficulties with these and other lines were described in Chapter 1.

In the last six months of 1861 receipts fell by just under £49,000, but[27]

[26] *Reports & Accounts*, 14 August 1861.
[27] *Ibid.*, 19 February 1862.

'Working expenses have been unusually heavy, . . . the expectation of an early arrangement of the unhappy differences in
America prevented for a time the reduction of Staff, etc. . . .'

Although the first half of the year had been a good time for traffic,
the result of the inaction of the Board over working expenses was
that, while in 1861 gross traffic receipts declined by only £22,000, net
traffic receipts fell by £67,000. Making matters worse for the holder
of ordinary stock was the increasing proportion of preference and
guaranteed stock in total paid-up capital. If, six months earlier, the
Company had thought that it was a most unsatisfactory business to
dismiss workers immediately receipts started falling off, it soon had
to change its mind. The fall in gross traffic receipts was very considerable in 1862 and it represented a reduction of 12 per cent over
the already low figure of 1861. But by now the Board was taking
steps to cut the cost of running the railway, and working expenses
were cut by the same margin.

The crisis had been restricted to Lancashire; in Yorkshire the
traffic was steadily maintained, and the woollen industry benefited
from the cotton industry's misery. In 1863 there was a fairly substantial recovery of receipts. This was not due to any increase in mileage,
which remained at 362, and the same applied to 1864, when a very
large increase in gross traffic receipts was recorded. By now the
Company had more than made up the ground it had lost in 1861 and
1862, but even after the war had ended the cotton trade was subject
to frequent fluctuations, and it was not until early 1866 that the
directors believed the effects of the war to have ended. The rate of
return of net traffic receipts on total paid-up capital had fallen from
6 per cent in 1861 to 5·2 and 5·6 per cent in 1862 and 1863. In 1864
and in 1865 it averaged 6·3 per cent,[28] but the Company had suffered
because the rate of return would have been even higher if it had not
been unlucky enough to be mainly Lancashire company. From 1863
until 1866 it maintained a good rate of increase in gross traffic
receipts, compared with working expenses, and its dividends went up.
It was not until 1866, however that it shared fully in the boom that was
to have such unfortunate effects for so many companies, including
railways. Its gross traffic receipts increased by almost a quarter of a
million, and its net traffic receipts jumped by 12 per cent.

The expansion slowed down in 1867. The boom had broken after
the financial crisis of the previous year, and industry was less

[28] The network mileage increased to 403 in 1865, but this was only an apparent
increase: most of the mileage was that of the North Union and Preston & Wyre
companies, the receipts from which have been included in all the traffic receipts
given in the tables.

prosperous. The Company had, towards the end of 1866, increasingly felt the effects of the rise in wages, and in the prices of materials used in the maintenance of rolling stock. The increasing burden of working expenses was now to be felt, almost without break, until the end of our period. Costs rose so much in 1868 that their absolute increase exceeded that of gross traffic receipts; this had only happened three times before in the history of the Company. The increase in wages had been felt since later 1866. In 1867 they went up further, and for the second half of the year the wage increases for engine drivers and firemen alone cost the Company more than £5,000.[29] Fuel and such items as fodder for horses also cost much more.

In the period 1867 to 1873 inclusive there was only one year, 1869, in which working expenses did not rise faster than gross traffic receipts. This trend was to lead the Company into great difficulties in the later 1870s and 1880s, but after the recovery from the depression of 1869 the Company enjoyed four years of unexampled prosperity. In the six years between 1868 and 1873 only 25 miles of line were added to the network, and the bulk of the increase in traffic receipts was caused by the great economic expansion of 1870 to 1873. In both 1871 and 1872, gross traffic receipts increased by over a quarter of a million pounds: a figure which had been approached only once before, in 1866.[30] The ordinary shareholder at last came into his own, but his joy was to be short-lived. After the downturn in 1873, dividends fell, until in the 1880s 3 per cent was the order of the day.

Concern was expressed in the quiet of the committee rooms of the Company, as well as in the directors' Reports, about the course of working expenses. Time and again it was hoped that the rise in costs was at an end, but in 1873 they rose by £287,000: £133,000 more than gross traffic receipts. This 20 per cent increase was the greatest since the old days of 1847–50,[31] and it heralded the financial doldrums.

It is apparent that one of the major problems the Company faced in our period was the 'stickiness' of working expenses. It was suggested by one writer of the 1860s, who was quoted above on p. 38 that if there were a true allocation of expenses between capital and revenue accounts, the average proportion of expenses on the railways would be not far short of 60 per cent. If he meant gross expenditure on revenue account then, as the figures in Table 4 on

[29] *Reports & Accounts*, 19 February 1868.
[30] The increase in 1859 is to be discounted, since it resulted from an amalgamation of already operating lines.
[31] Again, the increase of 1859 must be discounted because of the amalgamation of the Lancashire & Yorkshire and the East Lancashire; and it was, in any case, less than the increase in gross traffic receipts.

p. 59 show, he was absolutely correct. But the ratios of working expenses given in Table 1 on p. 48 remain well below 50 per cent until the end of our period, and it is difficult to believe that the Lancashire & Yorkshire could have built its lines, as it undoubtedly did, and at the same time paid dividends from capital *over a long period*. In the later 1840s there is practically no doubt that fairly large sums were misapplied, but it is not believed that there was the same malpractice after 1850—if only because there was not the same scope. As it is, the 'stickiness' of costs, and their undue increase, caused a decline in net traffic receipts in six of the thirty-two years under review. In only two years did costs decline, and in 1873 they jumped to over 50 per cent.

The Revenue and Net Revenue Accounts

The basis of revenue was, of course, the traffic receipts, but gross revenue was rather larger. Also, we come nearer to the fortunes of the shareholder with our definition of gross expenditure on revenue account. This expenditure includes interest paid on loans and, later in the period, on Debenture Stock, and also the depreciation allowances that were made. Net traffic receipts were applicable to all these charges; by deducting them from gross receipts on revenue account together with other outgoings, including working expenses, we approach the amount the Company had left for the often unhappy shareholder. The net revenue figures were calculated (the reader is reminded that they are not figures issued by the Company)[32] to assess the *annual* fortunes of the Lancashire & Yorkshire.

Table 4 gives gross receipts, gross expenditure and net revenue together with the ratios of the last two to gross receipts. One of the first things that strikes one is the contrasting movements of gross expenditure and of working expenses[33] between 1842 and 1848. Working expenses increased as a proportion of gross traffic receipts throughout the 1840s, but gross expenditure declined as a proportion of gross receipts on revenue account from 1842 to 1848, after which it increased to its highest point of the period, in 1850. This is largely due to the decline in the interest burden in the years 1845 to 1848, inclusive, and then to its great rise in 1849 and 1850. More will be said on this later.

After the high point of 1850 the gross expenditure ratio declined

---

[32] He is also reminded that notes explaining the completion of all the tables are in the Appendix.

[33] See Table 1, p. 48.

TABLE 4

GROSS RECEIPTS AND GROSS EXPENDITURE ON REVENUE ACCOUNT, AND NET REVENUE, 1842 TO 1873

Year	Gross Revenue £000's	Gross Expenditure		Net Revenue	
		Amount £000's	% of Gross Rev. %	Amount £000's	% of Gross Rev. %
1842	232	174	75	58	25
1843	249	169	68	80	32
1844	291	189	65	102	35
1845	339	201	59	138	41
1846	341	180	53	161	47
1847	360	183	51	177	49
1848	446	231	52	215	48
1849	561	345	61	216	39
1850	752	561	75	191	25
1851	878	600	68	278	32
1852	923	635	69	288	31
1853	1,000	651	65	349	35
1854	1,048	645	61	403	39
1855	1,091	685	63	406	37
1856	1,209	728	60	481	40
1857	1,255	770	61	485	39
1858	1,242	810	65	432	35
1859	1,754	1,078	61	676	39
1860	1,956	1,137	58	819	42
1861	1,943	1,179	61	764	39
1862	1,725	1,122	65	603	35
1863	1,839	1,132	61	707	39
1864	2,039	1,183	53	856	47
1865	2,162	1,268	59	894	41
1866	2,408	1,392	58	1,016	42
1867	2,499	1,469	59	1,030	41
1868	2,570	1,497	58	1,073	42
1869	2,554	1,462	57	1,092	43
1870	2,675	1,527	57	1,148	43
1871	2,918	1,662	57	1,256	43
1872	3,185	1,823	57	1,362	43
1873	3,333	2,111	63	1,222	37

irregularly until the mid-1850s, partly because the interest burden was decreasing, and partly because costs were no longer absorbing such a high proportion of the increase in gross traffic receipts. The influence of the interest burden is clearly brought out by a comparison of the movement of the ratios of working expenses, and of gross expenditure year by year. They by no means move identically in the 1850s. In the early 1860s there is a much closer conformity between the proportions of working expenses and gross expenditure. This is caused by the steadiness of the interest burden, and throughout the 1860s, in fact, gross expenditure moved directly with working expenses. In 1870, 1871 and 1872, however, the ratio of gross expenditure to gross revenue remained constant. The interest burden declined in 1870, and in 1871 and 1872 it rose at a much slower rate than did working expenses. This helped, so far as net revenue was concerned, to mitigate the effects of the steep rise in working expenses. In 1873, however, the rise in working expenses was so steep that it swamped a decrease in the interest burden and pushed up the proportion of gross expenditure from 57 to 63 per cent.

The annual fluctuations and rates of change in gross revenue, gross expenditure and net revenue are shown in Table 5 on p. 61. There are some contrasts between the movement of these figures and those in Table 2 (p. 49). Gross expenditure on revenue account declined more often than working expenses; the same number of times, in fact, as net revenue. In contrast, net traffic receipts fell in six years, working expenses in only two. It may also be noticed that net traffic receipts and net revenue did not always decline in the same years. On the other hand, gross revenue and gross traffic receipts moved in much the same way throughout the period. The close conformity of the patterns of gross traffic receipts and gross revenue is explained simply by the overwhelming preponderance of traffic receipts in gross revenue. The same does not apply to gross expenditure and working expenses. While the latter were the most important element in expenditure on revenue account, the interest burden was also important, and its fluctuations at times offset movements in working expenses. For instance, in 1846 working expenses rose by more than gross traffic receipts, and net traffic receipts therefore declined. But gross expenditure on revenue account fell by 10 per cent, and net revenue increased by 17 per cent, in spite of the failure of gross revenue to rise.

Offsetting, however, the benefit derived from this decrease in the interest burden chargeable to revenue in some years is the fact that annual increases of gross expenditure absorbed, or nearly absorbed, annual increments of gross revenue rather more often than working expenses absorbed traffic receipts. The most serious examples of this occurred in 1849 and 1850. In 1849 gross traffic receipts rose by £110,000, and net traffic receipts by £45,000; gross revenue increased by £115,000, but gross expenditure absorbed the

TABLE 5

ANNUAL FLUCTUATIONS IN GROSS REVENUE
AND GROSS EXPENDITURE ON REVENUE ACCOUNT,
AND IN NET REVENUE, 1842 TO 1873

Year	Annual Change in Gross Revenue Amount £000's	%	Annual Change in Gross Expenditure Amount £000's	%	Annual Change in Net Revenue Amount £000's	%
1842	—	—	—	—	—	—
1843	17	7	− 5	− 3	22	38
1844	42	17	20	12	22	27
1845	48	16	12	6	36	35
1846	2	0	− 21	−10	23	17
1847	19	5	3	2	16	10
1848	86	24	48	26	38	21
1849	115	26	114	49	1	0
1850	191	34	216	62	− 25	−11
1851	126	17	39	7	87	45
1852	45	5	35	6	10	3
1853	77	8	16	2	61	21
1854	48	5	− 6	− 1	54	15
1855	43	4	40	6	3	1
1856	118	11	43	6	75	18
1857	46	4	42	6	4	1
1858	− 13	− 1	40	5	− 53	−11
1859	512	41	268	33	244	56
1860	202	11	59	5	143	21
1861	− 13	− 1	42	4	− 55	− 7
1862	−218	−11	− 57	− 5	−161	−21
1863	114	7	10	1	104	17
1864	200	11	51	4	149	21
1865	123	6	85	7	38	4
1866	246	11	124	10	122	14
1867	91	4	77	5	14	1
1868	71	3	28	2	43	4
1869	− 16	− 1	− 35	− 2	19	2
1870	121	5	65	4	56	5
1871	243	9	135	9	108	9
1872	267	9	161	10	106	8
1873	148	5	288	16	−140	−10

whole of this increase, and net revenue was stationary. The following
year, 1850, was even worse. Gross and net traffic receipts went up by
£187,000 and £111,000 respectively; but while gross revenue in-

TABLE 6

RETURN ON PAID-UP SHARE CAPITAL, 1842 TO 1873

Year	A Paid-up Share Capital £000's	B Net Revenue £000's	B as % of A
1842	1,336	58	4·3
1843	1,339	80	6·0
1844	1,368	102	7·4
1845	1,613	138	8·5
1846	3,271	161	4·9
1847	5,180	177	3·4
1848	6,879	215	3·1
1849	8,032	216	2·7
1850	8,462	191	2·2
1851	8,654	278	3·2
1852	8,925	288	3·2
1853	9,253	349	3·8
1854	9,474	403	4·2
1855	9,506	406	4·3
1856	9,518	481	5·0
1857	10,170	485	4·8
1858	10,353	432	4·2
1859	13,935	676	4·8
1860	14,292	819	5·7
1861	14,731	764	5·2
1862	14,839	603	4·1
1863	15,088	707	4·7
1864	15,254	856	5·6
1865	15,554	894	5·7
1866	16,751	1,016	6·0
1867	16,851	1,030	6·1
1868	17,076	1,073	6·3
1869	17,369	1,092	6·3
1870	17,634	1,148	6·5
1871	17,904	1,256	7·0
1872	18,383	1,362	7·4
1873	19,162	1,222	6·4

creased by £191,000, gross expenditure soared from £345,000 to £561,000, an increase of £216,000. The result was that net revenue dropped £25,000, or 11 per cent. The existence of the loan debt was obviously a mixed blessing, but the absolute decline in the interest burden after 1851 to some extent compensated the shareholders for the poor financial return they had had in the preceding years.

Fluctuations in the interest burden were henceforth not to have the influence they exercised between the years 1842 and 1851.

Next we turn to the rate of return of net revenue on all forms of share capital—ordinary, preference, and guaranteed. Many of the influences which governed this rate of return have already been fully explained in the chronological discussion of traffic receipts and of expenditure and revenue on revenue account, but there are some additional remarks to make about Table 6. The average rate over the whole period was obviously far from princely: for exactly half the period it was under 5 per cent, and in seven years it was less than 4. In only eleven years did it reach 6 per cent, or more, and eight of these were concentrated between 1866 and 1873. An important cause of these poor results was the well-known tendency of nineteenth-century capitalism to concentrate capital investment in limited sectors of the economy during the expansion phases of the decennial trade cycles. With the upswing of the cycle, schemes would be proposed and investment decisions made; the bulk of the capital would be raised and most of the building would take place during the decline, and it would not be until the peak of the next trade cycle that the economy would catch up with the facilities provided. One can see this trend in the receipts and the return on capital. The expansion of the 1840s was, however, exceptional because the economy took longer to catch up. Even so the buoyancy of the British economy of the nineteenth century triumphed in a comparatively short time, considering the amount of investment in railways between 1844 and 1852. By 1857 there was need for further facilities on the Lancashire & Yorkshire network, but the financial stringency between 1846 and 1850 caused a revolt among the shareholders against the amount of capital expenditure undertaken by their Company. Committees of investigation were formed, and one of them bluntly said:[34]

> 'It would be a dereliction of duty not to state that they do not look with confidence to the future prosperity of the Lancashire and Yorkshire Railway Company under its present system of management.'

Whether all the charges made by some of these committees were true (other committees reported favourably on the conduct of the Board, and on the management of the Company) is not as important as the effect that they had. From the point of view of investigators the period was exceptional; but then it was from most points of view. Never before had there been such expansion of the railway system

[34] *Report of the Committee of Consultation: Appointed by the Meeting of Shareholders . . . March 6th 1850* (*1850*).

and so enormous a concentration of capital expenditure on one sector of the economy. If there had been much more capital expenditure, receipts and net revenue might never have caught up with the capital expansion. This may be an exaggeration, but it must be remembered that the Company achieved a modest 5 per cent return on paid-up share capital only once in the fourteen years between 1846 and 1859.

Dividend and Interest Payments

So far two sets of figures representing rates of return have been tabulated: net traffic receipts on total paid-up capital, and net revenue on total paid-up *share* capital. The Appendix explains that the purpose of the net revenue figures is to discover what sort of return the Company made, taking the revenue year by year. But there were surpluses—money carried forward, and sums set aside for depreciation which the Company unwisely used from time to time to meet dividend payments. The net revenue figures do not contain any surpluses. The amounts the Company disposed to meet dividends and depreciation were termed 'Balances Applicable to . . .'[35] and from these balances the dividends on ordinary and on guaranteed and preference capital were paid.

In Table 7 the amount of money paid as dividend is expressed as a percentage of all paid-up share capital, some of which was not, however, receiving a return. The object of the table is to determine the return on capital over the whole period. These percentages therefore differ from the *declared* dividends (which are to be found in Table 8 on p. 68). Nevertheless, although paid-up capital was supposed to qualify for payment only when lines were completed and in operation, problems arise because this principle was sometimes ignored between 1846 and 1849. The interest on loan capital is treated in a similar way, and similar problems are involved. Until 1846 the figures show fair returns on capital. In the first three years, between 1842 and 1844, paid-up share capital increased by only £32,000, and since business was increasingly prosperous until late 1845, the amount paid out in dividends was quite a good return. In 1844 loans had been obtained for as little as $3\frac{1}{4}$ per cent, and the drop in the average rate paid to 4·3 per cent in 1845 was a genuine reduction in the total interest burden. The hopes of the directors of the Manchester & Leeds were being fully realised.

In 1845 came the decision to replace the mortgage debt of the

[35] See Appendix, Table VII, p. 182.

TABLE 7

DIVIDENDS AND INTEREST PAID, 1842 TO 1873

Year	A Paid-up Share Capital £000's	Dividends Paid Amount £000's	% of A	B Paid-up Loan Capital £000's	Interest Paid Amount £000's	% of B
1842	1,336	75	5·6	1,627	80	4·9
1843	1,339	85	6·3	1,761	88	5·0
1844	1,368	101	7·4	1,837	92	5·0
1845	1,613	115	7·1	1,817	78	4·3
1846	3,271	172	5·3	1,677	53	3·2
1847	5,180	204	3·9	2,374	39	1·6
1848	6,879	215	3·1	2,393	34	1·4
1849	8,032	227	2·8	2,612	63	2·8
1850	8,462	183	2·2	3,163	134	4·2
1851	8,654	260	3·0	3,116	144	4·6
1852	8,925	306	3·4	2,843	133	4·7
1853	9,253	347	3·7	2,797	123	4·4
1854	9,474	387	4·1	2,799	117	4·2
1855	9,506	422	4·4	3,186	129	4·0
1856	9,518	475	5·0	3,302	138	4·2
1857	10,170	483	4·7	3,376	145	4·3
1858	10,353	440	4·2	3,336	150	4·5
1859	13,935	674	4·8	4,311	191	4·4
1860	14,292	806	5·6	4,524	188	4·1
1861	14,731	765	5·2	4,527	194	4·3
1862	14,839	611	4·1	4,620	190	4·1
1863	15,088	698	4·6	4,575	186	4·1
1864	15,254	872	5·7	4,798	191	4·0
1865	15,554	880	5·6	4,830	202	4·0
1866	16,751	1,012	6·0	5,336	215	4·0
1867	16,851	1,034	6·1	5,601	235	4·2
1868	17,076	1,075	6·3	5,671	241	4·3
1869	17,369	1,087	6·3	5,675	239	4·2
1870	17,634	1,134	6·4	5,654	235	4·1
1871	17,904	1,272	7·1	5,998	239	4·0
1872	18,383	1,364	7·4	5,971	246	4·1
1873	19,162	1,224	6·4	6,171	243	3·9

Company by stock (the £20 Preference Fifths) which should have a preference for a limited period. The amount of paid-up loan capital declined in 1845 and 1846, and the paid-up share capital increased by a large amount in 1846. The new policy was short-lived because the amount borrowed rose steeply in 1847, but its effects were to last for

F

much longer. From 1845 the returns, both of dividend and interest, on a rapidly expanding total paid-up capital, decreased sharply during the next five years. To repeat, not all the paid-up share capital was legally eligible for dividends. The large amounts raised in 1846, 1847, and even in 1848, were 'unproductive'[36] for a while: they represented lines which were not built or not completed until the years 1848–50. The Company was in fact paying out dividends on the Preference Fifths, which were largely 'unproductive' or 'non-productive'.[37] It is almost certain that it was also paying either interest on calls, or a bonus dividend, on the shares of some of the companies which it had taken over.

The rate of return on the loan capital is certainly understated in 1846, 1847 and 1848, and probably also in 1849. The Company was servicing a considerable proportion of its loan debt out of capital. This it was legally entitled to do, if that proportion was genuinely 'unproductive',[38] but it seems certain that in 1848 some of the 'productive' loan capital was serviced from capital receipts. It is true that the amount of 'productive' loan capital may well have decreased or risen only moderately in 1847 and 1848, because the rise in total loan capital was the result of borrowing under the powers of the many Acts obtained in the years 1845–47 and much of this capital would still be serviced from capital receipts in 1847 and 1848 pending the completion of the lines, and because the receipts on the Preference Fifths were now coming in and these shares were replacing the old mortgage debt. But the figure of £34,000 for 1848 is extremely low, and in these years the opportunities for misapplying capital receipts were so numerous and the accounts so confused and inadequate (most probably deliberately so) that the verdict must go against the Company.

In 1849 and 1850 practically all the capital became 'productive' and still the rate of return on share capital was very poor. In 1850 it fell as low as 2·2 per cent, which corresponds almost exactly with the declared dividend of 2 per cent. After 1850 the figures are, in comparison, perfectly comprehensible.

Over the whole period the shareholder was better off by 1·3 or 1·2 per cent per annum. This was, however, a small differential considering the nature of the investments, and it must be remembered that many shareholders who entered the market for the first time in

[36] 'Productive', 'unproductive', and 'non-productive', were all terms used by the Board. See Appendix, pp. 189–90.
[37] See Appendix, pp. 189–90 and 191–92.
[38] In contrast to the treatment of unproductive *share* capital, none of which should have received any return at all, unproductive *loan* capital was conventionally serviced from capital receipts. See Appendix, pp. 193-95.

the mid-1840s must have suffered considerable losses. Until the gradual conversion of debentures into Debenture Stock, which did not become important until the later 1860s, the debenture holder could regain his capital unimpaired at the end of his debenture term. Most held their debentures for three or five years; and yet on the average they received only 1 per cent or so less than the shareholder, who could only regain his capital—possibly considerably reduced—by selling his shares. There were many years in which it would not have been wise to sell. Relative to the debenture holder, the shareholder only came into his own in the early 1870s, and even this prosperity was of brief duration; by the 1880s the ordinary stock of the Company was less valuable than it had been in the 1850s.

Average paid-up share capital, 1842–73,[39] including 1846–48	£11,192,000
Average paid-up share capital, 1842–73, excluding 1846–48	11,821,000
Average dividend, including 1846–48	594,000
Average dividend, excluding 1846–48	635,000
Average dividend per cent, including 1846–48	5·3
Average dividend per cent, excluding 1846–48	5·4
Average paid-up loan capital, 1842–73, including 1846–48	3,821,000
Average paid-up loan capital, 1842–73, excluding 1846–48	3,994,000
Average interest, including 1846–48	155,000
Average interest, excluding 1846–48	167,000
Average interest per cent, including 1846–48	4·0
Average interest per cent, excluding 1846–48	4·2

So far we have not distinguished between the ordinary and the preference and guaranteed shareholders. The rates of return and the dividend declared on ordinary stock are given in Table 8. The return calculated as a percentage of paid-up ordinary capital is identical with the dividend declared by the Company in 1842 and 1843, and almost identical in 1844, when the paid-up share capital of the Company increased by a very small amount. In 1845 the great rise in capital began, and the difference between the dividend and the rate of return on ordinary stock is caused by the legitimate omission by the Company of the new capital from the dividend. It may once again be remarked how good were the prospects of the Manchester & Leeds at this time. 1844 was far from being a boom year; but it

[39] The inclusion or exclusion of the awkward years of 1846–48 makes very little difference to the percentages, but the two sets of figures are given because of the unreliability of the accounts for those years.

was a prosperous one, and the Manchester & Leeds paid a 7½ per cent dividend, which next year rose to 8 per cent. Until 1845 the guaranteed and preference capital of the Company was limited to the amount paid up on the 1841 preference £25 shares, and the business and finances of the Manchester & Leeds were in a sound and uncomplicated state.

TABLE 8

DIVIDENDS ON PAID-UP ORDINARY, AND GUARANTEED AND PREFERENCE CAPITAL, 1842 TO 1873

Year	Ordinary Stock			Declared Div. %	Guaran. and Pref. Stock		
	Capital £000's	Dividend £000's	%		Capital £000's	Dividend £000's	%
1842	1,299	71	5·5	5½	37	4	10·0
1843	1,300	81	6·2	6¼	39	4	10·0
1844	1,329	97	7·3	7½	39	4	10.0
1845	1,574	111	7·0	8	39	4	10·0
1846	2,752	98	3·6	7	519	74	14·2
1847	4,552	130	2·8	7	628	74	11·8
1848	5,163	143	2·8	5½	1,716	72	4·2
1849	6,042	182	3·0	3½	1,990	45	2·3
1850	5,823	116	2·0	2	2,639	67	2·5
1851	5,848	188	3·2	2½	2,806	72	2·6
1852	7,599	234	3·1	3	1,326	72	5·4
1853	7,927	275	3·5	3⅜	1,326	72	5·4
1854	8,147	315	3·9	3¾	1,327	72	5·4
1855	8,193	350	4·3	4⅛	1,313	72	5·5
1856	8,464	409	4·8	4¾	1,054	66	6·3
1857	8,892	415	4·7	4⅝	1,278	68	5·3
1858	9,246	369	3·9	3⅞	1,107	71	6·4
1859	12,065	570	4·7	4¾	1,870	104	5·6
1860	12,078	695	5·7	5¾	2,214	111	5·0
1861	12,080	635	5·2	5¼	2,651	130	5·0
1862	12,081	469	3·9	3⅞	2,758	142	5·1
1863	12,082	544	4·5	4½	3,006	154	5·1
1864	12,083	710	5·9	5⅞	3,171	162	5·1
1865	12,085	710	5·9	5⅞	3,469	170	4·9
1866	12,609	816	6·5	6¾	4,142	196	4·7
1867	12,429	825	6·6	6½	4,422	209	4·7
1868	12,694	857	6·7	6¾	4,382	218	5·0
1869	12,694	857	6·7	6¾	4,675	230	4·9
1870	12,694	889	7·0	7	4,940	245	4·9
1871	13,335	1,025	7·7	7⅞	4,569	247	5·4
1872	13,335	1,117	8·4	8⅜	4,948	247	5·0
1873	13,335	950	7·1	7⅛	5,827	274	4·7

Partly acting on their own initiative, and partly responding to the pressure of events, the directors of the Manchester & Leeds now embarked upon the projecting, amalgamating, and financial dabbling that have already been discussed, and from 1846 until 1852 there is great confusion about preference and guaranteed stock and dividends. The low percentages of return on guaranteed and preference stock between 1848 and 1851 really represent only the *bonus* dividend on the Preference Fifths, in addition to some genuine preference dividend, as on the 1848 6 per cent preference shares, and on the Sheffield & Barnsley stock, payment on which started in 1850. In 1846 and 1847, on the other hand, the very large percentages include a proportion paid on the nominal amount of Preference Fifths, a nominal amount which is not, of course, included in the figures for *paid-up* guaranteed and preference share capital in Table 8. An approximation to the correct percentages of return on guaranteed stock for the years 1848 to 1851 might be obtained if the percentage returns on ordinary shares and on guaranteed stock were added together. Although the original intention, stated in 1845, was that there were to be no payments on the nominal unpaid money once the ordinary dividend fell below 5 per cent, this promise was abandoned in 1847.[40]

Since the bulk of the new capital became 'productive' in 1849 and 1850, the difficulties do not last very long. Already in 1849 the return on the total of paid-up capital on ordinary shares was close to the declared dividend: 3 to $3\frac{1}{2}$ per cent. In 1850 the two percentages are identical at 2 per cent. The fiddling with the Preference Fifths continued and the discrepancy between the declared dividend and the calculated figure for 1851 is almost certainly due to some double counting in the accounts, but in 1852 the bulk of this capital went into consolidated stock. Omission of the years 1849, 1850 and 1851 when averaging the figures of paid-up guaranteed and preference capital, and of dividends, makes a difference of 0·3 per cent. Over the whole period, then, the problem reduces in significance, but while the muddle was on, and while the dividends were being paid on nominal amounts, the ordinary shareholder suffered if he was not also a holder of the Fifths.

From 1852 the ordinary dividend recovered, and for the rest of our period the return on paid-up capital and the dividend declared by the Company are, in every year, almost exactly the same. For years the ordinary share capital of the Lancashire & Yorkshire expanded very slowly, except in 1859, when the Company amalgamated with the East Lancashire. Indeed, between December 1859 and December

[40] See Appendix, pp. 189–90.

1865, the increase was negligible, and since the bulk of the new share capital was preference capital, which received 4½ or 5 per cent, the ordinary shareholder benefited after 1863 from the growing tendency to issue preference or guaranteed shares.

In the 1850s the proportion and absolute amount of preference and guaranteed stock had declined as it was absorbed in consolidated stock. The amalgamation of 1859 pushed up both the absolute amount and the proportion, and from then on there was a steady expansion. In 1861 there was a large 4½ per cent preference issue, and more followed in 1865, 1868, 1870 and 1872. The rub came after 1873, when a guaranteed 4, 5 or 6 per cent became riches compared with the ordinary dividend. In the thirty-two years from 1842 to 1873, the average dividend on ordinary capital was 5·4 per cent; the average dividend on guaranteed and preference capital was 5·2 per cent (excluding 1849, 1850 and 1851 from the averages). On the whole, therefore, as with the comparison between shareholders and debenture-holders, the ordinary shareholder was slightly better off than the holder of guaranteed and preference shares. But, once again, the differential was small relative to the amount of risk-bearing. After 1873, the real effects of the increased proportion of guaranteed and preference capital began to be felt.

The Structure of Capital

The trends in the proportions of Table 9 are clear. In 1842, 1843 and 1844, the proportion of paid-up ordinary capital, in total paid-up capital declined, as a result of the decision to borrow as much as possible at the low rates of interest prevailing in those years. The idea was to enhance dividends, assuming a basic rate of return on total paid-up capital well in excess of 5 per cent, by having half the capital of the Company on loan at 5 per cent or less. The increase in the proportion of loan capital was caused particularly by the issue of bonds, the security for which was the unpaid portion of the share capital. Gladstone's Act of 1844 set a limit of five years on the life of these bonds, and this, together with the mania for buying shares in 1845, resulted in a dramatic change in policy. From 1845 to 1851 the proportion of loan capital declined, and the proportion of share capital increased. Both ordinary and preference and guaranteed capital rose, but it was the latter which increased quickly, as a result of the issue of the Preference Fifths, from 1 to 24 per cent. By 1851 the proportion of loan capital had fallen from 53 to 26 per cent.

The proportion that loan capital could bear to total paid-up capital was limited by law, but early in the period it was believed that

TABLE 9

PROPORTIONS OF ORDINARY, GUARANTEED AND PREFERENCE, AND LOAN CAPITAL, 1842 TO 1873

Year	Total Paid-up Capital £000's	Ordinary Capital % of Total	Guaran. and Pref. Capital % of Total	Loan Capital % of Total
1842	2,963	44	1	55
1843	3,100	42	1	57
1844	3,205	41	1	58
1845	3,430	46	1	53
1846	4,948	56	10	34
1847	7,554	60	8	32
1848	9,272	56	18	26
1849	10,644	57	19	24
1850	11,625	50	23	27
1851	11,770	50	24	26
1852	11,768	64	11	25
1853	12,050	66	11	23
1854	12,273	66	11	23
1855	12,692	64	10	26
1856	12,820	66	8	26
1857	13,546	66	9	25
1858	13,689	67	8	25
1859	18,246	66	10	24
1860	18,816	64	12	24
1861	19,158	63	14	23
1862	19,459	62	14	24
1863	19,663	61	15	24
1864	20,052	60	16	24
1865	20,384	59	17	24
1866	22,087	57	19	24
1867	22,452	55	20	25
1868	22,747	56	19	25
1869	23,044	55	20	25
1870	23,288	54	21	25
1871	23,902	56	19	25
1872	24,254	55	20	25
1873	25,333	53	23	24

it was legal to issue bonds for loans on the security of the part of the share capital that remained unpaid. At this time loan capital could be as much as 64 per cent of the total. With the increasing emphasis on loan capital in 1842, 1843 and 1844, we find that its proportion was approaching this maximum; in 1844 it reached 58 per cent. Bonds were legalised to the extent that they could exist for five years from July 1844, or for the period which had been contracted for in the case of bonds issued before the 1844 Act; but thereafter, the maximum percentage of loan capital would be 40 per cent. The proportion of loan capital went down to 27 per cent in 1850, at which date the bonds had practically disappeared. By this time, also, the maximum of 40 per cent had become a theoretical maximum, since it was only possible if a company had called up the bare half of the share capital which had to be raised before borrowing on mortgage could commence. Once all the share capital had been called, and paid up, the legal maximum proportion of loan capital was 25 per cent,[41] and it will be seen from Table 9 that between 1852 and 1873 this proportion was, in fact, exceeded in only two years, and that by only 1 per cent.

With the conversion of the Preference Fifths the proportion of guaranteed and preference paid-up capital declined from 24 per cent in 1851 to 8 per cent in 1858, when the proportion of ordinary paid-up capital reached its peak of 67 per cent. The amalgamation of 1859 was accompanied by the comparatively small drop of 1 per cent in the proportion of ordinary capital, but this decline was to continue. The increase in the proportion of preference and guaranteed stock was slow but steady. With slight ups and downs, it grew from 8 per cent in 1858 to 23 per cent in 1873. This increase was of a different order from that of the period 1845 to 1851; there was rarely any question of the new preferences being temporary.

The structure of the Lancashire & Yorkshire's capital apparently compared very favourably with many other companies' structures. Henry Ayres' study of railway finances, published in 1868, showed that few companies of any note had a higher proportion of ordinary capital in December 1866, few paid a higher dividend, and few showed such a favourable comparison between growth of receipts and growth of capital.[42] This favourable proportion of ordinary capital—which, according to Ayres, was so important because of the very close correlation he found between low proportions of ordinary capital and poor financial results—was in fact already declining and had been declining since 1858. Nevertheless, even in 1873 the

---

[41] The figure of 64 per cent would be reached if total borrowing powers (which almost invariably amounted to one-third of share capital) were exercised; if half the share capital were paid-up, and if the remaining half of the share capital were used as security for bonds. The figure of 40 per cent would be attained if the total borrowing powers (one-third of share capital) were exercised; if only a statutory one-half of the share capital was paid up, and if no bonds were issued. The 25 per cent represents the proportion loan capital could be, if all the share capital and borrowing powers were exercised.

[42] Henry Ayres' analysis of railway finances is discussed below in Chapter 5, pp. 159–60.

Company still had over half its capital in ordinary stock, more than many railway companies had had in 1866. And the movement towards preference and debenture stock was nation-wide.

CONCLUSION

In the years between 1842 and 1873 the shareholder of the Lancashire & Yorkshire had many poor years, and some very good ones. If he bought his shares early in the history of the Company, and retained them for the greater part of our period, he received an average return of just under $5\frac{1}{2}$ per cent, and if he later bought preference shares he received about $5\frac{1}{4}$ per cent, with at times some additional amounts by way of bonus. The period was hardly one of tranquil prosperity for him, or for his Company. It covered the great mania and the great mid-Victorian boom, and he was no doubt concerned in the heart-searchings, criticisms and direct attacks on the conduct of his directors. It is known that he was at times so uneasy about the finances of the Company that he wrote to the Board asking for assurances that there was a proper allocation of expenses, that borrowing powers were not being exceeded, that dividends were not being paid out of capital.

The great period of such enquiries was the later 1840s and early 1850s, when there was no doubt that some dividends had been paid from capital, and after years in which the amount of capital flowing into the Company had been so great that there was much scope for mistakes or for deliberate misapplication. (See the figures of receipts and expenditure on capital account in Table 10 on p. 000.) Some of the factors to be taken into consideration were mentioned early in this chapter. Directors of companies such as the Lancashire & Yorkshire should, no doubt, have resisted the pressure from shareholders expecting the crock of gold to fall in their laps at every dividend time, and it is clear that the lessons of the 1840s were not fully taken to heart. They were learned to the extent that in 1850 and 1851 dividends were as low as 2 per cent and that in the 1850s there was a greater financial rectitude, but another and probably more important restraint was the decline in capital receipts in this decade. In the nine years between 1850 and 1858 paid-up capital increased by only £2 millions, compared with just under £7$\frac{1}{2}$ millions in the five years between December 1844 and December 1849. In each of these years in the 1850s, paid-up capital increased by an average of less than £250,000, and this was clearly absorbed by capital expenditure. There was simply no scope for the misapplication that had been possible between 1845 and 1850.

TABLE 10

RECEIPTS AND EXPENDITURE ON CAPITAL ACCOUNT,
1842 TO 1873

Year	Total Receipts on Capital Acct. £000's	Annual Receipts on Capital Acct. £000's	Total Expenditure on Capital Acct. £000's
1842	2,997	219	3,050
1843	3,136	141	3,198
1844	3,246	118	3,294
1845	3,561	365	3,570
1846	5,031	(1,470)*	5,036
1847	7,626	(2,595)*	7,598
1848	9,460	(1,834)*	9,218
1849	10,722	1,263	10,818
1850	11,669	946	11,488
1851	11,862	194	11,683
1852	11,984	135	11,850
1853	12,237	153	12,029
1854	12,417	202	12,402
1855	12,837	419	12,892
1856	12,964	127	13,070
1857	13,662	419	13,620
1858	13,883	221	13,799
1859	18,519	168	18,549
1860	18,968	450	18,932
1861	19,390	422	19,393
1862	19,854	463	19,649
1863	19,978	124	19,960
1864	20,320	342	20,431
1865	20,984	664	21,114
1866	22,069	752	22,176
1867	22,528	459	22,709
1868	23,005	477	23,146
1869	23,222	217	23,466
1870	23,597	375	23,793
1871	24,209	612	24,330
1872	24,871	661	24,898
1873	25,449	578	25,552

* These figures are the differences between the cumulative totals of capital receipts: for four half-years in 1846, 1847 and 1848 the bi-annual accounts did not give the bi-annual receipts on capital account.

It may be noticed that there are discrepancies between the annual figures and the increases of the cumulative total. This is due, in the main, to amalgamations which brought already paid-up capital to the Company, but no actual cash in the year. Minor discrepancies are the result of rounding.

But in the middle-1860s the enquiries were renewed, and Mr. Hargreaves, a member of the Finance Committee, and obviously an awkward fellow, made several criticisms of the financial conduct of the Company. Early in 1865 he urged the cutting of capital expenditure, except on rolling stock.[43] In September of the same year, the following entry occurred in the Finance Committee minutes:[44]

> 'Mr. Hargreaves referred to the statement which had been made that the Great Eastern Company have borrowed money in excess of their powers to enable them to pay off loans falling due and enquired whether this Company has ever done the same.'

In October 1866 Hargreaves, and Blacklock, another director, strongly objected to capital expenditure being ordered without the money first having been raised under Parliamentary sanction.[45] Table 10 shows that in several years in the 1860s capital expenditure exceeded capital receipts. In November 1866 a Mr. Forbes wrote from Edinburgh suggesting that the auditors should give bi-annual certificates that there was no excess of debentures, no suspense accounts, and that the dividend had been fairly earned from traffic.[46]

The 1860s saw another boom and crisis intimately linked with railway promotion. Some companies were shown to be insolvent in 1866, and shareholders were afraid that they were in for another bad time. Those of the Lancashire & Yorkshire turned out to be comparatively lucky; but it is evident that their Company had been slipping from the position it had built up in the 1850s. At the end of 1860 the Treasurer told the Board that soon the Company would have spent about £200,000 in excess of its powers. It is also clear that in several years in the 1860s the Company paid part of its dividend directly out of capital receipts, but this was the product of a failure to maintain a rigid separation of capital and revenue accounts, rather than deliberate misapplication. In some years, there is evidence to show that capital expenditure was financed from revenue, because of a reluctance to call up money. When it was decided to exercise the capital powers, the capital receipts might well be devoted to the payment of a dividend. 1869 may be cited as a year in which this misapplication of revenue account receipts occurred.[47] In these years an unwillingness or inability to recognise that it was extremely important to keep the receipts and expenditure of the two accounts strictly separate once again emerged.

In spite of these irregularities, the Lancashire & Yorkshire

[43] Proceedings of the Finance Committee, 7 February 1865.
[44] *Ibid.*, 19 September 1865.   [45] *Ibid.*, 16 October 1866.
[46] *Ibid.*, 27 November 1866.   [47] *Ibid.*, 19 January 1870.

proprietary was more fortunate than the investors in many other enterprises, and the Company itself maintained a fairly clean record in this era of shaky financial practices. The returns of the 1860s and early 1870s were fairly good, when one remembers that the investment was comparatively secure, and that the railways rescued many an investor from the low yields on government stock especially in the early 1840s.[48] For many, the large shares of the better joint-stock banks were out of the question; the railways soon turned to shares of quite low denomination. On the other hand, many investors suffered badly from the violent fluctuations of share prices, considerable capital losses were sustained at times, and the ordinary shareholder who averaged his returns over, say, 1850 to 1880 or 1890 would indeed have had cause for complaint.

[48] Irving Fisher, *The Theory of Interest* (1930), p. 530, gives the interest yield on Consols at 725 pence per £100 investment—or £3 per cent—in 1844. Between 1839 and 1873 the yield exceeded 800 pence in only five years.

Part II

The Early Railway Capital Market

CHAPTER 3

The Sources of Loan Capital

FROM their beginnings British railways, like most other national networks, have been subjected to severe criticism of their financial practices. It is not uncommon to find examination questions asking for a judgement on the accusation that the development of railways in England was accompanied by widespread waste and extravagance, and it is true that there were enough fraudulent practices to lend support to charges of malpractice in almost every branch of railway finance and administration. Particular emphasis was laid by contemporaries on the high proportions of temporary and guaranteed capital, compared with ordinary capital. Money on loan was a vital part of every railway company's sources of capital and in this chapter an account is given of the motives of, and methods used by, railway directorates in raising temporary finance.[1] This account is followed by a survey of the sources from which the money was borrowed, and of the terms on which it was lent.

I

The methods of raising loans, unlike the sources, were few. Apart from bank advances, which are dealt with in the section on sources, only three are distinguished here: acceptance of money paid on shares in advance of calls; borrowing on bonds; and issuing mortgage debentures. Of these three, only one, mortgage debentures, proved to be of lasting significance throughout our period, although all were important at one time or another. Loans on mortgage debenture are called temporary finance because they could be withdrawn at the end of the mortgage period, but in fact much of this money remained permanently with the Company, and one of the financial characteristics of the later 1860s was the large-scale conversion of this debt into permanent stock, the famous 4 per cent Debenture Stock. The end of the period witnessed another significant

---

[1] Most of the primary source material is for the Manchester & Leeds and Lancashire & Yorkshire Railway Companies, but these methods were used by most, if not all, the companies of this period.

development in another method of raising money. In the 1860s, and particularly in the early 1870s, there is a very pronounced tendency for shareholders to pay up the full amount of their shares in advance of the calls because dividends were so high and they probably hoped to encourage the Company to make calls more quickly. Thus the second method of raising temporary money was important at both the beginning and the end of the period. The remaining method, borrowing on promissory notes or bonds, was important from an early date, but was affected in 1844 by legislation which restricted the legal life of the bonds.

PRE-PAYMENT OF CALLS

So much was written in the nineteenth century, as a result of the decennial crises between 1825 and 1866, on the financial scandals of the railways and on the vast sums that mounted up as arrears of calls on shares, that it is nice to record that at times shareholders paid up quite considerable sums on their shares before they were required to. This source, although much less important in total than the other two methods, was far from negligible, and may legitimately be regarded as a form of temporary finance, since those who paid more than was called for by the Company could always ask for repayment. Naturally, much of the money became permanent capital when further calls were made. The Proceedings of the Finance Committee show many internal transfers from advance call account to general account.[2] Between November 1837 and February 1841 more than £120,000 were transferred in this way.[3] There are also several references to the repayment of pre-paid calls between October 1839 and February 1841, when about £27,000 were repaid to directors and other shareholders of the Company.[4] Business conditions were extremely depressed in these years, particularly in Lancashire.

In March 1841, according to the biannual accounts, a total of more than £185,000 had been paid in advance of calls in the period up to December 1840.[5] Although over £145,000 of this had at various times gone to meet further calls, and although after December

---

[2] The minutes do not explain this process until October 1841, when it is explicitly recorded that the deposit on the 1841 preference shares was paid by some holders out of money already held by the Company.

[3] Proceedings of the Finance Committee of the Manchester & Leeds Railway, 15 November 1837 to 5 February 1841.

[4] Ibid., 25 October 1839 to 19 February 1841. This sum included interest.

[5] Reports & Accounts of the Manchester & Leeds Railway, 3 March 1841. Total receipts on capital account amounted to just over £2½ millions at this time.

1840 this source of receipts dried up for a time,[6] the confidence shown by the shareholders must have been very encouraging for the directors. Their experience contrasted very favourably with that of the Boards of some companies which had to threaten legal action to enforce the payment of calls in the depressed years of 1839 and 1840. Doubtless the intensifying depression of 1841 proved too much even for the wealthy merchants and manufacturers of Manchester.

This was not by any means the end of payment in advance, which continued throughout and beyond our period, although variations in business conditions and in the financial policy of the Company affected the amount which could be secured. Another simple limit to the amount of money that could be advanced was the proportion of shares that remained unpaid, and on this point the policy of the directors varied from time to time. We shall see how the Board changed its mind about the advantages and disadvantages of having a high or a low proportion of paid-up capital on shares, but here we may note that the attitude of the investors also had an effect. It has been said that the institutional investor, among others, was more interested in fully paid-up shares, that such investors were concerned more with dividends than with the possibilities of speculation.[7] In 1849 the Railway Commissioners referred to the 'great number of people' who knew little or nothing of commercial matters but who were 'only desirous to obtain a secure and advantageous invest-ment'.[8] Certainly the directors of the Manchester & Leeds thought that this was so:[9]

> 'Looking to the amount of capital that will be required . . . within the next two or three years' it was expedient to accept calls in advance, to a limited amount at a permanent rate of 5 per cent p.a.; 'and, as Trustees and many other parties seeking Railway investments give a preference in their purchases *to shares paid up in full. . . .*'

This was in the spring of 1847. What was to trouble the directors in the succeeding months was not the attitude of Trustees and similar investors, but the problem of calls in arrear. Even at this time money in advance of calls was being paid. The *Accounts* show £83,020 out-standing on this account at the end of December 1846, and in June

---

[6] *Ibid.*, 16 September 1841. There had been no money paid in advance of calls between December 1840 and June 1841.
[7] See, for example, J. B. Jefferys, 'Trends in Business Organisation in Great Britain since 1856' (unpublished Ph.D. thesis, London, 1938), *passim*.
[8] See below, pp. 171 and 72.
[9] *Reports & Accounts*, 10 March 1847; directors' italics.

G

1846 the amount outstanding had been £31,377.[10] Further, offers of prepayment totalling £30,000 have been traced in the Finance Committee minutes for 1847, but by now arrears were much more significant.[11]

The influence of the new attitude towards payment on shares may be seen in the biannual accounts of the 1860s and early 1870s. Prepayments totalling tens of thousands of pounds were made at times in the 1850s, and at one point in 1859 reached £61,516 on the £9 shares created in March 1857.[12] But these sums represented only a small proportion of the capital, and the number of new issues in this decade was small. In the 1860s, however, the influence may be seen clearly. At times, when calls were very numerous, there would naturally be little opportunity to prepay on shares, but in several years the outstanding balances were over £300,000, and in two, nearer £400,000.[13] In the early 1870s large amounts were again paid, and in December 1872 the balance was £497,805.[14] The prepayments would benefit from the rate of interest only, not from the rate of dividend, but the level of dividends was so high at this time and compared so favourably with the rate given on loans as to make the investor press for fully paid-up shares. From the second half of 1864 until the first half of 1876, dividend never fell below 6 per cent, and in the period 1870–73 it never fell below 7 per cent. For the second half of 1872 dividend was $9\frac{1}{8}$ per cent.[15] This was a boom period and it was soon to end, but it is obvious that while it lasted there was every incentive to ask for fully paid-up shares.

BONDS

Prepayment of calls was the first form of temporary finance which the Company used, but the supply of such money was dependent upon the capacity and confidence of a limited number of shareholders, and while these qualities were not lacking in the proprietors of the Manchester & Leeds, the Company, like every other, had to resort to other methods of raising money. Even so, many of the lenders were shareholders and several factors influenced the decisions the Board

[10] *Ibid.*, 9 September 1846. A balance remained throughout 1847, although it did decrease. Balances are referred to here because one of the many changes in the form of accounts occurred in 1847: from March 1847 to March 1849 the capital accounts were much abbreviated and did not separate the half-yearly receipts on capital account from the accumulated totals.
[11] Arrears reached a peak in June 1847 when they exceeded £500,000. Cf. Proceedings of the Finance Committee, 16 June 1847.
[12] *Ibid.*, 16 March 1859.
[13] See *Reports & Accounts*, August 1862 to August 1868.
[14] *Ibid.*, 19 February 1873.
[15] *Ibid.*, 1864 to 1873.

made when considering which type of temporary finance to concentrate on. Bonds were used at the same time as mortgage debentures, but they came upon the scene a little later and had a shorter career. At the third meeting of the shareholders in March 1838, the directors stated that they had 'the power of borrowing one-third the amount of capital *at any stage of their proceedings*' but they did not want to use that power until 50 per cent of the calls had been made and paid.[16] The reason they changed their minds is not known, but three months later a special general meeting sanctioned a proposal to mortgage the railway and its tolls, although capital receipts were less than two-thirds of the 50 per cent of the authorised capital.[17]

Bonds differed from mortgages in that their security was the unpaid portion of the share capital. According to the directors in 1840, their use had been 'suggested . . . by the fact of a large surplus having been tendered upon the mortgage loan'.[18] They had, in their report a year earlier, already stated that not only had the full £433,000 of borrowing powers provided by their Act of incorporation been contracted for, but further loans had been placed at their disposal. They believed that this illustrated the 'flattering opinion' which the public had of the Company.[19]

How important were these bonds? The total value issued was at first much smaller than that of debentures. For instance, in the period 30 June to 31 December 1839, mortgage loans amounting to over £200,000 were taken; bonds fetched only £72,802. These figures have to be put beside a total of £1,181,055 received on capital account.[20] By December 1840, the capital account totalled just over £2½ millions, and bonds were now over £500,000, that is, about 20 per cent. The Company had, at this date, overspent by almost £47,000.[21] In the next six months the expansion of capital slowed down considerably, with the debit balance at the banks growing to more than £100,000.[22] This was the period, it will be remembered, during which there were no further pre-payments of calls. By mid-1842, when prepayments were coming in again, bonds totalled £805,000. This was just short of the debenture total, and was 27 per cent of the total received on capital account.[23] In the next few

---

[16] *Ibid.*, 15 March 1838; directors' italics. The Board was apparently quite correct, as the act of incorporation of 1836 did not stipulate that half the share capital had to be paid up first, a restriction which was common in railway finance legislation.

[17] *Ibid.*, 17 September 1838.
[18] *Ibid.*, 12 March 1840.
[19] *Ibid.*, 18 March 1839.
[20] *Ibid.*, 12 March 1840.
[21] *Ibid.*, 3 March 1841.
[22] *Ibid.*, 16 September 1841.
[23] *Ibid.*, 1 September 1842.

months, bonds exceeded debentures for the first time, and in December 1843 they constituted just over 30 per cent of the total.[24]

In the meantime the directors were opening their minds to their shareholders, and they were full of optimism about the future. The years ahead would be rosy enough, but mortgages and bonds could make them even rosier:[25]

> '. . . the Directors believe that only one more *call of £5 per share upon the new half shares will be made, until payment of some of these bonds shall become due*. In consequence of such confidence of the public in this undertaking, half of the entire capital stock only will be paid up by the Shareholders, the other half being borrowed upon security, by mortgage or bonds, and the effect of this will be that every excess in the net receipts beyond 5 per cent upon the whole amount of capital expended will produce double that excess of dividend to the Shareholders.'

If net receipts were $7\frac{1}{2}$ per cent on the whole capital, half of which was to be borrowed at 5 per cent, the proprietors were assured of a 10 per cent dividend; 10 per cent, the magic figure of the Liverpool & Manchester and a few other lines. In view of all the later difficulties over the relative proportions of ordinary and guaranteed stock, and of loan capital, and of all the accusations that were levelled against railway directorates, it is interesting to see what the original motives of the Manchester & Leeds Board were. When this statement was made, the share capital consisted of ordinary stock only, and their intention was to assure the ordinary shareholders of a prosperous future.

The life of the Bonds had so far been limited to between two and five years, but it is obvious that the directors felt that they could be extended indefinitely at a rate of 5 per cent. Indeed, in March 1842 they were so sure of their future and of the attractions of their securities that they could prophesy a gradual fall in the interest burden.[26] A continual decline in the rate demanded was bound to come about as the 'confidence of capitalists in placing their money in railway securities' increased.[27] In fact, the rate on their bonds was down to 4 per cent in March 1843, and loans were being secured at $3\frac{1}{4}$ per cent in February 1844.[28]

[24] *Ibid.*, 14 March 1844.
[25] *Ibid.*, 17 September 1840; directors' italics. The new half shares were created in 1839: 2 & 3 Vict., c. 55, s. 114.
[26] *Ibid.*, 17 March 1842.
[27] *Ibid.*, 1 September 1842.
[28] Proceedings of the Finance Committee of the Manchester & Leeds, 2 February 1844.

In 1843 a new prosperity phase had begun to emerge, and in 1844 the cycle revolved more quickly. Early results were Gladstone's Select Committee and the 1844 Act. Doubts had long been cast upon the validity of the bonds which the railway companies were issuing for loans accepted in anticipation of calls.[29] In 1844 the Railway Regulation Act, clause 19, stated:[30]

> 'And whereas many railway companies have borrowed money in a manner unauthorized by their acts of incorporation or other acts . . . upon the security of loan notes or other instruments purporting to give a security for the repayment of the . . . sums . . . and whereas such loan notes . . . have no legal validity . . . but such loan notes . . . . issued . . . and received in good faith . . . in ignorance of their legal invalidity, it is expedient to confirm such as have already been issued. . . .'

The clause went on to say that in future it would be an offence to issue such notes; but that a company might renew any already issued for a period or periods not exceeding five years from the passing of the Act. Clause 20 provided that holders of these notes were entitled to demand repayment of their money when their notes became due. While the new Act sponsored by Gladstone made the existing notes legal documents, it limited their duration to five years, except for those contracted before 12 July 1844, which could run their full term, if this exceeded the five years from 9 August 1844, the date set by the Act. The directors now said that nearly all the uncalled portion of stock would have to be paid up in the next five years.[31] So much for their earlier hopes.

They had also changed their minds about debentures; in fact they attempted a complete reversal of financial policy in 1845, but this belongs rather to the story of debentures. They never made it clear whether or not it was intended to stop issuing bonds as well as mortgages, but all their intentions about loans were shelved at one time or another. In December 1846 and January 1847, bonds totalling £197,000 were due, and in the November it was decided to offer renewal at 4½ per cent for a period of about three years, until August

---

[29] According to Arthur Smith, *The Bubble of the Age*, p. 7: 'The Railway Companies previous to 1844, had borrowed without any legal authority, millions on loan notes; . . . the holders had no legal remedy whatever for the recovery of their money, either against the Company or the Directors. . . .'

[30] 7 & 8 Vict., c. 85, *An Act to attach certain Conditions to the Construction of Future Railways, authorized or to be authorized by any Act of the present or succeeding Sessions of Parliament; and for other purposes in relation to Railways*, s. 19.

[31] *Reports & Accounts*, 5 September 1844.

1849, 'being the time fixed by the Acts'.[32] A large number of bonds were renewed for the correct period of two and a half years, and a number for two years, but the Company was induced to ignore the provisions of the 1844 Act by two circumstances. First, 1847 was a year of crisis, calls were in arrear to the extent of some hundreds of thousands of pounds, and money was needed. Second, some bond-holders insisted not only on a higher rate of interest, but on a longer period.[33] The Finance Committee gave in to several demands for renewals of five years' duration,[34] and by the middle of 1847 were advertising for loans for three to five years at 5 per cent. They received hundreds of offers, and in one fortnight in June/July they accepted offers totalling over £129,000.[35] Most of this money was, however, for straightforward mortgages.

But this was the last fling with the bonds. In the 1850s mortgage debentures became the standard form of loan, and these in turn gave way to debenture stock in the late 1860s and early 1870s. In 1849 the amount of bonds outstanding was reduced from £501,812 to £65,500. By December 1850 the total bond issue was £24,000, and only £2,000 remained with the Company after 1851. This small sum disappeared from the accounts in 1857.[36]

MORTGAGE DEBENTURES

The legality of the bond had been questioned in the early 1840s, but even before the Act of 1844 the Manchester & Leeds could point to its act of incorporation, which seemed at least to give it permission to borrow £433,000 *over and above the amount of calls unpaid*.[37] Bonds would therefore appear to have come within the scope of the Company's Act, and it is obvious how the confusion of the early 1840s arose. But there were no doubts about the legality of mortgage debentures. The 1836 Act provided that, in addition to the share capital of £1,300,000, the sum of £433,000 (borrowing powers were usually one-third of the share capital) could be borrowed by means of mortgages, which could be transferable.[38] It has already been pointed out that money could be borrowed at any time, irrespective of the amount paid on shares (subsequent acts stipulated that half the

[32] Proceedings of the Finance Committee, 2 November 1846. It will be remembered that the legislation of 1844 had restricted the duration of bonds until 1849.
[33] This demand is rather surprising in view of the drawback to the bonds that they could not be transferred. Cf. Proceedings of the Finance Committee, 16 October 1846.
[34] *Ibid.*, 6 June 1847.   [35] *Ibid.*, 7 July 1847.
[36] *Reports & Accounts*, 1848 to 1858.
[37] 6 & 7 W. IV, c. 111, s. 200. But the clause is confused.
[38] *Ibid.*, s. 191.

share capital had to be paid up before borrowing could commence), but it was not until mid-1838 that the issuing of mortgages was sanctioned by the proprietors.

The amount of mortgages increased steadily. In June 1840 a total of £648,490 had been issued.[39] In 1839 the Company had secured another Act which allowed it to raise a further sum of £216,000, by either loan or mortgage, and so it now had total borrowing powers of £649,000.[40] The directors were therefore borrowing right up to the hilt. In contrast to the Act of 1836, the 1839 Act compelled them to call up half their new share capital before borrowing; so they were now running the law close, because their second call of £10 on the new issue was still coming in, in May 1840.[41] In December 1840 the law was, technically, being broken. Shareholders were in arrears to the extent of £8,390 on the new shares, although the amount was a very small proportion of the required sum of £325,000.[42]

In 1841, the directors deliberately defied the provisions of their new Act of that year. They did not alter the accounts: the evidence of the infringement is contained in the half-yearly statement of capital account published with their Report, in June 1841. The Company was not, compared with other concerns like the Eastern Counties, having a bad financial time: arrears of calls were reduced from £8,000 to £6,000, and this was in a very depressed year, but the Company was spending more than it was receiving on capital account, and owed the bankers over £100,000. On 18 May 1841, the Royal Assent was given to another bill, which authorised £487,500 in share capital, and £162,500 on loan when half the share capital was paid up.[43] In spite of this, now usual, stipulation, the Company's 'Stock Account' on 30 June 1841 contained the following entry:[44]

		Capital Authorised £	Amount to be Received £	Amount Received £
Shares	Act No. 4	487,500	487,500	—
Loan on Mortgage	18.5.1841	162,500	131,400	31,100

[39] *Reports & Accounts*, 17 September 1840.
[40] 2 & 3 Vict., c. 55, s. 118.
[41] Proceedings of the Finance Committee, 22 May 1840. The 1839 shares were half, or £50, shares. The second call of £10, together with the first, and the deposit of £5, would yield half the nominal share capital.
[42] *Reports & Accounts*, 3 March 1841. The share capital authorised in 1839 was £650,000.
[43] 4 Vict., c. 25, ss. 2 and 8.
[44] *Reports & Accounts*, 16 September 1841. The Act of 1841 was the fourth act obtained by the Company, but only the third which authorised additional capital.

£31,100 had, therefore, been accepted on mortgage before even one penny had been raised on the shares, before even the deposit had been paid, and the fact was calmly set out in the accounts. It is difficult to give the benefit of the doubt to the directors that the £31,100 might have been borrowed on bonds and wrongly assigned, although borrowing on bonds and not on mortgages had been the main purpose of securing the new authorisation.[45] The sum is assigned to mortgages in two different places, and the total of bonds is stated separately. In June 1842, with the total received on the new shares standing at only £37,404 (even this was £1,600 short of the total deposit on the 19,500 £25 shares), the amount borrowed on mortgage for 'Act No. 4' was £159,450.[46] No calls were made on the shares until their preference expired in 1846, by which time the Company had been breaking the law for years.

By mid-1842, then, it had been decided that mortgage debentures and bonds were to be the basis of the equity-holders' prosperity. At this date, debentures and bonds constituted about 55 per cent of the receipts on capital account, in almost exactly equal proportions. The proportion of loan capital continued to increase until it reached a peak of 58 per cent in 1844. At this time the directors were acting on certain roseate assumptions: that there would be no promotion mania, that financial results would be so good that dividends in excess of 5 per cent would always be possible, that there would always be an adequate supply of money on loan at 5 per cent or less. Since there would always be a reserve of unpaid share capital, bonds could be issued; and mortgages could be issued to the value of one-third of the nominal share capital.

The Manchester & Leeds had, in 1836, excellent prospects, and the claims of its supporters were not extravagant. It was to be built in an already highly industrialised district, and when it was built its Board recognised the peculiar nature of its potential traffic: much of both passenger and goods traffic would be short-distance, and the wisdom of cheap rates and third-class facilities was apparently appreciated. But the dreams of prosperity were soon dispelled by Gladstone and the mania, although once the directors were compelled to revert to

---

[45] *Reports & Accounts, loc. cit.* The new shares were to have a preference. A rate of 10 per cent per annum was to be given, but the burden of the preference was to be slight, the directors said, because it was intended that only £2 per share should be paid up in the first five years, after which time the preference was, in any case, to cease. The uncalled portion of the stock was to be used as security for bonds. From the outset there was evidently no intention of adhering to the Act in this respect. This, *pace* G. H. Evans, is a new slant on the motives for issuing preference shares; see the discussion in Chapter 2, pp. 70–72.

[46] *Ibid.*, 1 September 1842.

the original intention of building their lines with equity capital, the mania provided an opportunity to represent the new financial policy as one made possible by the public's desire to buy shares:[47]

'The disposition of the public . . . to [contribute] towards the share capital rather than towards loans as formerly, . . . no longer require[s] that the same policy which has hitherto marked their [the directors'] financial arrangements, should be continued. Your Directors are convinced, that by extending . . . the base from which the capital is eventually to be drawn, the number of those interested in the prosperity of the undertaking will be increased, ...'

There was to be a complete reversal of policy. At a special general meeting the proprietors passed a resolution which stated:[48]

'That it is advisable that provision be made for paying off the existing Mortgage Debts of this Company by the Creation of New Shares . . . to the sum of £2,071,300.'

The new shares were to be Fifths and were to have a preference, the nature of which was confused and complicated.[49] The new capital issue caused great trouble between 1846 and 1851, and the Board probably regrettted its new policy. The proportion of loan capital fell steeply from 53 per cent in December 1845 to 34 per cent in December 1846, and to 26 per cent in December 1848.[50] Of course, debentures were never eliminated from the Company's capital account, and the absolute amount of loan capital did not follow this pattern. It did decrease in 1845 and 1846 when the effort to pay off the loan debt was made, but in 1847 there was a sharp increase, and from 1848 onwards the proportion of loan capital remained steady at about a quarter of the whole.

In the years 1848, 1849 and 1850 the maturing of bonds was offset by the increase in the issue of debentures, and it must be remembered that the more or less constant proportion of loan capital was maintained while the total paid-up capital was increasing from £11½ millions in 1850 to £25¼ millions in 1873. In this period paid-up loan capital increased from just over £3 millions to just over £6 millions. Much of the increase in the later 1860s and early 1870s was in the form of permanent Debenture Stock which carried 4 per cent interest, and the conversion of debentures into Stock was stimulated by the financial scandals of the 1866 mania.[51]

[47] *Ibid.*, 3 September 1845.   [48] *Ibid.*, *loc. cit.*
[49] See above, Chapter 2, pp. 64–69; also Appendix, pp. 189–90.
[50] See above, Chapter 2, Table 9, on p. 71.
[51] See below, especially pp. 102, 104, and 109–11.

II

We now turn to the sources for loans of all kinds. It is extremely difficult to give a balanced picture of the sources of loan capital, and there can be no similarity between the treatment of loan capital and that of the sources of share capital which follows this chapter. For the sources of loans there is nothing comparable to the lists of names, addresses, and occupations contained in railway subscription contracts and Parliamentary Papers. Throughout the Proceedings of the Finance Committees of the Manchester & Leeds and Lancashire & Yorkshire Railways there are scattered thousands of names of creditors. Some are easily identifiable as shareholders or directors, or of well-known people; the majority are not. No addresses, no occupations are given. No attempt can be made to analyse information about creditors on the lines of Chapter 4.

We are, therefore, confined to the kinds of sources from which the Company obtained temporary capital. Even here we cannot end with a table containing the sources, each with a percentage against it. We cannot estimate, except in very broad terms, the relative importance of the sources examined. Some sources were obviously major, some equally obviously minor, and the latter are included as a contribution towards completeness and to show the wide field from which loans came. The sources have been grouped under the following headings:

1. Insurance Companies.
2. Banks with which the Railway had accounts.
3. Other Banks.
4. Shareholders and Directors of the Railway.
5. Private Individuals.
6. Other sources.

1. INSURANCE COMPANIES

It is well known that insurance companies have been large investors in British Railways, and the Lancashire & Yorkshire and its constituent companies found their willingness to invest very useful, especially in times of financial stringency. This is not to say that the companies were soft options. On the contrary, the Treasurer or a director sometimes had to negotiate directly with them, particularly with the larger London firms, which very often secured better terms than those first offered by the Finance Committee to investors in general.

The first loan was recorded in January 1847 and was from a local firm, the Yorkshire Fire and Life Insurance Company, which offered, on mortgage of the Wakefield Pontefract & Goole, £5,000 at $4\frac{1}{2}$ per cent for five years.[52] Other sums were borrowed in the same year, notably from the Royal Exchange Assurance Corporation, which advanced £66,000 to the Preston & Wyre, repayable in annual instalments.[53] In the 1850s and 1860s loans were to be nearer the Royal Exchange's scale than that of the Yorkshire Fire and Life. There were a few small loans but £10,000 was the usual minimum, and sums of £100,000 were not unknown. In 1852 two London companies, the Alliance Assurance and the London Life Assurance, negotiated loans of £50,000 and £100,000 respectively. Both were for five years, carrying $3\frac{1}{2}$ per cent,[54] and both remained with the Company for at least ten years, although the Treasurer of the Lancashire & Yorkshire had to make two trips to London in 1857 to secure renewal which, in that year of crisis, cost 5 per cent.[55]

Some companies, like the Globe, made brief appearances as creditors; others, like the Scottish Equitable Life Assurance Company loaned money from 1858 to 1873. We cannot even begin to estimate the total loan capital provided by these companies, since there are many examples of an insurance company appearing only once in the minutes against either a renewal or a repayment order. At other times a total of loans from a company would be given and previous entries did not add up to the total. The total of all the loans mentioned in the minutes in our period was, excluding renewals, just under £400,000. This is a small proportion of the loan capital in the 1860s, but the actual proportion must have been larger.

BANKS

Banks were an extremely important source of temporary capital. As far as the Lancashire & Yorkshire Railway is concerned, the banks with which it dealt may be divided into two categories: those with which it had accounts, and those which, so far as is known, did not handle any of the Company's business.

2. BANKS WITH WHICH THE RAILWAY HAD ACCOUNTS

As an almost constant source of temporary finance, these banks were, for fairly obvious reasons, by far the more useful: accounts with banks were a matter for negotiation and bargaining, and in the

[52] Proceedings of the Finance Committee, 6 January 1847.
[53] Ibid., 4 August 1847.
[54] Ibid., 22 March, 7 December and 21 December 1852. The Alliance had offered 'a large sum' for ten years at 4 per cent, but the Committee turned it down.
[55] Ibid., 4 November, 2 December and 16 December 1857.

allocation of its business the Company's Board would be swayed by such considerations as the commission charged on turnover, and the size of the advances offered. Another factor influencing the dealings with banks was the presence of bankers on the Board of Directors, or shareholders' lists.

The banks in this category were local to the Company's territory. The Lancashire & Yorkshire had accounts at various times with banks as far apart as Liverpool and Pontefract.[56] But the most important throughout the period were: Cunliffes Brooks and Company, the Manchester and Liverpool District Bank, and Loyd Entwistle and Company. The first was a very prosperous concern, and was the major bank for the Lancashire & Yorkshire. Samuel Brooks had been active in the promotion of the Manchester & Leeds, and had chaired the first meeting of the Board of Directors in November 1835.[57] This connection no doubt helped to establish the bank as the Company's main financial agent, but there is no evidence that it also involved preferential treatment. In fact, relations with the bank were often far from good. It sometimes refused to lend money.[58] It appears to have raised its charge on the account without warning,[59] and it added insult to injury by not answering letters of complaint from the Treasurer,[60] who on several occasions served notice on Cunliffes to terminate their arrangement, but each time the trouble was smoothed over.[61] In fact the bank, along with various others, was a valuable source of credit, especially at dividend time, when it was frequently necessary to overdraw the accounts at the various banks. During the 1850s and 1860s these accounts were almost always overdrawn biannually and as much as £130,000 was obtained from Cunliffes on one occasion alone,[62] although £100,000 was seldom exceeded from a single bank. In these two decades the various banks in our category provided credit to the extent of several millions but it is impossible to give an exact figure.

[56] In this category of banks there is only one example of a Liverpool company, and even here there is only one reference to the bank in the minutes. In 1847 the Royal Bank of Liverpool agreed to take the Liverpool & Bury's account. Cf. Proceedings of the Finance Committee, 6 January 1847.

[57] Proceedings of the Board of Directors of the Manchester & Leeds Railway, 23 November 1835.

[58] Proceedings of the Finance Committee of the Lancashire & Yorkshire, 14 March 1855.

[59] Ibid., 18 June 1855. The commission charged by Cunliffes on turnover, which at over £2¾ millions in 1865 was easily the largest of any of the Lancashire & Yorkshire's banks, was a constant source of friction.

[60] Ibid., 29 May 1861. This correspondence was over an incorrect allowance of interest on the Lancashire & Yorkshire credit balances.

[61] Notice to terminate was given in 1855, 1866 and 1868. In August 1868 the bank agreed to reduce the commission on the turnover.

[62] Proceedings of the Finance Committee, 21 March 1865.

There was, in the minutes, never any mention of the repayment of advances from Cunliffes. It may be that the bank would not agree to any particular sum being made available for a definite period; or that, since the bank was the Company's principal agent, it was sure of a quick reduction of the overdraft as receipts from traffic operation and other sources flowed in. Certainly the overdrafts never remained very large for long. Other banks put a definite amount at the disposal of the Company at, for instance, three months' notice; and at the same time they might grant additional credit when called upon. Practice varied in these matters. In 1856 the Manchester and Liverpool District Bank agreed to a fixed advance of £15,000 to £20,000 and, in an emergency, to another of up to £50,000.[63] The Yorkshire Banking Company offered, in March 1862, an advance of £20,000 to £30,000 at $3\frac{1}{2}$ per cent, payable at the railway company's pleasure, and also £25,000 at $3\frac{1}{2}$ per cent for three months certain.[64]

If Cunliffes Brooks was a very successful bank,[65] the Manchester and Liverpool District Bank (also called the District Banking Company) was outstanding. Established in 1829 it was apparently first among the provincial joint stock banks in 1876, with 53 branches, £14 millions of assets, and a 20 per cent dividend. It had helped to finance the Company at an early date—in 1845 and 1846 loans totalling £95,000 were repaid to the bank[66]—and in January 1847 it was also handling the business of the Manchester & Southport Railway, to which it advanced £30,000.[67] The first reference to Lancashire & Yorkshire *deposits* in the District Bank occurs in 1852, when the bank reduced interest on them to $1\frac{1}{2}$ per cent.[68] After that there is the entry already referred to, when the bank agreed to a fixed advance. This agreement was made on the occasion of a transfer of an account to the District Bank, and thereafter the bank's practice in giving advances appears to have followed that of Cunliffes.

There were several other banks with which the Lancashire & Yorkshire dealt. The Yorkshire Banking Company probably first entered into an arrangement with the railway company in 1852, when the Leatham Tew and Company's account was transferred to

[63] *Ibid.*, 30 January 1856.
[64] *Ibid.*, 12 March 1862 and 26 March 1862.
[65] One of the partners, Samuel Brooks, was believed to have left £2½ millions, even after disposing of much of his estate, when he died in 1864. Cunliffes was passed into the sole possession of William Cunliffe Brooks and was still functioning in 1877. Cf. Leo H. Grindon, *Manchester Banks and Bankers* (1878), pp. 199 and 214.
[66] Proceedings of the Finance Committee, 7 February, 1 August, 3 October and 5 December 1845; 3 July and 28 October 1846.
[67] *Ibid.*, 6 January 1847.
[68] *Ibid.*, 17 May 1852.

it.[69] It also absorbed the railway's account with Harris and Company of Bradford in 1857; it was charging ⅛ per cent commission compared with Harris's ¼ per cent.[70] The Yorkshire Banking Company's account appears to have been a valuable asset to the railway. The bank was often willing to step in when Cunliffes or Loyds were not being co-operative; its charges compared favourably with other banks, and it retained the custom of the railway until the 1870s at least. It never advanced large sums of £100,000 or so, as did Cunliffes and the District, but it could always be relied upon for £15,000 to £20,000 at dividend time, and over the two decades it advanced several hundreds of thousands of pounds.[71]

The list of banks which applied to the Lancashire & Yorkshire for a share of its business is quite long, and the directors obviously spread their business for a variety of reasons. With plenty of alternative sources for advances they would stand more chance of getting the £100,000 to £200,000 they so often needed. They would also have more freedom of choice in the matter of commission; and opening a new account could be the occasion for pressure on its other banks, particularly on Cunliffes. In 1868, for example, notice was served on Cunliffes to close the account because the Company had decided to grant requests from the Barnsley, Halifax Joint Stock, and the Manchester and Salford Banks for some of the railway's business.[72] In addition, the 1860s was a period of joint-stock banking expansion, and the emergence of new banks, like the Manchester and County, which was established in 1862, did put the directors in a favourable position. Another factor of some influence was the extensive area covered by the railway. It would not only be convenient to have banks scattered throughout the Company's territory; it would also help to foster the impression the directors hoped to convey that they were doing their utmost in more ways than one to promote the commerce of the district. Finally, there are the 'interlocking directorates', and the banker-railway investor. Many of the partners or directors of the banks we have mentioned were also either directors or shareholders of the Manchester & Leeds or Lancashire & Yorkshire. More will be said on these creditors on pp. 98–100.

[69] Proceedings of the Finance Committee, 21 June 1852. Leatham's was a Pontefract bank.
[70] Ibid., 22 April 1857. Harris's had been the bankers of the West Riding Union Railway.
[71] Ibid., 1852 to 1873, passim.
[72] Ibid., 15 April and 5 August 1868. Cf. also Proceedings of the Board of Directors, 29 April 1868. This notice, like its predecessors, was never confirmed.

3. OTHER BANKS

The Company obtained loans from numerous banks in addition to those already dealt with. At the outset we must raise the question of the true source of the loans shown against these banks. Was it the banks, or was it individuals upon whose behalf the banks were acting? It is not always possible to give a definite answer to this question. But the loans are worth recording because they show banks acting as channels of investment, as well as direct sources of credit.

Geographically the banks were widely scattered, although not quite so dispersed as the inclusion of a Bank of Australasia seems to indicate. Many loans were received from banks in Ireland, Scotland, the northern counties, London, and other areas. The earliest references to such banks were in 1844, when the Manchester & Leeds minutes mention the Manchester and Salford Bank, the North Wilts Bank, and the Leicestershire Banking Company. More loans came in the 1840s from Leyland and Bullins, and A. Heywood Sons and Company, both of Liverpool. Heywood's was a private bank and lasted from 1773 to 1883, when it was absorbed by the Bank of Liverpool.[73] It offered a £10,000 loan to the Liverpool & Bury in 1847.[74] This loan probably came from a client. Leyland and Bullins was another Liverpool banking concern which had an independent existence for a long time before it was absorbed in 1901.[75] Again, it is not known whether its loan of £20,000, which was repaid in October 1846,[76] was the bank's money, but Leyland and Bullins certainly acted as agents. In June 1855 the following entry occurred in the Finance Committee minutes:[77]

> 'Messrs Leyland & Bullins on the part of the Bondholders require repayment of the Loans as they have no difficulty in replacing the money at $4\frac{1}{2}$ per cent.'

The Lancashire & Yorkshire had offered renewal terms of $4\frac{1}{4}$ per cent for five years, and 4 per cent for ten years.

In the 1850s and 1860s a number of banks appear as either direct creditors or as channels for loans. Some were to make brief appearances in the minutes, some had come to stay. The former were the Wilts and Dorset Banking Company, Overend Gurney and Company (of 1866 crisis fame), the Huddersfield Banking Company, the

---

[73] John Hughes, *Liverpool Banks and Bankers, 1760–1837* (1906), p. 98.
[74] Proceedings of the Finance Committee of the Lancashire & Yorkshire, 17 March 1847.
[75] Hughes, *op. cit.*, p. 173.
[76] Proceedings of the Finance Committee, 28 October 1846.
[77] *Ibid.*, 6 June 1855.

London and Westminster Bank, the Nottingham Bank, the West Riding Union Banking Company of Huddersfield, the Birmingham Banking Company, and the Burton Bank.[78] Some of these were obviously acting as agents. In 1868 the Lancashire & Yorkshire accepted a solitary loan of £5,000 at 4 per cent for seven years from the Birmingham Banking Company; and in 1850 £5,000 at 4¼ per cent for three years from the Nottingham Bank.[79] It seems likely that these banks were negotiating loans on behalf of clients, since the amounts involved were small and isolated. In October 1866 the Nottingham Bank asked 'on account of a Mrs. Burnside' what rate of interest would be offered in January.[80] The next month a Mary Burnside loaned the railway £3,000, and there was no mention of the bank.[81] On the other hand there were some substantial sums loaned for such short periods that it is reasonable to suppose that the banks themselves were lending the money. In 1866 the London and Westminster Bank provided a temporary loan of £120,000 for three months,[82] and in 1851 Overend Gurney and Company had unsuccessfully attempted to renew a £14,000 loan for the same period.[83]

The Bank of England, the National Bank of Scotland, and the Commercial Bank of Scotland were frequently mentioned in the Finance Committee minutes. It would be interesting to know why and how a bank like the National came to be the channel for so much loan capital to the Lancashire & Yorkshire. Loans were usually for three and never less than two years, and varied from £400 to £17,500.[84] At least twenty-one loans totalling more than £98,000 were repaid to the bank between 1851 and 1873. The variation in the size of these loans indicates that they came from clients of the National. The Bank of England, it is known, loaned money to railways. According to Sir John Clapham:[85]

> '... in the young railway companies the Bank has already discerned more useful borrowers. By a vote of 5 May 1842, the Court ... decided ... [to] lend up to £250,000 upon deben-

---

[78] The Burton Bank and the West Riding Union Banking Company are examples of concerns which wished to keep loans on a fairly short term basis. The former advanced two sums of £20,000 each at 3 per cent in 1867 for 12 and 15 months; the latter £30,000 at the same rate, for 6 months. The Lancashire & Yorkshire was not happy about the short term. See *ibid.*, 18 September, 16 October and 27 November 1867; 30 September, 14 October, 11 November and 25 November 1868.

[79] *Ibid.*, 22 July 1868 and 18 October 1850.

[80] *Ibid.*, 30 October 1866.   [81] *Ibid.*, 13 November 1866.

[82] *Ibid.*, 24 July and 16 October 1866.   [83] *Ibid.*, 5 May 1851.

[84] *Ibid.*, 18 June 1873 and 26 March 1862 for these sums respectively. They were repayments.

[85] *The Bank of England: A History Vol. II, 1794–1914* (1944), p. 145.

tures "of the best description". The Governor had already
begun to do this when the vote passed. He had lent £100,000 to
the London and Brighton, and was considering other possibilities.'

By August 1851 the Bank's capital account showed over £3 millions
of railway and canal debentures. For many years the Bank engaged
in a considerable number of lengthy transactions with the Lancashire
& Yorkshire. Loans from the Bank were arranged through Messrs.
Mullens, Marshall and Company, the government brokers, and
usually they were for £50,000. More often than not the Lancashire &
Yorkshire had considerable difficulty in satisfying the Bank's conditions, and often had to agree to pay a higher rate of interest than
other creditors were receiving. The Central Bank acted as a creditor
early in the Company's career, in the later 1840s, and was still taking
part in negotiations at the end of our period.

One £50,000 loan from the Bank may be traced through more
than ten entries in the minutes over a period of twenty years. It was
initially accepted in 1852 at $3\frac{1}{2}$ per cent for four years.[86] In 1856
Mullens and Marshall, with the incentive of a $\frac{1}{4}$ per cent commission, managed to secure its renewal for five years at $4\frac{1}{2}$ per cent.[87]
When it was due for repayment in 1861 the Company tried to reduce
the interest rate to $4\frac{1}{4}$, but the Bank insisted on $4\frac{1}{2}$.[88] In 1864, when
the great majority of creditors had to be satisfied with $4\frac{1}{2}$ per cent,
the Bank successfully held out for $4\frac{3}{4}$ per cent for a five-year term.[89]
Again, in 1869, the Bank refused the Company's offer and would
only accept a reduced rate of 4 per cent if the loan was to last three
years.[90] If this is found to be a little puzzling, it must be remembered
that at this time the Company was more interested in 4 per cent
Debenture Stock than in long-term mortgage debentures.

Sometimes the Bank and the Company refused to come to terms,
as in 1860, when another loan of £50,000, which had been granted
in 1855 for five years at $4\frac{1}{4}$ per cent, was repaid because the Bank
refused a reduction to 4 per cent.[91] The Company had at least one
success, however, in its continual battle with the Bank, when the
latter agreed to the 1855 loan just mentioned after the Company
had, in May 1855, 'respectfully declined' (the only time such a
courteous form of rejection was used) an offer of £50,000 at $4\frac{3}{4}$ per
cent for five or seven years.[92]

[86] Proceedings of the Finance Committee, 23 November 1852.
[87] *Ibid.*, 17 and 31 December 1856.
[88] *Ibid.*, 18 December 1861 and 7 January 1862.
[89] *Ibid.*, 13 December 1864.
[90] *Ibid.*, 24 November, 8 December and 22 December 1869.
[91] *Ibid.*, 1 August 1855, 23 May and 20 June 1860.   [92] *Ibid.*, 9 May 1855.

H

The Bank provided another £100,000 on each of three occasions between 1867 and 1872 at a rate comparable with that given to other creditors.[93] In 1868 it was joined by another central bank, the Bank of Ireland, which at the end of our period seemed set to provide a comparably steady investment: the Bank's loan of £50,000 at 3¾ per cent for three years was renewed in 1871 at 4 per cent for a further three years.[94]

Banks played a vital part in providing temporary advances, especially when the Company needed money to cover the repayment of mortgages and dividend payments. This does not mean that such dividends were necessarily paid out of loan capital. Debit balances at banks just after the payment of dividends would soon be reduced by the normal flow of receipts on revenue account. It does show, however, that the railways were, and always have been, far from conforming or from being able to conform to the financial methods of most business concerns. The majority of industrial companies have required bank advances as part of their working capital, but few of any standing can have suffered from the constant pressure and sense of urgency felt by railway companies such as the Lancashire & Yorkshire. Some railways did finance some development, such as the tripling of track, from their own resources, that is, from revenue account, but they were far removed from the industrial concern, with its huge reserves.

4. SHAREHOLDERS AND DIRECTORS OF THE COMPANY

Shareholders and directors had a variety of motives in becoming creditors of the Company. Some merely had surpluses to place and, like employees, already had a convenient connection. Some, such as those who bought shares as an investment rather than as a speculation, lent sums on condition that future calls on shares could be paid from the loans. Others no doubt wanted to spread investments, and regarded a company over whose conduct they had some control, as a good subject for investment. Others wished to help the Company when it needed temporary finance—it is known that directors did so. The bankers who handled some of the Company's business, might have felt obliged to lend, when their own concerns were unwilling to advance further sums to the railway. Yet others felt that they could call on the Company to repay part or all of a loan if it was needed before it matured.

Examples can be found which illustrate most of these motives.

[93] *Ibid.*, 25 June 1867, 7 July 1869 and 20 December 1871.
[94] *Ibid.*, 10 June 1868 and 19 July 1871.

Whatever the reasons, the shareholders and directors did provide large sums on loan to the Company from the very first days of borrowing, which began halfway through 1838. Many remained as creditors for very long periods, renewing loans, or offering fresh ones periodically, and some left their money with the Company permanently. The names of, for instance, Edward Loyd, the banker, Ellis Cunliffe, Dr. Peter Wood (son of James Wood, one-time Chairman of the Company), Bernhard Liebert, Captain Binstead, and Lewis Loyd, constantly recur in the minutes. Some of these people were among the original shareholders of 1836. Between them, even these few provided many tens of thousands of pounds.

Prominent among these creditors were the banker-shareholders. Several of the large Cunliffe family, such as James, William and Ellis, were persistent creditors, as well as shareholders of the Company. Edward and Lewis Loyd have already been mentioned; Lewis Loyd Jnr. had managed the London business of his bank until 1848, when he handed over to Samuel Jones Loyd. He had become a very wealthy man and had been associated with the railway since the late 1830s.[95] He invested considerable sums in the Lancashire & Yorkshire and its constituent companies. Jones Loyd, who became Overstone in 1850, was also a substantial creditor, and in 1863 loaned £50,000 for ten years.[96] As a final example we may cite James Heald who was, with the possible exception of Ellis Cunliffe, the most constant creditor of the Company. He appeared at meetings of proprietors as early as 1840 and, with female relatives, figures as a creditor until the end of our period.[97] He was a managing director of the Manchester and Liverpool District Bank.

Most directors were at one time or another creditors of their Company. Manufacturers such as Henry Houldsworth (founder-director and one-time Chairman) and Joshua Radcliffe were prominent. In addition we find, as we would expect, merchant-directors fulfilling their time-honoured function of providing credit. To select a few: many loans, both short and long term, came from J. C. Harter, Robert Gill, James Wood (one-time Chairman), and James Hatton, all of whom were very well known and wealthy merchants. The Chairman of the Finance Committee, James Audus, himself advanced money when it was particularly needed, as in 1855 when he first lent £50,000 for six months and, a month later, another

[95] *Reports & Accounts of the Manchester & Leeds*, 17 September 1838.
[96] Proceedings of the Finance Committee, 6 October 1863.
[97] Cf. e.g., *Reports & Accounts*, 12 March 1840, and Proceedings of the Finance Committee, 19 June 1872. On the latter date it was reported that loans of £11,000 and £6,000 from James Heald and Margaret Heald respectively were to be repaid. They were subsequently renewed for three years.

£30,000.[98] It was in 1855 that the Company's bankers were refusing to advance any more money.

5. PRIVATE INDIVIDUALS

What is probably the most important category of longer-term creditors, that of private individuals, is the one about which we know the least. We may, however, in this section make some general remarks which, although they could be applied to other sources, will usually have particular relevance to loans from individuals. As might be expected, loans to the Company came from an immense variety of people. There were the shareholders, directors, and employees; among these would be merchants, manufacturers, bankers, clerks, landowners. Among private individuals we find bishops, a cardinal, generals (including Napier, who also found the railways useful for moving troops), naval officers, the famous Captain Galton of the Board of Trade, masters and scholars of schools and colleges, earls, viscounts, and, of course, Members of Parliament.

The many thousands of creditors employed various methods of placing their money with the Company, just as the Company employed various methods of obtaining loans. First of all there were many offers of loans or enquiries about terms, mostly from the individuals themselves, sometimes through intermediaries. The Company advertised extensively in railway journals like *The Railway Times* and *Herapath's*, and this was probably the most usual way in which borrower and lender contacted one another. Circulars were often sent to shareholders pointing out the beneficial terms on which money would be accepted. For the person who did not wish to negotiate personally with the Company, there were alternative ways of placing loans. The intermediary that first springs to mind is the broker. Brokers acted for large financiers who wanted to place considerable loans on short notice, and also for small clients who wanted a three- to ten-year mortgage. In 1855 £50,000 was offered through a London broker at ('after much negotiation') 4 per cent at three months' notice on either side.[99] Again, in 1868, £50,000 for twelve months came through London brokers.[100] The smaller creditor may be represented by the Misses Woodcock who loaned £4,200 through a London broker named Morris.[101] One feature of these transactions that is not always clear is the question of com-

[98] Proceedings of the Finance Committee, 20 June and 18 July 1855. It is, of course, possible that Audus was an intermediary.
[99] *Ibid.*, 15 August 1855.
[100] *Ibid.*, 18 August and 2 September 1868.
[101] *Ibid.*, 12 August 1869.

mission. When lengthy negotiations took place, they were often over the amount of commission which the Company was to pay the broker. If he charged commission to both sides he must have done well, but commission is not always mentioned, and it is likely that in these cases the loans were not solicited by the Company.

Banks also acted as intermediaries, again for small and large creditors. The activities of the National Bank of Scotland were described earlier, when it was suggested that the variations in the size of the loans, from £400 to £17,500, indicated that they were provided by customers of the bank. Some entries in the minutes did state that the banks were acting for clients. That solicitors were yet another medium is known from a Finance Committee minute when the 1873 crisis was brewing. The Company had been going all out for the conversion of it loan capital into Debenture Stock and 'the excited state of the Money Market' was linked with the possibility that 'a commission . . . of a ¼th per cent on Stock will have to be allowed in some cases where Solicitors & Bankers are the Mediums [*sic*] of Renewal'.[102] Finally, the directors acted for other people, particularly for relatives. One example of a director acting for a friend or acquaintance occurs in 1856, when Henry Wickham, Member of Parliament and Chairman of the Lancashire & Yorkshire from 1853 until he died in 1868, acted for Sir Charles Douglas in placing £9,000 with the Company.[103]

6. OTHER SOURCES

With the exception of a few very miscellaneous items, the remaining sources of credit were companies other than insurance and banking concerns; mortgages issued in payment or part-payment of accounts owned by the Company; trustees; and Company employees. Not a great deal can be said about any of these categories. There is on record a large number of loans from companies or firms the nature of which is unknown, and also from trustees. Frequently it was only because there were peculiar circumstances which gave rise to entries in the minute-books, that the true nature of some of the loans came to light. It was discovered, for instance, that loans from the Leeds & Liverpool Canal Company were misleadingly recorded against the names of individuals.[104] The same is true of some mortgages which were accepted in payment or part-payment of accounts owed by the Company. While most of these particular mortgages were issued to people from whom land had been purchased, and who were willing

[102] Proceedings of the Finance Committee, 20 November 1872.
[103] *Ibid.*, 9 April and 4 June 1856.
[104] *Ibid.*, 13 October 1869.

to leave it on loan, some were accepted by contractors such as George Miller, who appeared first as an individual accepting mortgages in 1847, and then as Geo. Miller and Company, contractors, accepting a mortgage of £30,000 at 4¼ per cent for three years as part-payment of an account of £40,000.[105] Not much more is known about these loans, but the published accounts show that quite a substantial amount of land-purchase money was left in the hands of the Company. This must have been a very welcome development for the directors, for land purchase was a heavy item of expenditure at times.

Finally there are the Company employees. It is pleasant to record that while the number of loans from comparatively lowly employees was very small, they were granted a higher rate of interest—usually a half per cent higher—than that commanded by the general run of mortgages. In 1860 the Company almost set up as a savings bank when it decided to allow its Clayton Bridge Station clerk to deposit his savings—'say £10 to begin with'—at 4½ per cent instead of the current rate of 4 per cent.[106]

III

Over the years there are few very noticeable trends in the size or duration of the loans. In the early and mid-1840s, loans were as small as £100 or as large as £10,000 or £15,000 from individuals, and £100,000 from banks and insurance companies. The larger loans from individuals came from wealthy merchants like the Ashtons and William Garnett, or from bankers like William Entwistle.[107] At the end of our period loans could still be in hundreds or in thousands of pounds. As for their duration, the periods varied from a month to fifteen years (and a few in perpetuity, before the issue of permanent Debenture Stock), and there is a noticeable difference in emphasis on long and short periods, as the Company's financial policy changed from time to time. There were very few loans, however, of more than seven years' duration, and the more usual periods were three to seven years. This, apart from the period of conversion to Debenture Stock in the 1860s and early 1870s, applies in almost any year. And even in the period of the great conversion, loans were still accepted for a term of years. The Company was very flexible in this matter, to its own confusion, and would in the same week or on the same day

105 *Ibid.*, 10 November 1847 and 2 December 1850.
106 *Ibid.*, 11 April 1860. On another occasion an employee was allowed to add to his security and receive 5 per cent. Most employees in positions of responsibility had to deposit a security of £100–200, or to find a guarantor.
107 For example, see *ibid.*, 3 January and 1 August 1845.

accept loans for periods of a few months, a year, eighteen months, two, two-and-a-half, three, four, five, six years and upwards.

How the rate of interest varied with the period of loan would depend partly upon the Company's general financial policy at the time, partly upon expediency or the placidity or staying power of creditors and, apparently, partly upon sheer inconsistency. Sometimes a lower rate would be offered to those who wanted to place money for longer periods of five or seven years; sometimes a higher rate would be given. Sometimes a loan for a very short period of a few months would command a higher rate of interest than the average, and at others it would command a lower rate. These variations cannot by any means be correlated with fluctuations in business conditions. These would always have some influence, especially on the general level of interest; they would, perhaps, determine whether it should be 4 to 5 or 3 to 4 per cent. But the interest differentials relating to variations in length would be in quarters of a per cent, and it would often be a matter of chance which rate was given or accepted.

Probably the major influence on the duration of loans and the interest differentials was the attitude of the Company to the question of loan versus share capital with a highly paid-up proportion. This attitude itself was naturally influenced by, and partly subject to, business conditions. In the early 1840s when the verdict was more loans and less paid-up share capital, the Company doubtless wanted loans for as long as possible, especially in 1844 when the rate of interest was down to $3\frac{1}{4}$ per cent and the yield on Consols was about £3 per cent.[108] Unfortunately we are unable to check this, as the early years of this decade are not covered in much detail in the minute-books. In the mid-1840s, when policy was reversed for a short time, and the emphasis was to be solely on paid-up share capital, the acceptance of loans was no doubt conditioned by the desire to end the loan debt. But this did not last long, and already in 1846 there was a slight tendency to give a higher percentage of interest on the longer loan. Later, in 1847, a major influence was the legal restriction on the life of bonds imposed by the Act of 1844, although even here, due to the pressure on the money market, the Company in some instances ignored the Act for a while, and yielded to demands for longer bonds.[109]

In the 1850s there was a greater willingness to accept offers of loans for seven, ten or even twelve years, and then in the 1860s another reversal took place. Now the effort was directed towards

[108] See above, pp. 83–84 and 88.
[109] See above, p. 86.

dissuading people who had money to lend, from asking for mortgages, and towards persuading them to take 4 per cent Debenture Stock, which was, of course, a permanent stock. The Company had great success here for some years, after the crisis of 1866 which was, among other things, a crisis of confidence in mortgage debentures. But already before the end of our period, in the increasingly troubled years of the early 1870s, the demand for Debenture Stock was dropping and mortgages were once again increasingly important.

This last trend was associated with the very high dividends, which reached a peak in 1872. Investors saw the high returns on shares, realised that a higher rate of interest might be demanded, and were not so enthusiastic about the figure of 4 per cent. For a short time the crisis conditions of 1873 encouraged mortgage debentures, but they also marked the beginning of the decline in dividends. This decline was to be almost permanent; a trend which the Company, not surprisingly, did not perceive, although misgivings about the great increase in working expenses were being more frequently expressed in 1872 and 1873. Dividends fell catastrophically in the 1880s. With returns on ordinary capital falling to 4 and 3 per cent, the permanent return of 4 per cent on the Debenture Stock once again proved attractive, and by 1888 the interest charge on temporary loan capital had almost disappeared from the Company's accounts. But before this happened, in spite of all the changes of policy and in spite of variations in economic conditions, there were always loans which were taken for almost any length of time from one to seven years.

One would have thought that for administrative convenience alone the Company would have been keen to get loans for as long as possible. Biannually, the Finance Committee was engaged in the long and often extremely complicated negotiations for renewal of loans which came due in June/July and December/January of each year, in addition to a few others which came due at various times. Twice a year the Treasurer was faced with the problem that several hundred thousand pounds (later in the period as much as half a million) might have to be repaid.[110] Resolutions on the rate of interest to be offered for renewal were passed and then ignored as it became apparent that creditors would not accept the rates. When creditors representing amounts of £150,000, for example, indicated their intention of demanding repayment, the Finance Committee thought again and offered better terms. At times they so obviously failed to keep track

---

[110] Joseph Lee Thomas, *A Letter on the Present Position of Railways* . . . (1867), p. 11n, said: 'It is estimated that the debenture debt of the Railways . . . amount[s] to 120 millions, and that from one-fourth to one-fifth of this amount has to be renewed annually.'

of the vagaries of the loan account, of the rates, varying between 3½ and 5 per cent, that were already being paid, and of the various rates to be offered for varying lengths of time, that they passed despairing resolutions leaving such matters to 'the discretion of the Treasurer'. One supposes that they always had the hope that if they did not accept a large amount of money for ten years at 4½ per cent they would find the following year, or the year after, that the interest rate had fallen to 3½ per cent, and they would then be able to cut the interest burden. They were always anxious to do that, as there were many charges that the holder of ordinary share capital suffered on behalf of the guaranteed stockholders and the debenture holders. It has already been pointed out that the Company kept changing its policy towards temporary capital *vis à vis* permanent capital.

Sometimes the Company would, with a few exceptions, successfully renew loans at the rate decided before negotiations started, but often the rate would have to be increased when the results of the first offer proved unfavourable. By the time it had increased its rate from 4 to 4½ per cent it had already concluded negotiations on some of the loans at the lower rate. For instance, in the first half of 1859 it was first decided to offer 4 per cent for the renewal of loans due at the mid-year.[111] The rate of 4 per cent was confirmed two months later,[112] but four weeks later it was decided to offer 4½ per cent for three years.[113] The result was that in the month of June, of about £270,000 due for repayment, renewals were made as follows:[114]

£		%		Years
39,400	at	4½	for	3
9,550		4¼		3 and 5
76,360		4		3, 5, 7 and 10
550		3¾		5

Obviously this particular loan negotiation was not very successful. This was not entirely a typical result, but the rest of the story does apply to most biannual negotiations. Whether or not the Company lost goodwill when it became known that the rate had been increased, it is impossible to say, but those who renewed at 3¾, 4 and 4¼ per cent must have been annoyed to learn that others had received up to ¾ per cent more.

The Parliamentary legislation of the early railway age must bear its share of the blame for the complications, malpractices and

---

[111] Proceedings of the Finance Committee, 2 February 1859. Since, in February, the half-yearly negotiations would only just be completed, the business of renewal was almost constantly before the Committee.
[112] *Ibid.*, 13 April 1859.   [113] *Ibid.*, 11 May 1859.
[114] *Ibid.*, 8 June 1859.

difficulties of the railways over debentures. The companies have been much criticised for their actions; for the suffering caused to bond and debenture holders. It is true that at first the companies' authorised share capital was based on the estimates of the cost of construction, but it was soon clear that no railway could keep within those estimates and some rethinking should have been done. It is also true that the companies themselves had exaggerated ideas of what they could achieve by manipulating the proportions of the different types of stock. But the whole business of allowing railway companies to sink temporary capital into fixed assets of a highly specialised kind was mistaken and unsound.[115] The railways and the investing public suffered from this, particularly in 1866 and after. It was this period which saw the effort made to avoid the tortuous negotiations described above by the conversion of the mortgage debt into permanent Debenture Stock.

An outstanding characteristic of the rate of interest on loans in this period is its steadiness. One might almost say that even for so long a period of more than thirty years there was a conventional rate of interest. There is nothing new about this idea. Walter Bagehot, who was writing at the end of our period, took 5 per cent as the rate aimed at by those who wanted safe investment:[116]

'An Englishman—a modern Englishman at least—assumes as a first principle that he ought to be able to "put his money into something safe that will yield 5 per cent; . . . ." '

Keynes considered that:[117]

'It might be more accurate, perhaps, to say that the rate of interest is a highly conventional, rather than a highly psychological phenomenon. . . . *Any* level of interest which is accepted with sufficient conviction as likely to be durable *will* be durable'; subject to fluctuations in a changing society.

Apart from the early 1840s and early 1850s, when the Company was obtaining money on loan for as little as $3\frac{1}{4}$ per cent for a term of years, and when the accumulation of capital had reached explosive stages,[118] the cost of loans was never outside the $3\frac{1}{2}$ to 5 per cent range. Keynes believed that there was:[119]

[115] At least one writer of the 1860s recognised this. See Anon., *Railway Debentures and How to Deal with Them* (1867), pp. 7–8.
[116] W. Bagehot, *Lombard Street* (14th Edn., 1920), p. 126. Bagehot began his book in the autumn of 1870 and published it in the spring of 1873.
[117] J. M. Keynes, *The General Theory of Employment Interest and Money* (1936), p. 203.
[118] The explosions happened in the mid-1840s and mid-1850s.
[119] Keynes, *op. cit.*, pp. 307–8.

'evidence that for a period of almost one hundred and fifty years the long run typical rate of interest in the leading financial centres was about 5 per cent, ...'

The evidence afforded by the Lancashire & Yorkshire seems to support that belief, provided that 'about 5 per cent' is taken as nearer 4 per cent, since, on the whole, the rate was more often pushed nearer 4 than 5. This point is unimportant, however, since there is no doubt that 5 per cent was accepted as conventional. In the later 1830s the Company, as we have seen, was basing its optimism partly on the expectation that money could always be borrowed at 5 per cent or less.[120] Their hopes were more than realised in the early 1840s; even in early 1844 loans could still be had at $3\frac{1}{4}$ per cent.[121] Soon the boom was to push the rate up, but not excessively. In early 1846 money was obtained for 4 per cent, and throughout the year the rate given varied from 4 to $4\frac{1}{2}$ per cent, with *some* (but only some, the Company was very inconsistent) indication that the longer term commanded the higher rate: the only loan to receive 5 per cent in 1846 was the only loan accepted for ten years.[122] The typical loan was accepted for three or five years at $4\frac{1}{2}$ per cent.

TABLE 11

LONDON RATES OF INTEREST, 1841 TO 1874

Year	Interest Rates Market %	Bank %	Year	Interest Rates Market %	Bank %	Year	Interest Rates Market %	Bank %
1841	4·9	5·0	1853	3·7	2·7	1865	4·6	4·8
1842	3·3	4·3	1854	4·9	2·1	1866	6·7	6·9
1843	2·2	4·0	1855	4·7	2·9	1867	2·3	2·6
1844	2·1	2·5	1856	5·9	6·1	1868	1·8	2·1
1845	3·0	2·7	1857	7·1	6·7	1869	3·0	3·2
1846	3·8	3·3	1858	3·1	3·2	1870	3·1	3·1
1847	5·9	5·2	1859	2·5	3·7	1871	2·7	2·9
1848	3·2	3·7	1860	4·1	4·2	1872	3·8	4·1
1849	2·3	2·9	1861	5·5	5·3	1873	4·5	4·8
1850	2·2	2·5	1862	2·4	2·5	1874	3·5	3·7
1851	3·1	3·0	1863	4·3	4·4			
1852	1·9	2·2	1864	7·4	7·4			

Source: Irving Fisher, *The Theory of Interest*, p. 520.

[120] See above, pp. 83–84.
[121] Proceedings of the Finance Committee, 2 February 1844.
[122] *Ibid.*, 4 December 1846.

This movement of the Lancashire & Yorkshire loan rate may be compared with the movement of the average market and Bank rates in Table 11 on p. 107. The latter increased in 1845 and 1846, but even the market rate was below 4 per cent in 1846, while Bank rate did not rise above 3½ per cent between May 1842 and January 1847.[123] The financial crises of spring and autumn 1847 are reflected in the rate given by the Company. In early March 1847, loans were still commanding only 4½ per cent.[124] (Bank rate was not raised from 4 to 5 per cent until 8 April), but by the 17th the Company's rate was up to 5 per cent, and there it remained for months, with very few loans indeed being accepted for less. The severest pressure on the money market, which came at the end of April and again in October and November, when Bank rate was 8 and 7 per cent, did not affect the Company's rate for loans, which were accepted for periods varying from three to seven years; it never exceeded 5 per cent. According to Fisher's figures, the average market rate in 1847 was 5·9 per cent.

Bagehot wrote at some length on the saying 'John Bull can stand many things, but he cannot stand two per cent'.[125] The Lancashire & Yorkshire never obtained loans for as little as that, although for some time in the early 1850s its shareholders had to put up with just that rate of dividend. On the other hand it is just as obvious that John Bull could not for long stand, or would not countenance, a rate on long-term loans which exceeded 5 per cent. After the 5 per cent of 1847 the rate of interest on the Lancashire & Yorkshire loans sank to 3½ and 3¼ per cent in 1852 and, apart from 1868, the average market rate in London reached its nadir in the same year. Bank rate also fell to 2 per cent in 1852, one of the few years in this period when it did so. Rates on the Lancashire & Yorkshire mortgages never again went so low in our period but, at the other end of the scale, they only once went as high as the 1847 level. In another crisis year, 1857, 5 per cent was paid on loans totalling £105,000, almost half the renewals of the loans which were due for repayment in December 1857 and January 1858.[126]

For the rest of this period the interest rate on the Company's mortgages varied between 3½ and 4¾ per cent, with the rate normally standing at 4 per cent. What is striking in the years between 1840 and 1870 is the marked tendency, associated with the course of the mid-nineteenth-century trade cycles, for the rate to be low in the early

[123] Clapham, *Bank of England*, p. 429.
[124] Proceedings of the Finance Committee, 3 March 1847.
[125] W. Bagehot, *op. cit.*, p. 133.
[126] Proceedings of the Finance Committee, 30 December 1857.

years of a decade and for it gradually to increase in the middle years, reaching a peak usually in the seventh or eighth year of each decade. (This movement may also be seen in the tabulation of London interest rates on p. 107.) But later in the period there seems to have been a secular movement downwards. From late 1867 the normal rate was 4 per cent, with $3\frac{3}{4}$ per cent quite regularly paid. A very slight upward tendency is discernible in 1873, when there were fewer loans being accepted or renewed at $3\frac{3}{4}$ per cent, but the tendency is very slight. For more than six years 4 per cent dominated the loan terms, and this was due to the decreasing importance of loans on mortgage and to the increasing importance of the conversion into 4 per cent Debenture Stock. There were very few loans accepted in, for instance, 1871. But the Company could only issue the Stock if the public would take it; the Stock could not have caused the decline in the interest rate.

1873 saw a change in the attitude towards mortgages because the money market was, to use the Lancashire & Yorkshire Treasurer's word, 'unsettled'. Bank rate was up to 7 per cent in the October, 8 per cent the next month, and the press for Debenture Stock had most definitely slackened off. The amount of loans due at the end of the year was £282,121, and this total was composed of the following sums, carrying the rates shown:[127]

£		%
13,000	at	$4\frac{1}{2}$
5,500		$4\frac{1}{4}$
254,959		4
8,662		$3\frac{3}{4}$

The Treasurer was to endeavour to renew the whole amount at 4 per cent. In the years immediately preceding 1873 the efforts of the Company had been to reduce, at the biannual repayment time, mortgage debt and substitute Debenture Stock. Now loans were once again assuming a greater importance.

It is true, then, that 5 per cent was a dominant rate of interest. Early in our period, in the later 1830s, it was taken for granted that 5 per cent should be paid on calls in advance, and charged on calls in arrear. The standard rate for loans was, in any statement on financial policy by the directors, always assumed to be 5 per cent. But this rate tended to dominate as the *upper* limit, even when the Usury Laws were relaxed. Later on the rate paid on calls in advance was down to $4\frac{3}{4}$ and then $4\frac{1}{2}$, and even 4 was suggested.[128] And we have seen

[127] *Ibid.*, 8 October 1873.
[128] *Ibid.*, 11 March 1857 and 10 February 1858.

how the rate on loans declined to 4 per cent, which was the norm for many years.[129] This decline was secular and national as the following figures, given by Irving Fisher, indicate:[130]

	Market Rate	*Bank Rate*
	%	%
1825–34	3·4	4·2
1834–39	4·0	4·4
1839–52	3·4	3·7
1852–57	4·7	3·8
1858–64	4·2	4·4
1864–70	4·1	4·3
1870–73	3·5	3·7

After 1852, the market rate of interest in London shows a steady decline.

IV

This account of bonds and debentures, of the conversion into Debenture Stock in the 1860s, and of the sources of loan capital, applies in general to English railways in the early and mid-Victorian decades. Expediency, legislation and the state of the capital market governed railway companies' changes of financial policy. The financial practices of the Lancashire & Yorkshire were *comparatively* sound, yet its directors must have countenanced the deliberate infringements of their Acts. The unconscious infringements were excusable; the Proceedings of the Finance Committee contained examples of genuine lack of knowledge on the part of the directors as to just what was, and what was not, permitted by their Company's Acts—which is not surprising in view of the numbers of statutes obtained by every railway company.[131]

Apart from overdrafts on bank accounts, mortgage debentures were the most constant source of temporary capital the railways could draw upon. For decades there was little question of their security, but after the crisis of 1866 the permanent Debenture Stock began to take its place, and by the 1880s the mortgage debenture was

[129] The only exception to these remarks is the decision of the Board, at a special general meeting in 1857, to charge 6 per cent on arrears. Cf. Proceedings of the Board of Directors, Special Meeting, 1 July 1857.

[130] Irving Fisher, *op. cit.*, p. 527.

[131] Many of the directors had a high moral sense. The members of the Board decided to fine themselves if they turned up late to meetings, and in March 1840 three of them (Jas. Wood, Chairman, Jas. Heald and John Burton) resigned over the decision to allow Sunday travelling; their resignation was 'founded on conscientious motives'. (See *Reports & Accounts*, 2 March 1840).

comparatively rare. It made little difference (although for the Company the change eliminated a biannual nightmare when the renewal of mortgages had to be tackled) because after 1866 it was only too clear to investors that while the mortgage certainly gave them prior claim on the revenue of a company, it was of little or no value when a company went bankrupt; the assets of a company were useful only as a railway and the only course open to debenture holders was to change the Board. Few holders would want the responsibility of actively participating in the management. The Debenture Stock performed the same function as the mortgage—it gave a return of roughly 4 per cent. It is only necessary to add that conversion also meant stable charges for the Company, although stability in the later 1870s and during the 'Great Depression' was at the expense of the ordinary shareholder, who was down to 3 per cent dividends.

CHAPTER 4

The Sources of Share Capital

I

GEOGRAPHICAL SOURCES

IN answering the question 'Where did the railways' share capital come from?' use is made of the simple and familiar concept of 'interested' counties. The location of all our companies[1] within, roughly, south Lancashire (that is, the area between the Mersey and the Ribble) and the West Riding, facilitates comparison of the relative contributions of 'interested' counties over the period of about ten years from 1835 to 1845. Any classification of counties or areas into 'interested' and 'non-interested' is bound to have defects. The criterion of 'interest' should be the expectation of direct commercial or industrial benefit from any given railway. The Lords Committee on the Manchester and Leeds Railway Bill in 1836 took Lancashire and Yorkshire as locally interested areas, although it did distinguish those subscribers residing in Manchester and Leeds and within four miles of the projected line:[2]

> 'The Shareholders having a local Interest are—428 Persons residing in Manchester and Leeds, or within Four Miles of the Line, ... 176 Persons besides, residing in Lancashire and Yorkshire, ...'

It is, however, quite likely that a subscriber who lived in York, for example, would have had no particular interest, as defined, in the railway, while subscribers in north-west Derbyshire or in Kendal

---

[1] Lists of subscribers, in the shape of manuscript or printed copies of subscription contracts, original Parliamentary deeds, or lists in British Parliamentary Papers, exist for only some of these companies. Furthermore, contracts for the Preston & Wyre, which were at first included in the analysis, are omitted here because there were special circumstances affecting them, and because these circumstances necessitated continual and tedious qualification. This bestowed undue emphasis on the Preston & Wyre contracts which were for very small amounts of capital.

[2] B.P.P. 1836 (House of Lords, 147) XII: *Report of the Lords Committee on the Manchester and Leeds Railway Bill*, p. 40.

might.[3] But such a refinement of analysis would not significantly modify the results. It is reasonable to take, as locally interested, for the Manchester & Leeds, the Liverpool, Ormskirk & Preston, and the Liverpool & Bury Railways, those subscribers living in Lan-

TABLE 12

GEOGRAPHICAL DISTRIBUTION OF SUBSCRIPTIONS

Company	Date of Contract	Percentage Contributions*				
		Lancs.	Yorks.	Chesh.	London	Other
I Manchester & Leeds	1835–36	71	20	1	5	3
II *Manchester & Leeds*†	*1838*	*60*	*8*	*5*	*10*	*16*
III Manchester & Leeds	1839–40	66	7	5	10	13
IV Ashton, Stalybridge & Liverpool Jc.	1844	50	10	nil	30	11
V Bolton & Preston	1837	98	nil	nil	—	2
VI Blackburn & Preston	1844	71	16	(1)	nil	12
VII Manchester, Bury & Rossendale	1844	96	3	nil	nil	1
VIII Blackburn, Burnley, Accrington & Colne	1844–45	85	10	(1)	—	4
IX Liverpool, Ormskirk & Preston	1845	48	30	2	9	11
X Liverpool & Bury	1845	72	3	2	12	11
XI Blackburn, Darwen & Bolton	1845	96	nil	nil	3	1
XII Wakefield, Pontefract & Goole	1844–45	56	42	nil	—	2
XIII Huddersfield & Sheffield Junction	1845	12	83	(1)	2	2

* To the nearest per cent. Note: (i) A dash (—) means that there were subscriptions amounting to less than one half per cent; (ii) The bracketed figures under Cheshire are not included in the totals of Table 2.
† Line II is an analysis of *Shareholdings*.

Sources: I B.P.P. 1836 (House of Lords, 147) XII, Appendix, pp. 45–48;
    II *Circular to Bankers*, No. 509, 13 April 1838;
    III three parliamentary deeds (British Transport Historical Records Office);

    IV ⎫
    VI ⎬ printed or manuscript copies of subscription contracts (House of
    VII ⎭ Lords Records Office);
    V B.P.P. 1837 (95) XLVIII;
VIII–XIII B.P.P. 1845 (317 and 625) XL.

The printed copies of the contracts for VIII, XI, and XII were consulted (House of Lords R.O.) in addition to the B.P.P. cited. This facilitated a quick check of the figures derived from the 1845 Papers, which contain some 700 pages of names, occupations, addresses and subscriptions, and it was found that discrepancies were small.

[3] In fact, to take this example, Kendal had long had intimate trade connections with south Lancashire, and it crops up quite regularly, if on a small scale, in

I

cashire, Yorkshire and Cheshire; and for the Ashton, Stalybridge & Liverpool Junction, the Blackburn & Preston, the Manchester, Bury & Rossendale, the Blackburn, Burnley, Accrington & Colne, the Wakefield, Pontefract & Goole, and the Huddersfield & Sheffield Junction Railways, those residing in Lancashire and Yorkshire. There were no Yorkshire or Cheshire subscribers to the Bolton & Preston and the Blackburn, Darwen & Bolton Railways; nor were there any Cheshire subscribers to the Ashton, Stalybridge & Liverpool Junction.

Table 12 on p. 113 sets out the percentage contributions to each contract of the 'interested' counties, of London, and of other areas. It is important to note that Lines I and II are not, strictly speaking, comparable with the rest. Line I, the analysis of the Manchester & Leeds contract of 1835–36, covers only those subscribers who signed for £2,000 or more: the Appendix to the Report of the Lords Committee which considered the Company's Bill does not include the rest.[4] More importantly, Line II represents an analysis of *shareholdings* in the Manchester & Leeds as of 1 February 1838. It has been included in order that the geographical distribution of actual holdings might be compared with the distribution of subscriptions in 1835–36 and 1839–40. This provides one test of the reliability of the lists of subscribers as evidence of capital sources.

The preponderance of the 'interested' counties is more obvious from the combined percentages of Lancashire, Yorkshire and Cheshire, which are given in Table 13 on p. 115. The consistently high proportions of the capitals subscribed by 'locally interested' people are striking. But there is a noticeable decline in the Manchester & Leeds figures for those counties between 1835–36 and 1844.[5] The analysis of shareholdings in 1838 indicates that there was a marked reduction in the relative weight of Lancashire and Yorkshire of approximately 18 per cent between 1835–36 and 1838,[6] and that London's share increased from 5 to 10 per cent. Other areas

---

the contracts we are considering. For Kendal's trade connections see, for instance, G. H. Tupling, *The Economic History of Rossendale* (1927), and T. S. Ashton, *An Eighteenth Century Industrialist* (1939).

[4] *Lords Committee Report*, B.P.P. *loc. cit.*, Appendix, pp. 45–8. Subscriptions of £2,000 or more amounted to £628,700. The total is wrongly given in the Appendix as £530,000. The subscriptions of the directors, which amounted to £100,000, were listed separately, but there is a further discrepancy of £1,300. The total of *all* subscriptions was £1,059,400: *Ibid.*, p. 39.

[5] To some extent the Ashton, Stalybridge & Liverpool Junction may be regarded as supplying a contract for the Manchester & Leeds series. It will be remembered that this company was a branch of the Manchester & Leeds.

[6] This conceals an increase in Cheshire's relative interest: see Table 12.

TABLE 13

THE CONTRIBUTIONS OF 'INTERESTED' COUNTIES

Railway		Per cent.
Manchester & Leeds	Lancs., Yorks. and Cheshire	92
Manchester & Leeds	Lancs., Yorks. and Cheshire	73
Manchester & Leeds	Lancs., Yorks. and Cheshire	78
Ashton, Stalybridge & Liverpool Jc.	Lancs. and Yorks.	60
Bolton & Preston	Lancs.	98
Blackburn & Preston	Lancs. and Yorks.	87
Manchester, Bury & Rossendale	Lancs. and Yorks.	99
Blackburn, Burnley, Accrington & Colne	Lancs. and Yorks.	95
Liverpool, Ormskirk & Preston	Lancs., Yorks. and Cheshire	80
Liverpool & Bury	Lancs., Yorks. and Cheshire	77
Blackburn, Darwen & Bolton	Lancs.	96
Wakefield, Pontefract & Goole	Lancs. and Yorks.	98
Huddersfield & Sheffield Jc.	Lancs. and Yorks.	95

Since some addresses were inadequate, it is possible that these figures very slightly underestimate the weight of the 'interested' counties. Proportions are given to the nearest per cent.

also gained an additional share of some 13 per cent.[7] It is possible that some of the changes were merely a result of the marketing of the remainder of the £1,300,000 worth of shares after the subscription contract—which totalled only £1,059,400—had been submitted to Parliament, but even on the questionable assumption that Lancashire and Yorkshire absorbed none of the additional shares, other areas had still gained. So there is no doubt that the capital market for the Manchester & Leeds had broadened after it was incorporated. The slump after 1836, far from causing a withdrawal of the possibly more

[7] The difference between the total subscribed in 1835/36 (£1,059,400), and the amount signed for by those subscribing £2,000 or more (£628,700), could not materially affect these conclusions. Fortunately the Lords Committee Report (B.P.P. *loc. cit.*, p. 40) gave the combined subscriptions from Lancashire and Yorkshire in 1835/36, which were £983,100, or just under 91 per cent of the total already contracted for. Since the corresponding percentage for the subscriptions of £2,000 or more is 91 (see Table 12, p. 113) no serious distortion can result from basing comparisons on them. There is, in any case, no alternative, because neither the House of Lords Record Office nor the British Railways Board has a copy of the contract.

impersonal London investors, was accompanied by an increase in their ranks. The experience of the Manchester & Leeds was therefore the reverse of the Liverpool & Manchester's in 1826.[8] In this period, moreover, the Manchester & Leeds did not indulge in practices which might have attracted such impersonal investors. It paid no interest on deposits or called-up money, unless the latter were paid in advance.

The very close correlation between the geographical distribution of subscriptions in 1839–40, and of shareholdings in 1838, suggests that the investors had kept their shares. The new half-shares of 1839,[9] were offered on a *pro rata* basis to existing shareholders, who were circularised.[10] The Company did not, apparently, invite applications from the general public.[11] The subscription contract was drawn up in a year which was not very favourable to new enterprise. Compared with 1838, the proportion preference shares bore to new shares more than doubled in 1839, and their nominal value rose seven-fold.[12] Yet the Manchester & Leeds directors did not consider it necessary to make the new issue preferential.[13] It is true that the new bill authorising the additional capital was conceived long before the spring crisis of 1839, but the business cycle which reached its peak in the March of that year 'never reached full employment and was marked by chronic financial stringency, falling prices . . .'[14] The index of railway share prices constructed by Gayer, Rostow and Schwartz shows a slightly irregular decline of seventeen points between March and December 1839,[15] and on the whole the Manchester & Leeds £100 shares followed this trend.[16] Yet the Company's Parliamentary Deeds contain a considerable number of

---

[8] Cf. H. Pollins, 'The Finances of the Liverpool and Manchester Railway', *Economic History Review*, Second Series, V, No. 1, 1952.

[9] 13,000 £50 shares were to be issued: *Reports & Accounts*, Directors' *Report* to Special General Meeting, 17 January 1839.

[10] *Ibid.*; the circular was dated 17 January 1839.

[11] A search of *The Railway Times* issues of 1839 did not reveal advertisements inviting applications. This periodical was a favourite medium for companies, including the Manchester & Leeds, which advertised anything from loan tenders to timetables.

[12] G. H. Evans, *British Corporation Finance*, p. 48.

[13] The directors were, in the period up to 1842, continually complimenting the shareholders, especially for the 'extraordinary punctuality' with which calls were paid. See *Reports & Accounts*, particularly 17 September 1838.

[14] Gayer, Rostow and Schwartz, *Growth and Fluctuation*, I, p. 242.

[15] *Ibid.*, p. 375. The prices of the Manchester & Leeds shares are included in the sample upon which this index is based.

[16] Cf. *The Railway Times* share prices lists in 1839. The Manchester & Leeds £100 shares (£50 paid-up) declined, irregularly, from 70½ to 60 between January and June. In December the price stood at 67–68, but £60 were now paid-up.

subscriptions dated from March onwards.[17] This, and the steadiness of the price of the new shares, suggest that there was little, if any, speculation.[18]

From a comparison of the two lists of subscribers to the Manchester & Leeds in 1835/36 and 1839/40 we can learn whether those who financed the original project continued to support the Company.[19] Of the 162 names in the first contract,[20] 64 recur in the 1839/40 list. Forty-seven were accompanied by the same, or very slightly different,[21] descriptions and addresses; 14 by either a different address or a different description; and 3 by both different addresses and different descriptions. Several of the last two groups of names were so distinctive and/or were the same as those of directors or of those who turned up regularly at meetings, that it may be assumed that they related to the same people.[22] A fairly conservative estimate of the number who subscribed £2,000 or more in 1835/36, and subscribed again in 1839/40, would therefore be one-third. As the existing shareholders were given first refusal of the new shares, at least one-third of a substantial section of the original subscribers retained their shares until 1839, paying up £50 per share in the meantime, and then took up new half-shares. Further, to those who still held their shares in the later year must be added those who did not take advantage of the new offer. Unfortunately, the Finance Committee Minutes of the Manchester & Leeds do not contain very many additional names of holders who had subscribed in 1835/36. Of the 28 people who are in the first contract and whose names occur in the minutes from 1838 to 1845, 25 have already been included in the above total of 64 who contributed in both 1835/36 and 1839/40. What the minutes do help to confirm is the validity of the one-third estimate. Almost all the entries come under such headings as repayment of prepaid calls and repayment of calls paid twice by mistake.[23]

By their very nature, these entries would refer to only a comparatively small minority of the shareholders. It must not be supposed

---

[17] The original deeds were used. The indenture is dated 23 January 1839. Most of the entries in the three deeds were made in 1839, a few in 1840, and only one in 1841.

[18] Cf. *The Railway Times* share prices lists in 1839. The new £50 shares first appear in the lists in May, priced at 11 (£5 paid-up). For three months after the week ending 1 June, the price was steady at 9 to 9½.

[19] Unfortunately, a full comparison is impossible because only those subscribing £2,000 or more are listed in the Appendix to the Lords Report of 1836.

[20] Some were probably duplications, but none of these appeared in the 1839 lists.

[21] E.g. Manchester and Chorlton; silk manufacturer and manufacturer.

[22] E.g. the Honourable Thomas Best (director); John Milligen Laws (manager).

[23] Proceedings of the Finance Committee of the Manchester & Leeds, 1837 to 1845.

that the Finance Committee dealt with all the details of calls on shares; it met primarily to approve and confirm payments by the Company, to accept loans and similar business. A list of people who are stated to have paid, for instance, the first instalment of the eighth call, would not, regrettably, be a list of all those paying their calls. The entries almost certainly represented internal transfers from the account which dealt with money paid in advance of calls, because the people mentioned are the same as those who are listed, in other minutes, as recipients of interest due on this money. At all events, the minutes confirm the conclusions drawn from the comparison of the contracts of 1835/36 and 1839/40. So 1835/36, although a year in which speculation was increasing, was also a year in which many of the subscribers of the Manchester & Leeds desired to invest rather than to speculate.

It would have been of great value if the trend towards a geographically wider capital market for the Manchester & Leeds could have been tested by a comparison of the 1839/40 contract with the list of subscribers to the Company in 1841, when the first preferential issue was made.[24] But this list cannot be traced. We are therefore unable to pursue the interesting subject of ordinary versus preferred shareholders, and the opinion that preference shares were designed to appeal to a different type of investor. The Ashton, Stalybridge & Liverpool Junction Railway issue of 1844, which was made by the Manchester & Leeds, was not preferential. But it is of some use in continuing our comparison of the trend in the relative weights of the 'interested' counties of Lancashire and Yorkshire, and of London.[25]

In Table 13 (p. 115) the percentage contributions of the 'interested' counties decline from 92 per cent to 78 per cent between 1835/36 and 1839/40, with the decline apparently confirmed by the figure of 73 per cent of shareholdings in 1838. Conversely, the weight of the London investors increased from 5 to 10 per cent between 1835/36 and 1839/40.[26] At first sight it appears that this decline continued, for the figures in 1844 for Lancashire and Yorkshire, and for London, are 60 and 30 per cent respectively. This seems to confirm the view that railways were drawing their capital from ever-widening sources in the early 1840s, compared with previous decades, and the figures do conform to the pattern observed in the years 1835/36 to 1839/40, although a jump from 10 to 30 per cent from London is very steep.[27]

---

[24] 4 Vict., c. 25, *An Act for enabling the Manchester and Leeds . . . to raise a further Sum of Money.* Clause 3 authorised the issue 'in such Manner, for such Prices' as a meeting ordered.
[25] There were no subscriptions from Cheshire.
[26] See Table 12, p. 113.
[27] It should be realised that expressing comparisons in this way does not permit

It is possible that an analysis of the 1841 subscribers might show intermediate changes—but that is purely conjecture.

Are we able to come to any conclusions by pursuing the kind of comparisons made between the lists of 1835/36 and 1839/40? One difficulty is that the contract of 1844 contains the names of those who were subscribing for £25 shares of the Ashton, Stalybridge & Liverpool Junction, whereas the Manchester & Leeds, after absorbing the former company, offered sixteenths to existing shareholders on a *pro rata* basis.[28] To this extent, therefore, we cannot be certain that those who subscribed in 1844 were actually shareholders in the Manchester & Leeds at the time. But it is reasonable to assume that the people who subscribed in both 1839/40 and 1844 were. This assumption is reinforced when we bring in those who subscribed in 1835/36, as well as in the later years: 14 occur in all three contracts.[29] One more subscriber signed in 1835/36 and again in 1844, but not in 1839/40; while another 12 subscribed in 1839/40 and 1844, but not in 1835/36. Thus 27 of the 70 subscribers of 1844 were almost certainly already investors in the Manchester & Leeds.[30] Of the 27, 9 were Londoners, and their subscriptions were about 9 per cent of the total subscribed. The other London subscribers were well-known and wealthy people such as the Grenfells and Kennards. Whether their status should lead us to place reliance upon their subscriptions is, perhaps, a moot point. At least they were not 'men of straw' or fictitious characters. And at least one of the Kennards held shares in the Manchester & Leeds after 1844 and was apparently wealthy enough to be careless about his investments. John Peirse Kennard received a payment of £193 from the Company because he paid his calls twice by mistake.[31] In the same year that this payment was made, Charles Pascoe Grenfell became a director of the Company.[32] The inclusion of Kennard and Grenfell brings the total of what we may regard as valid London subscriptions to about 17 per cent of the amount of the contract; and if we were to regard the three remaining Kennards, together with Pascoe St. Leger Grenfell, as *bona fide* investors, we have accounted for almost the whole of the 30 per cent.

There is further evidence to intimate connections with, and sustained interest in, the Manchester & Leeds of many of the

---

any distinction between the contracts on the basis of amounts. The total subscribed in 1844 was much smaller than in 1835–6 and 1839–40.

[28] *Reports & Accounts*, 5 September 1844.
[29] A number of these were directors at various times.
[30] Many of them appear in the Proceedings of the Finance Committee.
[31] Proceedings of the Finance Committee, 1 May 1846. There are many examples of this peculiar mistake.
[32] *Reports & Accounts*, 9 September 1846.

subscribers to the 1844 contract. We have already seen that 29 of the 70 people who signed it had this interest or these connections. Apart from the 4 of the remaining 41 who have been mentioned above (the three Kennards and P. St. L. Grenfell), there were Joseph Hegan, Christopher Woodhouse, R. J. Badge, Lot Gardiner, John Jellicorse, W. McKerrow, Samuel Schuster and Sigismond Stern, all of whom can be shown to have had a much more substantial connection with the Manchester & Leeds than the mere function of filling up a subscription contract. Joseph Hegan of Liverpool was elected a director of the Company in 1844 and again in 1848.[33] Lot Gardiner and Christopher Woodhouse were concerned with resolutions at the half-yearly general meeting in September 1840.[34] R. J. Badge and John Jellicorse were employees of the Company: Jellicorse was the secretary, and Badge evidently was a shareholder in the Manchester & Leeds before 1844.[35] W. McKerrow paid calls twice by mistake in 1845,[36] while Sigismond Stern and Samuel Schuster both had relations with the Company and supported its projects. Stern was chosen to sign at least three subscription contracts. The term 'chosen' is used advisedly, since even when it was not stated, the intention seemed to have been to sign merely *on behalf* of the Company. Stern was one of the two subscribers to the contract which was drawn up for the 1844 bill authorising the Company to buy land upon which the Heywood branch had been built without Parliamentary sanction.[37] (The other subscriber was a director.) He is included in Schedule B of the Wakefield, Pontefract & Goole Railway Subscription Contract, in the indenture of which the signatories of Schedule B undertook to turn the shares over to the Manchester & Leeds in the event of the Wakefield, Pontefract & Goole obtaining the sanction of Parliament.[38] He performed a similar function for the Manchester & Leeds in another contract of 1845.[39] Samuel Schuster was also one of the Schedule B subscribers to the Wakefield, Pontefract & Goole.

Taken all together, these details of the subscribers to the three contracts of 1835/36, 1839/40 and 1844 show that a very substantial

[33] *Reports & Accounts*, 5 September 1844 and 1 March 1848.
[34] *Ibid.*, 17 September 1840.
[35] Proceedings of the Finance Committee, e.g. 25 September 1839, in which Badge is down as having paid calls.
[36] *Ibid.*, 4 April 1845.
[37] Printed Copy of the *Manchester and Leeds and Heywood Branch Railway Subscription Contract*. Two subscribers signed for £1,000 each, on which they had paid £200.
[38] *Wakefield, Pontefract and Goole Railway Subscription Contract for 1845.*
[39] This contract or, rather, list of subscribers, is in B.P.P. 1845 (317) XL. There were ten subscribers, each of whom signed for £34,000; six of them were directors of the Company, and a seventh, Samuel Brooks, had been Chairman.

proportion of them were *bona fide* investors, and that any conclusions based upon an analysis of the contracts are reliable. Since so many of the 1844 subscribers had a continuing interest in, or connections with the Manchester & Leeds, it would be surprising if more than a minority subscribed only to speculate. There is, moreover, one further comment on the London element in these contracts. Apart from the fact that the 1844 list is not a list of Manchester & Leeds shareholders as such, and therefore that the increase in London's participation from 10 to 30 per cent between 1839/40 and 1844 cannot be accepted as an incontrovertible reflection of the disposal of shares by Lancashire and Yorkshire holders, there are the Lancashire connections of some London subscribers. In the 1844 contract at least one subscriber giving a London address was a Lancashire man: William Entwistle, who subscribed from Manchester in 1839, was a Member of Parliament in 1844. This qualification does not seem to be very serious for the 1844 list but in others banker-subscribers such as Loyd, Cunliffe, and Brooks might give London addresses, but they were north-country people.

To sum up this analysis of the Manchester & Leeds' capital sources, we can point to one very definite conclusion. At least one-third of the original subscribers of £2,000 or more, to the Company's first issue of stock, not only kept their shares between 1835/36 and 1839/40, thus paying up half of what they had promised, but also established themselves as a body with a continued interest in the railway by buying more shares in 1839/40. The addition to their liabilities took place, moreover, at a time when railway share prices were declining. While the new half-shares of 1839 were at a premium (the price was 9 to $9\frac{1}{2}$ when the amount paid-up was £5), the steadiness of the price does not suggest that any great speculative activity was centred around them. In addition to the third who subscribed in both years, it is possible that there were some shareholders who did not take advantage of the new offer. This is more than likely, in view of the circumstances of the year, which was one of comparative depression in trade and industry.

The 30-odd per cent of subscribers of 1835/36 who invested again in 1839/40 were mainly Lancashire people, and they represented a very strong body of supporters for the Company; the directors themselves commented on this fact.[40] At the same time it is evident that the Manchester & Leeds was, in 1839, drawing upon a geographically wider market for its capital, although the Lancashire and Yorkshire interest was still sufficiently strong to justify the term 'local' company in 1839.

[40] *Reports & Accounts*, 15 March 1838.

The greater proportion of the subscribers of 1844 were either past or future shareholders of the Manchester & Leeds, or had such connections with the Company that it seems likely that they were maintaining their role as suppliers of capital. According to the Chairman, in March 1842, there were 736 proprietors, 64 per cent of whom resided in Lancashire.[41] Now it is clear that these holders might have held more or less than 64 per cent of the shares of the Company; but it is worthwhile comparing the numbers, as distinct from the amounts of subscriptions, of Lancashire subscribers at the various dates. In 1835/36 the number was 113 out of 162;[42] in 1839/40 it was 201 out of 449; in 1844, 36 out of 70. These figures represent percentages of 70, 44 and 51, while the percentages of subscriptions coming from Lancashire at those dates were 71, 66 and 50. Whether the percentage of subscribers is reflected in the proportion of subscriptions as exactly in 1842 as it is in 1835/36, or understated as it is in 1839/40, it is still a high figure. That the shareholders of 1842 may have been different people from those in 1835/36 or 1839/40 is as irrelevant as it is unlikely. The fact remains that Lancashire was still providing the greater part of the Company's support.

The rest of the contracts are more unsatisfactory objects of analysis, since apart from the Manchester, Bury & Rossendale and the Blackburn, Burnley, Accrington & Colne, they do not present series similar to those of the Manchester & Leeds. And the Manchester, Bury & Rossendale and the Blackburn, Burnley, Accrington & Colne were sanctioned too close together to yield very useful conclusions about sources of capital. They are not, therefore, compared in any great detail; but they are used with the rest of the contracts in tests of the validity of these lists.

The subscriptions from some Lancashire towns and villages to the nine remaining railways are listed in Table 14 on the next page. A comparison of the contributions of particular towns to the various railways points to a much greater interest in the lines which were to serve those towns. It is thought legitimate, in this context, to regard Liverpool and Manchester as special cases. Liverpool's role in the sphere of railway financing is well known, while Manchester was the headquarters of the Manchester & Leeds and its successor, the Lancashire & Yorkshire. In any event, both towns, with their great

[41] Proceedings of the Proprietors, 17 March 1842.
[42] The reader is reminded that we are able to consider only those who subscribed £2,000 or more in 1835/36.

TABLE 14

SUBSCRIPTIONS FROM SOME LANCASHIRE TOWNS[43]

SUBSCRIPTIONS TO EACH RAILWAY (£100's)[44]

	Bolton & Preston	Black. & Preston	Man. Bury & Ross.	Black. Burnley Acc. & Colne	Liver. Ormskirk & Preston	Liver. & Bury	Black. Darwen & Bolton	Wake. Pon. & Goole	Hudds. & Sheff. Jc.
Turton	—	—	—	—	—	—	165	—	—
Darwen	—	19	—	—	6	—	224	—	—
Clitheroe	—	—	12	152	6	—	240	—	—
Blackburn	—	418	—	109	696	50	1307	—	10
Burnley	—	—	5	51	16	—	10	—	—
Accrington	—	20	2	61	169	—	57	—	—
Colne	—	—	—	130	17	10	—	—	—
Bury	2	2	787	1635	19	72	12	—	25
Rawtenstall	—	—	74	29	—	—	2	—	—
Padiham	—	—	—	62	—	—	2	—	—
Haslingden	—	—	75	65	—	—	—	—	—
Bacup	—	—	—	—	—	—	5	—	—
Tottington	—	—	50	92	—	—	—	—	—
Pleasington	—	—	—	—	25	—	1	—	—
Chorley	47	3	—	—	—	10	—	—	—
Bolton	615	—	27	6	—	102	85	—	—
Wigan	69	—	—	—	22	615	67	—	—
Warrington	135	22	—	—	39	20	—	—	--
Preston	—	47	—	15	132	25	132	—	—
Ormskirk	—	—	—	—	65	—	—	—	—
Burscough	—	—	—	—	4	—	—	—	—
Lancaster	15	1	—	—	22	25	17	—	—
Oldham	10	—	—	60	37	25	—	—	32
Rochdale	5	—	—	88	51	—	7	—	10
Liverpool	264	50	703	217	966	1651	24	—	180
Manchester	312	25	641	985	163	1750	395	1510	265

commercial interests, would be interested in practically any project affecting the transport communications of Lancashire and Yorkshire. Yet even Manchester and Liverpool show variations in their support for different lines, variations which suggest motives similar to those adduced for the other towns on the list. On the other hand, it appears that some of the merchants and manufacturers of Manchester were also swayed by the policy of the Manchester & Leeds. For the moment it is proposed to set aside the 'big two', and turn to the rest

[43] Note that (a) nearby places are included in the totals for several towns and villages, e.g. in Turton, in Wigan, in Accrington, and in Bolton; (b) as with previous tables, the possibility of error must be admitted for those figures compiled from B.P.P. 1845 (317, 625) XL, although any errors would be comparatively slight, and would not modify the general picture; (c) so far as is known, with the exception of those for the Wakefield, Pontefract & Goole, these figures represent subscriptions made by individuals, and do not include contributions by railway companies. By far the greater part of Manchester's figure for the W.P. & G. (XII) represents subscriptions made on behalf of the Manchester & Leeds Railway.

[44] All figures to the nearest £100; for the full names of the railways compare with Table 12, p. 113.

of the centres which gave initial financial support to these railways.[45]

The main interest of Turton, Darwen, Clitheroe, Blackburn and Preston was in the Blackburn, Darwen & Bolton. Turton was on the projected line, and this was the only railway to which its residents, and those of the nearby villages included with it, subscribed. It is, in fact, a good example of a railway interest being confined to the one line which would bring direct facilities—this particular project would give access to Manchester as well as Bolton and Blackburn. Among the subscribers of Turton were several members of the Ashworth family, with one of whom (Henry Ashworth, a cotton manufacturer who promised £1,250 to the railway) William Cooke Taylor stayed while on his 'Tour'.[46]

Clitheroe, while it was not to be provided with a line, would at least have one brought nearer to it. In fact, in the year that the Blackburn, Darwen & Bolton was sanctioned, the Blackburn, Clitheroe & North-western Junction Railway was floated to build a line from Blackburn through Clitheroe to Chatburn. Its Act of 1846 empowered it to lease or sell to the Blackburn, Darwen & Bolton.[47] Like Turton, Clitheroe was an expanding town: between 1831 and 1841 its population increased by about 30 per cent,[48] and the railways were to provide outlets for the cotton goods produced by 'Extensive cotton manufactories, and print-works, which [were] yearly increasing', as well as the lime turned out from the kilns which drew their raw material from 'an almost inexhaustible bed of limestone' in the neighbourhood.[49]

The participation of Blackburn and Darwen in the initial financing of this company needs little explanation. For Darwen, as for Turton, the concentration of subscriptions is clear; of about £25,000 to these nine companies, over £22,000 was to go to the Blackburn, Darwen & Bolton. The two Darwens (Over and Lower) boasted a rapidly growing population, up by almost 30 per cent in the 1830s, and were without railway facilities. Blackburn showed a considerable interest in more than one of these projects, but all the railways it supported to a substantial extent were expected to be of direct benefit. The

---

[45] That is, those in Table 14, which is not of course a comprehensive list of all centres which backed these nine lines.

[46] W. Cooke Taylor, *Notes on a Tour in the Manufacturing Districts of Lancashire* (2nd Edn., 1842), Letters II and VIII. 'The . . . valley is studded with factories and bleach works.'

[47] 9 & 10 Vict., c. 265, s. 39.

[48] All population statistics are taken from the following: for 1831, S. Lewis, *A Topographical Dictionary of England* (4th Edn., 1840); and for 1841, *The Population Abstract* in B.P.P. 1843 (496) XXII, pp. 182–92: 'County of Lancaster'.

[49] Lewis, *Dictionary*.

town was, however, comparatively unenthusiastic about the Blackburn, Burnley, Accrington & Colne, and what we do have to explain is the preference for the Blackburn, Darwen & Bolton, when both these companies were to provide it with facilities. If the reason was speculative, what was the especial attraction of the Darwen company? The Blackburn, Burnley, Accrington & Colne was destined for absorption by the Manchester, Bury & Rossendale from the start, and would surely have been a better speculative bet. In fact, the B.D. & B. was to link Blackburn with a more heavily industrialised and more densely populated area; and, moreover, it would provide a direct route to Bolton, and from there a rather quicker access to Manchester. The large sum promised to the company did not come from a few promoters: the number of subscribers from Blackburn was over 200.

Blackburn supported the Blackburn & Preston and the Liverpool, Ormskirk & Preston for fairly obvious reasons. The Blackburn & Preston, together with the North Union line from the Liverpool & Manchester to Preston, which had been opened in 1838, meant access to both Liverpool and Manchester. By the time the Liverpool, Ormskirk & Preston was floated, the Blackburn & Preston had been sanctioned, and these two lines offered not only an alternative but a more direct route to Liverpool. Whether Blackburn could afford all this support which, for the four companies we have considered, amounted to just over £250,000, is hard to say. Certainly the Blackburn district was already a great manufacturing area; as early as 1838 the returns of the Factory Inspectors put the number of cotton operatives in Blackburn parish at over 10,000,[50] while the population of the parish, and of the town, had reached over 71,000 and 36,000 by 1841. In 1840, and it should be remembered that we are discussing projects which were sanctioned in 1844 and 1845, the value of calico, muslin and cotton goods alone 'exclusively of dyeing and printing, is estimated at more than £2,000,000 sterling per annum'.[51] In addition, there were large factories for printing, dyeing, bleaching, and other processes connected with the manufacture of cotton goods throughout the entire parish.[52] The commercial and industrial classes—the merchants, manufacturers and bankers—supplied 56 per cent of the total subscribed to the Blackburn & Preston, 60 per cent to the Liverpool, Ormskirk & Preston, 75 per cent to the Blackburn, Burnley, Accrington & Colne,

---

[50] S. J. Chapman, *The Lancashire Cotton Industry: A Study in Economic Development* (1904). This figure would not, of course, take into account non-factory workers.
[51] Lewis, *Dictionary*.   [52] *Ibid.*

and 57 per cent to the Blackburn, Darwen & Bolton.[53] The 370 or so subscribers (and this is not allowing for duplication) to the companies in question were not a large proportion of the population; and the lines were built.

Preston is an interesting example of variation in the financial support given to companies in the initial stages of their promotion. The town's residents, who numbered about 50,000 in 1841, an increase of more than 17,000 since 1831, concentrated on only two of our companies. In round figures, £13,200 was subscribed to each of the Liverpool, Ormskirk & Preston and the Blackburn, Darwen & Bolton Railways. But what is more noticeable is the general lack of subscriptions coming from the town, not only for the railways of Table 14, but also for the other lines. A possible explanation of this is the comparatively good system of communications enjoyed by Preston at an early date. By June 1843, traffic could be sent by rail to both Liverpool and Manchester via the North Union and the Liverpool & Manchester Railways and, in addition, the Bolton & Preston provided an alternative route to Manchester in conjunction with the Manchester & Bolton. There were also canal facilities: the River Douglas had been made navigable to near Ormskirk,[54] where the Leeds & Liverpool Canal could be taken, and the Lancaster Canal passed near the town.[55] Thus Preston was in a much better position than most of these Lancashire centres. Another factor might be that many commercial people were already financially concerned with the North Union, although the Bolton & Preston did not receive one subscription from Preston in 1837. The Bolton line was, however, promoted in opposition to the North Union, which later absorbed it, and if some of Preston's inhabitants had backed the North Union they would not have supported a competitor. But this motive could hardly have had universal appeal in a relatively large town. At all events, the Liverpool, Ormskirk & Preston, and the Blackburn, Darwen & Bolton were lines which would improve Preston's communications. The former's attraction is obvious, while the Blackburn & Bolton would complete a chain of railway communication between Preston and Manchester, via the Blackburn & Preston and the Manchester & Bolton.

Apart from Preston's lack of interest, the Bolton & Preston Railway is a good illustration of our point. A glance at Table 14

[53] See below, Table 17, p. 139.
[54] Thomas Baines, *History of the Commerce and Town of Liverpool*, . . . (1852), p. 401. As early as 1720 an Act had been passed for making the Douglas navigable from the Wigan coalfield to the mouth of the Ribble.
[55] James Wheeler, *Manchester: Its Political, Social, and Commercial History* (1836), p. 277. The canal ran through Preston from Kendal to West Broughton.

(p. 123) will show the main areas from which the Bolton & Preston drew its initial support. Bolton, in which are included Halliwell and Farnworth, subscribed more to this one railway than to all the others put together, and was alone responsible for over a third of the total promised. It was, of course, *par excellence* the expanding cotton town. Between 1831 and 1841 its population grew from 41,000 to not far short of 50,000, and cotton and engineering were increasingly important. Subscriptions came from nine bleachers (£15,500); from Benjamin Dobson, the machine maker (£3,750); and from iron-founders, reflecting the main industries of the Bolton area, since there were apparently 10 iron foundries which were chiefly engaged in producing steam engines for the cotton factories, while 'Machinery of all kinds, . . . are made to a great extent'.[56]

Like Bolton, Warrington was far more enthusiastic about the Bolton & Preston than any other railway. The town was noted for its varied manufactures and widespread commercial connections, which included trade relations of long standing with Preston and centres farther north, such as Kendal.[57] Since the Bolton & Preston would be an alternative route to Preston, and indirectly to Kendal, the presence of 29 Warrington people in the contract is not surprising. Chorley, again, subscribed most to the Bolton & Preston, which was to include the town in its route. Wigan did not take a great part in the financing of the companies, and only the Liverpool & Bury commanded substantial support. The main line of this railway was to pass through Wigan, providing an excellent alternative to the North Union–Liverpool & Manchester route. The new project, which was promoted by the Manchester & Leeds in opposition to the Liverpool & Manchester, would also link Wigan with the M. & L. at Bury, to which the latter was planning to extend the Heywood Branch from its main line.

As instances of a completely exclusive interest in a particular railway we may cite Ormskirk and Burscough, which subscribed only to the Liverpool, Ormskirk & Preston. Both were small places, it is true, and one would not expect their inhabitants to have promised capital to projects which did not touch them directly. But this applies only if we do not look to speculative motives. The one line to which the residents of the towns subscribed was the one which was to provide direct railway facilities. The Liverpool, Ormskirk & Preston drew much of its initial support from the two groups of places at the bottom and top of Table 14. Centres like Blackburn, Pleasington,

---

[56] Lewis, *Dictionary*.
[57] Cf. Ashton, *Eighteenth Century Industrialist*, especially the chapters on 'The Market' and 'The Carriers'.

Burnley, Accrington, Colne and Lancaster all stood to benefit from its construction. But most were also committed to the Blackburn, Burnley, Accrington & Colne, and to the Manchester, Bury & Rossendale. Not only these towns, but Bury, Rawtenstall, Padiham, Haslingden and Tottington all subscribed more to these two companies than to any other of the group, and all were to be served by them. The relations between the M.B. & R. and the B.B.A. & C., which amalgamated in 1845, have been explained, and they account for the prominence of Bury, which was the headquarters of the companies. Bury, as well as the Rossendale area, was still noted for its woollen manufacture, and this industry involved it in intimate connections with Rochdale and the West Riding. Woollen manufacturers of Bury and Rawtenstall, woollen merchants of Rochdale, and merchants and manufacturers of the West Riding wool trade, were conspicuous as promoters of and subscribers to the companies. Bury businessmen like the Grundys (woollen manufacturers), and John Robinson Kay (cotton manufacturer and spinner) were promoters and directors of both railways.[58] Kay remained a director until 1859, when he took a place on the joint Board of the Lancashire & Yorkshire and East Lancashire companies.[59]

While it is true that Kay was a shareholder in the Manchester & Leeds before the Manchester, Bury & Rossendale was projected, and Edmund Grundy, Jnr., subscribed to the Liverpool & Bury in 1844/45, the population of Bury was little attracted by the rest of the projects. The Manchester & Leeds and the Bury caucus were not on good terms (it will be remembered that the Rossendale company was a product of Bury's dissatisfaction with the Manchester & Leeds' plans for the area) and this is no doubt one of the reasons for the lack of support for the Liverpool & Bury. It is also possible that the merchants and manufacturers of Bury decided they had taken on enough with the B.B.A. & C. and the M.B. & R., which were both promoted in less than two years.

Oldham and Rochdale, though they contributed rather more substantially to the Blackburn, Burnley, Accrington & Colne than to the other railways, are something of an enigma. If anything, Oldham illustrates better than Bolton the effects of the industrialisation of north England. It has been estimated that in 1770 it contained fewer than 3,000 souls,[60] and it was only after 1790 that the town achieved any sort of prominence. In the 1830s the increase in population had

---

[58] 7 & 8 Vict., c. 60, Preamble and s. 76; 8 & 9 Vict., c. 35, ss. 3 and 10.
[59] *Reports & Accounts of the Lancashire & Yorkshire Railway*, 31 August, 1859. The East Lancashire had been the outcome of the expansion of the Manchester, Bury & Rossendale.

been about 10,000, and textiles and mining were rapidly expanding industries. According to Samuel Lewis's *Topographical Dictionary*, the number of steam engines in use was considerably more than 200. Yet the list of subscriptions from Oldham is unimpressive, especially when compared with the activity of other Lancashire towns in the sphere of railway finance. It is unlikely that the inhabitants were satisfied with the facilities afforded by the Oldham and Rochdale Canals, and there was too much industrial enterprise for lack of capital to be a convincing explanation. There was, furthermore, a great deal of building and provision of public utilities.[61] Even the Manchester & Leeds gained little support: only £5,000 in 1835/36,[62] and there was not a single subscription in 1839/40.

Rochdale is also near Manchester and was on the Manchester & Leeds' main line, but it did not subscribe to the Company and its population promised a smaller total to all the railways than Oldham. However, the town had close links with the woollen trade of Rossendale and Bury and it is apparent that the Blackburn, Burnley, Accrington & Colne was in greater favour, for well over half the total subscribed went to this company. It had long been the market for the woollen products of the Rossendale area, which was one of the last districts in Lancashire to succumb to the cotton manufacturing industry, and its merchants had been concerned in the flotation of the Rochdale Canal Company, which was sanctioned in 1794.[63] Although the control of the Rochdale merchants over this trade was weakening in the early nineteenth century, as Manchester became more important; and although the woollen manufacture itself was declining in the face of competition from cotton,[64] the Rossendale–Rochdale links had not vanished. According to Tupling, 'the Rossendale dealers did not wholly forsake the Rochdale market',[65] and in the 1840s the woollen trade was by no means extinct in Bury, Rossendale, or Rochdale. There were 36 woollen mills in the Rochdale area about 1844, besides 4 mills 'manufacturing both wool and cotton'.[66] In 1840 it was noticed that while 'calicoes and strong

---

[60] A. P. Wadsworth and J. De L. Mann, *The Cotton Trade and Industrial Lancashire 1600–1780* (1931), p. 311.

[61] Lewis, *Dictionary*.

[62] That is, from those subscribing £2,000 or more; there may have been subscriptions of less than £2,000.

[63] A. Redford, *Manchester Merchants and Foreign Trade 1794–1858* (1934), p. 174. Even here Manchester merchants were the mainstay.

[64] G. H. Tupling, *Economic History of Rossendale*, pp. 201–2.

[65] *Ibid.*, p. 201n: 'The trade reports in the Manchester newspapers of the 'thirties frequently mention "goods of the Rossendale manufacture" in the Rochdale market.'

[66] *Ibid.*; these figures are not given by Tupling in his text—they have been counted from the map facing p. 212.

K

cotton goods are made to a very considerable extent and within the last few years, [and] the spinning of cotton has been introduced with success' in Rochdale [parish?] itself, the woollen trade still gave employment to about 12,000 people.[67]

Since '. . . the practice of visiting Manchester twice or thrice a week was as well established in the third decade of the century among the woollen as among the cotton manufacturers'[68] of Rossendale, it is not surprising that those manufacturers supported the Manchester, Bury & Rossendale, and that Rochdale was hostile. By the time the Blackburn, Burnley, Accrington & Colne was projected, however, the Manchester & Leeds was proposing an extension of the Heywood branch to Bury. These new lines would give Rochdale improved access to its old markets, and this may explain the town's greater interest in the Blackburn, Burnley, Accrington & Colne. But the paucity of financial backing from both Rochdale and Oldham remains rather puzzling.

There are, then, qualifications to an argument which seeks to explain the subscriptions of particular towns to particular railway schemes in terms of direct commercial interest in the lines which were to serve those towns. There is the peculiar position of Oldham and Rochdale; Bacup, in this view, should have supported the B.B.A. & C., if not the Manchester, Bury & Rossendale; and the role of Liverpool and Manchester obviously cannot be explained solely by reference to this factor. And it may be thought that there is a contradiction between this argument, and the view stated in the Introduction and in Chapter 5 that it is the influence of Lancashire in the national railway capital market that should be emphasised, rather than the prevalence of local finance. But it was most probably the surpluses from Manchester, Liverpool and from a few other large towns like Birmingham, which flowed over the country. Lancashire railways alone could not absorb the excess of capital. For the smaller centres of Lancashire the 'home' railways probably provided opportunity enough; certainly most of the towns considered (and not only those listed in Table 14) concentrated on those railways which were to provide them with facilities.

Finally in this section the part played by Liverpool and Manchester in the initial financing of our companies is considered. Their primary importance was indicated by the figures in Table 14 (p. 123), and no account of capital sources would be complete without

[67] Lewis, *Dictionary*. This figure may well be exaggerated.
[68] Tupling, *Economic History of Rossendale*, p. 201.

discussing and emphasising this predominance. With only an occasional exception the towns, singly or jointly, were responsible for a large proportion of the money subscribed for each capital issue.

TABLE 15

TOTAL SUBSCRIPTIONS FROM MANCHESTER
AND LIVERPOOL

Company	Date of Contract	Total of Contract (£)	Manchester £	%	Liverpool £	%
Manchester & Leeds	1835–36	628,700	343,000	55	55,000	9
Manchester & Leeds	1839–40	650,000	328,500	50	22,500	3
Ashton, Stalybridge & Liverpool Jc.	1844	117,500	54,250	38	6,100	5
Bolton & Preston	1837	174,750	31,200	18	26,400	15
Blackburn & Preston	1844	90,350	2,500	3	5,000	5
Manchester, Bury & Rossendale	1844	285,200	64,100	22	70,350	25
Blackburn, Burnley, Accrington & Colne	1844–45	461,600	98,450	21	21,650	5
Liverpool, Ormskirk & Preston	1845	513,950	16,300	3	96,650	19
Liverpool & Bury	1845	609,250	175,000	29	165,100	27
Blackburn, Darwen & Bolton	1845	296,100	39,500	13	2,400	1
Wakefield, Pontefract & Goole	1844–45	269,100	151,000	56	—	—
Huddersfield & Sheffield Junction	1845	451,600	26,500	6	18,000	4
Totals		4,548,100	1,320,300	29	489,150	11

N.B.—Sums are to the nearest £50; percentages are to the nearest per cent.

The role of Liverpool in the early railway capital market has received the notice it deserves. But it is rare that Manchester receives even a degree of the stress placed upon Liverpool, and for these companies at least, Manchester was in total a much greater source of primary support than Liverpool. This is not so very surprising when we remember that the metropolitan area of Manchester had a larger population than Liverpool: their populations in 1841 have been estimated at 417,000 and 330,000 respectively.[69] Liverpool, moreover, felt the impact of migration to a much greater extent than Manchester in the 1830s and 1840s, and since Manchester took in

[69] Edwin Cannan, 'The Growth of Manchester and Liverpool, 1801–1891', *Economic Journal*, Vol. 4 (1894), pp. 111–114. In Manchester were included Manchester, Salford, Prestwich, Barton and Chorlton registration districts, together with four sub-districts. In Liverpool, the districts of Liverpool, Toxteth Park, West Derby and Birkenhead.

more of the Lancashire-born migrants, and Liverpool more of the Irish-born immigrants as residents,[70] it seems probable that Manchester gained in wealth *per capita*. Taken together the two centres were, more than any other, the true origins of the railway system of England. The role of Lancashire in the national railway capital market will be considered in more detail in Chapter 5, and here we are concerned only with the extent to which Manchester and Liverpool participated in the initial financing of our companies.

The amounts subscribed from Manchester and Liverpool to each railway are given in Table 15 on p. 131; in round figures, the total amount subscribed by these two towns[71] to the contracts was £1,800,000 out of just over £4½ millions, or approximately 40 per cent. This is a striking result, but no less impressive is the greater importance of Manchester, which supplied almost three times as much as Liverpool. Manchester, it is true, was more intimately concerned with some of the companies than Liverpool. The Manchester & Leeds was a Manchester company; the Liverpool & Bury, the Wakefield, Pontefract & Goole, and the Ashton, Stalybridge & Liverpool Junction were sponsored by the Manchester & Leeds; and it is these projects which commanded the greater amount of capital from Manchester. There is also the fact that the subscriptions from Manchester to the Wakefield, Pontefract & Goole were of a special nature, which will be explained later. At the same time, it is clear that Liverpool was more interested in the two companies (the Liverpool & Bury and the Liverpool, Ormskirk & Preston) with which it was directly associated, and it is worth looking at these variations in support more closely.

Liverpool was noted for its very active promotion of the national railway network, support for which cannot be explained by purely local commercial interest, but in Lancashire there was much greater support for the companies which extended its railway facilities. The largest totals of subscriptions went to the Liverpool & Bury, the Liverpool, Ormskirk & Preston, the Manchester, Bury & Rossendale, and the Manchester & Leeds. In a sense practically all the companies listed in Table 15 would benefit a commercial centre like Liverpool, and the large amount promised to the M.B. & R. must come under the heading of general commercial interest. But the other companies were to provide direct facilities. The Liverpool & Bury and the Liverpool, Ormskirk & Preston would be new and alternative routes

[70] *Ibid.*, p. 114.
[71] In the totals for Manchester have been included subscriptions from places such as Pendleton, Crumpsall and Chorlton, as well as from the more important Salford. Liverpool includes Everton, Kirkdale and other nearby places, but not Birkenhead.

from Liverpool to Wigan, Bolton, Bury and Preston. It is legitimate to emphasise the twin motives of providing access to towns, and of breaking a company's monopoly. But unless it can be shown that the merchants who were supporting a line which was to provide an alternative route were either not financially concerned in the existing railway or had more to gain from the advent of a competitor, monopoly-breaking may only be put forward as a tentative explanation. It is not known, for instance, whether the shareholders of the Liverpool & Manchester Railway subscribed to the Liverpool & Bury, which was promoted to compete with the older line; and there is, in addition, the speculative motive. A merchant-shareholder in the Liverpool & Manchester might think it profitable to subscribe to the Liverpool & Bury in the hope of disposing of the shares at a profit, even at the risk of an ultimate depreciation of his L. & M. holding. However, the new line would give a less tortuous connection with Wigan, Bury and intermediate industrial centres, as well as an alternative route between Manchester and Liverpool, and it is more than likely that commercial advantage would outweigh these other considerations.

The Manchester & Leeds was a natural object of interest, because it would achieve complete railway communication between Liverpool and Hull. But the support from Liverpool was comparatively weak in view of the benefits to be gained, not only from improved communications with Hull, but also, *inter alia*, with the West Riding. The Manchester & Leeds was, however, definitely a product of Manchester enterprises as well as finance, and its Board no doubt exercised control over access to its subscription contract.[72] It is also possible that by the time the contract was drawn up the Liverpool investors were too deeply involved in other schemes.[73] Their backing for the Bolton & Preston, though only slightly larger than that for the Manchester & Leeds in 1839/40, represented a much larger proportion of the contract: 15 per cent compared with 3 per cent. The town ranked, in fact, third after Bolton and Manchester. The Bolton & Preston, besides providing an alternative to the North Union's route to Preston, would also give access to places between Bolton and the junction with the North Union line at Farington Junction.

[72] Railway boards always wanted to show Parliament that their projects were receiving local financial support, but their success naturally depended on the availability of local capital and, as Chapter 5 shows, in many parts of the country this supply was inadequate. Often Lancashire was then called upon to make good the deficiency.
[73] See below, Chapter 5. Many of these schemes were major lines in widely scattered parts of the country.

The contributions to the remaining companies may be briefly examined. The Blackburn, Burnley, Accrington & Colne probably commanded support for the same reasons as the Liverpool, Ormskirk & Preston, which was to join the Blackburn & Preston at Farington Junction, and would therefore be a part of a line extending from Liverpool to Colne. The Blackburn, Darwen & Bolton would, on the face of it, have been attractive since it connected Liverpool with the important manufacturing area between Bolton and Blackburn for the first time, yet it received the promise of a mere £2,400. Since the amount subscribed by Manchester was also quite small, it is likely that the promoters of the Bolton–Blackburn line successfully kept the contract in the hands of those who lived in the towns local to the line. The proportions of subscriptions coming from Lancashire in general, and from those towns in particular, were very high indeed. The lack of interest in the Blackburn & Preston may be explained by a similar argument, since it contrasts with the support for the Liverpool, Ormskirk & Preston. But it is impossible to say how far the control the companies exercised over the composition of their contracts affected the distribution of subscriptions. It is most probable that some of the methods of disposing of shares would have enhanced the proportion of subscriptions coming from local sources. Several applicants for shares in the Manchester & Leeds in the early months of 1836 pointed out that they possessed property affected by the projected line, and one asked for 10 or 20 shares 'previously to signifying his assent'.[74] The Secretary of the Company was directed to inform these applicants that a portion of the shares was 'reserved for the use of the Landowners and others whose property' was involved, and that their claims would receive the best consideration when the allotting of shares took place.[75] It was subsequently decided that an allotment was to be made if the line passed through the land of another person who was applying for shares.[76] This does not mean that these applicants received shares on preferential terms in the monetary sense. There is no evidence to support the view that they obtained free shares or shares at a discount.

So far as Liverpool is concerned, we may dispose of the two Yorkshire companies in a few words; nothing was subscribed to the Wakefield, Pontefract & Goole, and the amount that went to the Huddersfield & Sheffield Junction was only 4 per cent of the total. Manchester was more important in the initial financing of these companies, but in fact its role has been over-stated because the bulk

---

[74] Proceedings of the Directors, 4 February 1836. This application was later withdrawn.
[75] *Ibid., loc. cit.*   [76] *Ibid.,* 11 February 1836.

of the subscription to the Wakefield, Pontefract & Goole was made on behalf of the Manchester & Leeds. (This is not shown by the 1845 Parliamentary Papers from which the subscriptions were taken, and anyone using that source must be careful that he is not crediting individuals with a greater amount of financial support than is justified.) £145,000 of the £151,000 included in Table 15 as Manchester's contribution is contained in a separate schedule to the contract, the indenture of which states that the subscribers named in the schedule undertook to turn the shares over to the Manchester & Leeds. Since the latter was a Manchester concern, and since the subscription to the Yorkshire company would have to be financed by a Manchester & Leeds stock issue, there is some justification for including it under Manchester,[77] whose overall percentage would only be reduced to 26 by its omission. But it is not surprising that none of the big towns is well represented in the contract, since well over half the total came from another railway company: there was little scope for the independent subscriber. The Huddersfield & Sheffield Junction contract seems to stand in a class of its own. This railway was most certainly a 'local' line; over 80 per cent of the total subscribed in 1845 was from Yorkshire, and well over half that proportion from Huddersfield, Holmfirth, and nearby towns and villages. But it may be remembered that the Manchester & Leeds gave no support to this line and felt obliged to take it over in 1846 as a defensive measure.[78]

It would obviously be quite wrong to identify the interests of such a large centre as Manchester with those of a particular company, in spite of the large amounts subscribed to the Manchester & Leeds in both 1835/36 and 1839/40, and the strong support shown for the Liverpool & Bury, which was floated with the support of the M. & L. The numbers of subscribers were large on these occasions; 76 residents of Manchester and its satellites each contributed £2,000 or more in 1835/36, 122 subscribed in 1839/40, and the Liverpool & Bury was supported by 89 Manchester people in 1845. Many of the subscribers of 1835/36 signed for shares again in later contracts (31 of the 76 reappear in the 1839 contract), and were therefore still shareholders three years after their original subscriptions, forming a body of investors concerned to protect the interests of the company in which they held shares. Practically none of these subscribed, for instance, to the Manchester, Bury & Rossendale in 1844,[79] when it

[77] See the Act incorporating the W.P. & G.: 8 & 9 Vict., c. 172, ss. 6 and 7.
[78] See above, pp. 22, 32.
[79] Only three of the 35 Manchester names in the Manchester, Bury & Rossendale contract are in either of the Manchester & Leeds contracts, and two of these are almost certainly the same person.

was promoted in opposition to the Manchester & Leeds, and this may have been the reason for the abstention of M. & L. shareholders. But 22 per cent of the contract of the Rossendale company was subscribed from Manchester. Clearly there was an independent collection of people interested in improving communications between Manchester and the Rossendale area, and of the 35 Manchester names in the contract, 19 were those of merchants and manufacturers.

The results of this analysis of geographical sources of share capital will be used in Chapter 5, which attempts a reassessment of the early railway capital market.

II

FUNCTIONAL SOURCES

The contracts are now used to throw light upon the classes from which the companies received financial support. The usefulness of an analysis showing the functional sources of share capital depends not only upon the general validity of the subscription contracts, a question which was dealt with in the previous section, but also upon the accuracy with which the subscribers were described. The genuine investor described as 'esquire' may well have been a landowner; on the other hand, he may have been a person of no occupation, but of independent means, who adopted what was already a courtesy title—although this type one would normally expect to be described as a 'gentleman'. Against this difficulty may be set two considerations. First, the purpose, and it was known, of requiring a description was to determine the status or occupation of the subscriber, and if a contract is regarded as reliable there is no reason to suppose that an individual would have given a false description. Second, a number of those who were described as 'esquire' possessed addresses such as '—— Hall' and/or 'near ——', which indicate landowning status. This, however, is far from conclusive proof of accuracy and to add to our difficulties the dividing line between a merchant and a manufacturer was, in practice, not at all rigid.

The subscribers to the twelve contracts have been grouped into eight categories, six of which are classed as 'occupational', and two as 'non-occupational'. The six occupational categories are: *Trade*, which includes merchants, carriers, brokers, grocers, innkeepers, shopkeepers, and similar tradesmen; *Industry*, which includes all types of manufacturers, and a very few coal-proprietors; *Land*, which includes esquires (and, therefore, probably the most unsatisfactory category), yeomen, and farmers; *Banking*, consisting of bankers only; *Law*, which includes solicitors, attorneys, barristers, and a few agents; and *Miscellaneous*, which includes all types of clerks, clergymen not excepted, professional people, other than those grouped under *Law*, members of the armed services, and certain other groups. The two non-occupational categories are: gentlemen; and gentlewomen, which includes gentlewomen, spinsters, and widows. There will be anomalies in any grouping that has to be limited to a fairly small number of categories if it is to be manageable, and the inclusion of shopkeepers and innkeepers in *Trade* tends to make it rather heterogeneous. But a 'grocer', for instance, might well perform wholesale as well as retail functions, and the category does include those whose interests were broadly similar in that they were all traders of a sort.

Table 16 on p. 138 gives the percentage contributions of the two main groups of occupational and non-occupational categories. The occupied classes naturally subscribed by far the greater proportion of the capital, and the maximum variation in the relative proportions is not very great. But if Table 16 is compared with Tables 12 and 13 on pp. 113 and 115, it may occur to the reader that a number of the contracts show an inverse relation, admittedly not very consistent, between the proportions of capital coming from 'interested' counties, and the proportions of non-occupational capital.[80] It is not suggested that this inverse relation is so close that a low relative contribution from the 'interested' counties must necessarily be accompanied by a relatively high proportion of subscriptions from subscribers described as gentlemen and gentlewomen. While the interested counties subscribed a *comparatively* small proportion to the Ashton, Stalybridge & Liverpool Junction, the non-occupational group contributed only 4 per cent of the total amount, the lowest proportion of any contract.

On the other hand, it will be seen that the highest percentages of subscriptions derived from the non-occupied classes most often occur in those contracts in which the relative weight of the 'interested' counties is 80 per cent or under. The most important contracts, the ones about which we know the most, were those of the Manchester & Leeds, and these lists of 1835/36 and 1839/40 showed a clear trend towards a wider geographical dispersion of the Company's shares between the two dates. In the same period, the increase in the relative weight of the non-occupational group in the Manchester & Leeds is very noticeable. There is some indication, here at least, of the growth

---

[80] In Table 16, and in subsequent tabulations of the functional distribution of subscriptions, there is no set of figures which can be compared with the analysis of shareholdings in the Manchester & Leeds in 1838, line II in Tables 12 and 13.

TABLE 16

OCCUPATIONAL AND NON-OCCUPATIONAL
DISTRIBUTION OF SUBSCRIPTIONS

Company	Date of Contract	Occupational %	Non-occupational %
Manchester & Leeds	1835–36	90	10
Manchester & Leeds	1839–40	83	17
Ashton, Stalybridge & Liverpool Junction	1844	96	4
Bolton & Preston	1837	89	12
Blackburn & Preston	1844	93	7
Manchester, Bury & Rossendale	1844	89	11
Blackburn, Burnley, Accrington & Colne	1844–45	91	9
Liverpool, Ormskirk & Preston	1845	85	15
Liverpool & Bury	1845	83	17
Blackburn, Darwen & Bolton	1845	94	6
Wakefield, Pontefract & Goole	1844–45	86	14
Huddersfield & Sheffield Junction	1845	91	9

For the sources from which this and subsequent tables are derived, see Table 12, p. 113. Figures are to the nearest per cent.

of the rentier class, but the proportion of the 'local', more personally concerned, interest remained high.

Table 17, p. 139, shows the relative contributions of the six categories of the occupied classes. The steady preponderance, as a single group, of *Trade* is obvious: with only one exception their subscriptions totalled between one-third and one-half of the contracts. This is not, of course, an unexpected result. The merchant class was more than any other interested in improved transport communications, and its role in promoting and financing railways has been rightly emphasised. Newmarch may have been exaggerating when he said 'that the Railway Excitement of 1844–5 . . . enabled this country to pass almost at one step, and by a single sharp and effectual effort of self-denial on the part of the Middle Classes, into the possession of the most complete system of railway possessed by any country',[81] but it is true that the basic network of railways was projected and constructed in the short space of twenty years, from 1830 to 1850, and the merchant class played a crucial role in the process.

TABLE 17

ANALYSIS OF THE OCCUPATIONAL GROUP

Company	Trade %	Industry %	Law %	Land %	Banking %	Miscellaneous %
Manchester & Leeds	54	25	3	1	5	4
Manchester & Leeds	34	10	5	17	5	11
Ashton, Stalybridge & Liverpool Junction	42	9	4	23	12	7
Bolton & Preston	39	32	9	nil	3	6
Blackburn & Preston	38	16	5	18	2	14
Manchester, Bury & Rossendale	47	30	6	4	—	3
Blackburn, Burnley, Accrington & Colne	33	41	4	5	1	7
Liverpool, Ormskirk & Preston	42	15	6	7	3	11
Liverpool & Bury	41	16	10	10	1	5
Blackburn, Darwen & Bolton	26	30	8	16	1	13
Wakefield, Pontefract & Goole	43	4	4	18	2	15
Huddersfield & Sheffield Junction	43	29	5	1	2	12

Figures are to the nearest per cent; — means less than half a per cent; rounding has resulted in slight discrepancies between Tables 16 and 17.

The role of the manufacturer is, however, equally obvious from Table 17, and it is not so often stressed. The category *Industry* consists almost entirely of manufacturers of various kinds. In two of the contracts the subscriptions from *Industry* were more important than those of *Trade*, which, moreover, is a very broad category. Manufacturers certainly received attention from contemporaries such as Tooke and the contributors to the *Circular to Bankers* for the part their surplus capital played in financing railway development, and, generally speaking, the railways in which they displayed the greatest relative interest were those which were to run through the most highly industrialised regions. Their share of the subscriptions to the Manchester & Leeds in 1835/36 was 25 per cent, although it had declined considerably by 1839/40, as had that of *Trade*. The

[81] T. Tooke and W. Newmarch, *A History of Prices* ... (1857), V, p. 389.

other examples are clearer. The Bolton & Preston, the Manchester, Bury & Rossendale, the Blackburn, Burnley, Accrington & Colne, the Blackburn, Darwen & Bolton, and the Huddersfield & Sheffield Junction, to which *Industry* made percentage contributions of 32, 30, 41, 30 and 29 respectively, were all to serve more highly industrialised areas than the other railways.

If we combine the percentages subscribed by *Trade* and *Industry*, we find that their interest varied from between 44 per cent in the Manchester & Leeds in 1839/40, to 77 per cent in the Manchester, Bury & Rossendale in 1844, and 79 per cent in the Manchester & Leeds in 1835/36. The average for the combined categories is 63 per cent (41 for *Trade* and 22 for *Industry*) of the total of known subscriptions to the twelve contracts.[82] Thus these two classes supplied easily the greater proportion of the promised capital. It is argued in Chapter 5 that it is the role of Lancashire in the national railway capital market, and not 'local finance' that should be stressed. In view of its extensive participation in the financing of railways in all parts of Britain,[83] it is interesting to find, especially, that manufacturers directed surpluses into railways.[84] It remains to be seen whether they participated to anything like the same degree in non-Lancashire and non-Yorkshire lines, but it is worth noting that in an age when 'ploughing back' was necessary for the expansion of business,[85] and when this factor, and the low productivity of labour, are generally regarded as being among the causes of the low level of wages, mercantile capital certainly, and industrial capital possibly, should have been so widespread an influence in railway financing.

The desire for improved communications, and the wish to break the costly monopoly of the canals, two motives which are seen to perfection in the rise of the Manchester & Leeds, are well-known and probably adequate explanations of the interest in the lines of Lancashire and Yorkshire. But participation in the financing of companies farther afield is sometimes not attributable to these motives. It is, of course, possible that individuals in these two classes subscribed to take advantage of premiums, and that shares, once on the market, flowed to a different type of investor, who supplied the

---

[82] Two points must be noted here. First, the averages are weighted, and not simple, averages of the figures in Table 17, that is, averages of the total amount of the contracts. Second, the subscriptions signed for by a number of the subscribers to the Wakefield, Pontefract & Goole are not included in the calculations for that company's contract; see footnote 87 to p. 141.

[83] See below, pp. 160–64.

[84] Even if they were all mere speculators, buying for a rise, they still had to risk the 5 or 10 per cent deposit on the shares; and it cannot be supposed that many of the pre-mania subscribers were paid, as were some in 1845, to sign contracts.

[85] Cf. A. K. Cairncross, *Home and Foreign Investment, 1870–1913* (1953), p. 98.

bulk of the calls. This must have happened to some extent, and such a flow is suggested by the comparison of the geographical and functional distribution of the subscriptions to the Manchester & Leeds in 1835/36 and 1839/40, and of shareholdings in the intermediate year 1838. But the constant preponderance of *Trade* and *Industry* in the great majority of our contracts, over a period of ten years, and what we know of industrial and social development at the time, render it unlikely that this flow was on a large scale. Moreover, most of those who subscribed to the Manchester & Leeds in both 1835/36 and 1839/40 and who, therefore, held shares at the later date, and had paid up £50 per share, were merchants and manufacturers. At all events, and more will be said on this subject in Chapter 5, it seems certain that the view that there was a great amount of capital seeking investment in this period should be broadened to include industrial capital, capital held by still active industrialists.[86]

With the exception of the Ashton, Stalybridge & Liverpool Junction, the *Land* category did not figure very prominently in the contracts, even when the unsatisfactory description of 'esquire' was taken to indicate a landowner.[87] Generally speaking, one finds that, as with gentlemen, 'esquires' were more frequently found in places other than Lancashire and Yorkshire. It is known that in Lancashire the large landowner, with the substantial and prosperous tenant farmer, was not so common as in other parts of the country. In 1815 it was reported that more than half the cultivated land of the county was divided into farms of from 8 or 10 to 100 customary acres.[88] Do the percentages given in Table 17 under *Land* conform to this picture of the agriculture of Lancashire? The figures for the Manchester, Bury & Rossendale and the Blackburn, Burnley, Accrington & Colne are very small. But the Blackburn, Darwen & Bolton received 16 per cent of its subscriptions from *Land*, and it is obvious that this capital could not have come from outside Lancashire, since

---

[86] This view is supported by some remarks made by Tooke, and by the contemporary *Circular to Bankers*. See below, pp. 162–64.

[87] The total of subscriptions for the Wakefield, Pontefract & Goole was first calculated from B.P.P. 1845 (317, 625) XL. The percentage contribution from *Land* was 62. But it was found, from the printed copy of the Wakefield, Pontefract & Goole contract in the House of Lords Record Office, that there were two schedules. Schedule B was signed by nine prominent people connected with the Manchester & Leeds, who described themselves as 'esquires', presumably because they regarded the description, in the circumstances, a neutral one. They were signing on behalf of the Manchester & Leeds, to which they were to hand over the shares. Elsewhere they put down their correct descriptions.

[88] R. W. Dickson, *General View of the Agriculture of Lancashire* (1815), p. 116. Quoted in Tupling, *Rossendale*, p. 228.

its inhabitants promised 96 per cent of the amount of the contract. Some of the subscribers describing themselves as 'esquire' were: Joseph Feilden of Wilton House, and William Feilden of Feniscowles, near Blackburn; J. F. Hindle of Woodfold Park, near Blackburn; Daniel Hornby of Raikes Hall, Blackpool; John Hornby, M.P.; the Kays of Turton Tower, near Bolton; James Simpson of Foxhill Bank, near Blackburn, an investor in, and director of, the Manchester & Leeds from 1835—all very substantial people who account for about 13 of the 16 per cent. Simpson, however, was a merchant when he signed the 1835/36 contract of the Manchester & Leeds, and had obviously retired by the time of the Blackburn, Darwen & Bolton contract of 1845,[89] and there are other examples of subscribers changing their descriptions upon retirement. This complicates the analysis, but the very fact that we are able to trace these changes means that their connexions with our companies were continuous.

It is clear from Table 17 that no judgement is possible on the accepted view that landowners gradually changed from opponents to avid supporters of railways. Herbert Spencer, when writing of the 'illegitimate agencies' in railway promotion, maintained that[90]

'Conspicuous amongst these is the self interest of landowners. Once the greatest obstacles to railway enterprise, owners of estates have of late years been amongst its chief promoters.'

The landed interest dominated Parliament, hence the change in the attitude of the legislature from one of opposition to one of support.[91] But David Spring's statement:[92]

'In spite of the approval and even the promotion of the early railroads by some of the gentry, the evidence would suggest that landed gentlemen did not figure conspicuously as investors in railway stock. . . . [They] took slowly to investment in railways, as the Parliamentary Returns of 1845 and 1846 might suggest.'

is confirmed by the results of an analysis of the Lancashire & Yorkshire companies' contracts. Only 1 per cent of the Manchester & Leeds contract of 1835/36 was taken up by the *Land* group, while it subscribed 17 per cent to the Manchester & Leeds in 1839/40. In 1844/45 the category is responsible for 18 per cent of the Wakefield,

[89] Simpson was also described as 'esquire' in the 1839/40 contract of the Manchester & Leeds.

[90] 'Railway Morals and Railway Policy', *Edinburgh Review*, October 1854, p. 428.

[91] *Ibid.*, pp. 429–30.

[92] 'The English Landed Estate in the Age of Coal and Iron: 1830–1880', *Journal of Economic History*, Vol. IX, No. 1 (1951), pp. 6–7.

Pontefract & Goole's contract, and a mere 1 per cent of the Huddersfield & Sheffield Junction's in 1845.

It is not, therefore, possible to say whether there was increasing support from landowners as the railway system was extended in the 1840s. The high contribution from landowners to the Wakefield, Pontefract & Goole may be explained by the nature of the country through which the railway was to pass. Much more than any of the other lines, this company was to serve an agricultural area, since Wakefield was a noted wheat market at the time, and was the centre of an extensive wheat growing district. According to Lewis' *Topographical Dictionary*, published in 1840, corn and wool were the staple commodities of Wakefield, and the trade in corn had greatly increased, while a considerable number of warehouses had been built, in addition to a new corn-exchange.[93] Associated with the local malting establishments was the cultivation of barley. Pontefract and its surrounding districts were essentially an agricultural area, which was also noted for its manufacture of Pontefract cakes. A more extensive participation of landowners is reasonable, therefore, especially when we remember that well over 90 per cent of the *individual* subscriptions to this Company came from Yorkshire. The comparative absence of manufacturers, who subscribed only 4 per cent of the contract, is very noticeable against the higher proportion from the landowners.

The remaining contracts to which the *Land* group subscribed more than 10 per cent were those of Manchester & Leeds in 1839/40, the Ashton, Stalybridge & Liverpool Junction, the Blackburn & Preston, and the Liverpool & Bury. The geographical dispersion of the Manchester & Leeds £100 shares between 1835/36 and 1839/40 might be associated with the very steep rise in the *Land* percentage from 1 to 17 per cent. The proportion of scrip held by residents of Lancashire and Yorkshire was 91 per cent in 1835/36, but by 1839/40 London and areas other than Lancashire, Yorkshire and Cheshire accounted for 23 per cent of the subscriptions. In addition to London and places outside England and Wales, there were subscriptions from people in 27 English and Welsh counties, who were placed in the *Land* group much more frequently than were subscribers in Lancashire, Yorkshire and Cheshire.

Those bearing the vague description of 'esquire' must obviously be treated with great care, but whatever the validity of the *Land* category, the agricultural interest was comparatively unimportant in the initial financing of these railways. Included in this group are

---

[93] The Wakefield wheat-market was important enough in the 1830s to be quoted by the *Circular to Bankers*, No. 479, 15 September 1837.

farmers and yeomen who were not, of course, necessarily land-owners, but of whom there were very few indeed. And when a yeoman or a farmer did subscribe, it was usually for a small amount: very often the minimum, depending upon the denomination of the shares. It is likely that this paucity of farmers reflects the state of agriculture rather than the farming community's lack of knowledge of the possibilities of investment and speculation in railway shares.

Since some of the 'gentlemen' might have been landowners it is advisable to consider the contributions of this class of subscribers in this connection. Even combining the 'gentlemen' with the 'esquires', the farmers and the yeomen, does not, generally speaking, greatly enhance their relative importance. The percentages they subscribed are tabulated in Table 18. *Land* supplied 8 per cent, and gentlemen 10 per cent of the total amount of all contracts. Thus *Land* was responsible for less than a tenth of the total amount promised to our companies, while the combination promised less than a fifth. This figure, which certainly exaggerates the influence of the landed interest, nevertheless contrasts with the three-fifths and more promised by *Trade* and *Industry*.

TABLE 18

TOTAL SUBSCRIPTIONS OF 'GENTLEMEN' AND *LAND*

Company	*'Gentlemen'* %	*Land* %	*Total* %
Manchester & Leeds	9	1	10
Manchester & Leeds	13	17	30
Ashton, Stalybridge & Liverpool Jc.	2	23	25
Bolton & Preston	7	Nil	7
Blackburn & Preston	4	18	22
Manchester, Bury & Rossendale	10	4	14
Blackburn, Burnley, Accrington & Colne	8	5	13
Liverpool, Ormskirk & Preston	14	7	21
Liverpool & Bury	15	10	25
Blackburn, Darwen & Bolton	3	16	19
Wakefield, Pontefract & Goole	12	18	30
Huddersfield & Sheffield Junction	8	1	9
Averages	10	8	18

The averages are of the absolute totals.

The rest of the categories serve to emphasise the paramount importance of the merchants and manufacturers in the financing of the railways. The category *Law* was separated partly for the reason that its activities in the railway sphere have received considerable emphasis. While its percentage contributions were not very high they do compare very favourably with those of *Banking* which, one would have thought, was a more wealthy class. The 10 per cent subscribed by *Law* to the Liverpool & Bury is perhaps the most noteworthy figure. It represents £59,000, which was easily the highest total subscribed by the group to any contract, and was substantial for such a limited category. Since the number of solicitors and attorneys would not be anything like the number of merchants and grocers, their subscriptions may be regarded as relatively important. It would not be true to say that people like solicitors were necessarily the speculative London type. Almost without exception the subscribers in this category who signed, for instance, the Liverpool & Bury contract, were residents of Lancashire or Yorkshire. Some, like Henry Bury and Samuel Darbishire, were closely associated with the Manchester & Leeds.

Linked with the solicitors in the descriptions of the flotation of railways, and especially in the accounts of the railway manias, are engineers and surveyors. Most of the comment on the Stephensons is eulogy. For example, R. M. Martin said:[94]

> 'The successful establishment of the "Liverpool and Manchester" Railway, ... great credit is due to the enterprising spirit of Lancashire capitalists' who backed 'The bold and comprehensive genius of George Stephenson, ...'

But few writers failed to castigate the 'pettifogging attorneys and rejected engineers' who were 'the true authors, ... of three fourths of the railway schemes before the world at this moment [1845]'.[95] Morier Evans, Herbert Spencer, James Locke writing to Huskisson, John Francis, all burst out against this breed from 1829 onwards. But in our contracts, the engineers and surveyors were few in number.

Bankers were never prominent numerically in the contracts, although the Ashton, Stalybridge & Liverpool Junction managed to attract 12 per cent of its subscriptions from this class. On the whole it was the same few bankers who appeared in the contracts of our companies, and some of them were very wealthy men. Samuel Brooks, of Cunliffes, Brooks & Company, a director of the Manchester & Leeds, and one of the original promoters of the line, was evidently most fortunate in that 'Everything he touched brought him

---

[94] *Railways—Past, Present, & Prospective* (1849, 2nd edn.), pp. 6–7.
[95] *The Bankers' Magazine*, September 1845, quoted in D. M. Evans, *The Commercial Crisis 1847–1848* (1848), p. 14.

L

revenue'.[96] According to Grindon, he disposed of the greater part of his real and personal estate before he made his will, but still left an estimated £2½ million when he died in 1864.[97] Like Brooks, Edward Loyd, the head of the Manchester section of Jones, Loyd & Company, was a director of, and a prominent subscriber and lender to, the Manchester & Leeds and various other companies of the Lancashire & Yorkshire network. He had, it was said, not 'the slightest taint of avarice', and was 'Indifferent to speculation, the desire to get rich by leaps, which, being a disorderly thing, he constantly discouraged'.[98] Others of these firms, notably Roger and James Cunliffe (London), and Lewis Loyd were constant subscribers. It is the continual reappearance of these men as subscribers that largely makes up the contribution of the banking class, although other Lancashire bankers were not entirely absent, and we find steadfast subscribers from farther afield—Timothy Rhodes Cobb of Banbury is one example. The Proceedings of the Finance Committee of the Manchester & Leeds show, moreover, that they were more than mere subscribers: for many years they appear not only as payers of money in advance of calls, but also as substantial lenders on mortgage.[99]

The *Miscellaneous* group is a fairly wide category, and what is surprising, therefore, is not that occasionally it subscribed about 15 per cent of a contract, as with the Wakefield, Pontefract & Goole, but that more often its weight was really insignificant. Surprising, that is, when we bear in mind what has been said of the activities in railway finance of those who comprise the group. The majority of the subscriptions in this category came from surgeons, physicians, accountants, book-keepers, clergymen, engineers, surveyors, clerks, teachers, and army and navy officers. It follows that the impecunious clerk, whose speculative participation in the manias of 1836 and 1845 has received much emphasis, was comparatively unimportant even in the 'mania' contract of 1835/36. The percentages are not very large for such a broad category and the mere clerk was certainly not very conspicuous, either for the frequency with which he appeared or for the amounts which he subscribed, although the group did increase somewhat in relative importance in 1844 and 1845.

In addition, it should be mentioned that the 'clerk' was often a clergyman. While many describing themselves as clerks prefixed the explanatory 'Reverend' to their names, there are examples of

[96] Grindon, *Manchester Banks and Bankers*, p. 208.
[97] *Ibid.*, pp. 199 and 214.
[98] *Ibid.*, p. 151.
[99] Proceedings of the Finance Committee of the Manchester & Leeds, *passim*.

so-called 'clerks' being entered in a contract with no indication that they were in holy orders. The entry 'Richard Bassnett, clerk, Gorton', occurred twice in the Manchester & Leeds contract of 1839/40. The Reverend Richard Bassnett figured in a resolution at the special general meeting of the Company's proprietors in January 1839, that is, before the contract was drawn up.[100] Other examples of what are almost certainly misleading entries in the same contract are the following: Thomas Butt, clerk, Trentham, Staffordshire—the Reverend Thomas Butt is mentioned several times in the Manchester & Leeds Finance Committee minutes;[101] Miles Formby, clerk, Melling, near Liverpool—the Reverend Miles Formby is entered in the Finance Committee minutes for the meeting of 1 April 1842; James Balfour, clerk, Cheltenham—the Reverend James Balfour was mentioned in connection with a dividend cheque for October 1841, in the Finance Committee minutes of 1845.[102]

The clergy themselves have received considerable attention for their speculative activities in the mania periods. In 1845 *The Times* coined the amusing phrase, that the clergy were almost 'forsaking scripture for script'.[103] But the four mentioned above were all *bona fide* investors. To these may be added further clergymen who signed the 1839/40 contract, who put themselves down as Reverends, and who are mentioned in the Finance Committee minutes in connection with shareholdings: James Cawley, Samuel Best, and James Edwards.[104] The majority of the clergymen who subscribed in 1839/40 were investors, to the extent that they kept their shares for a sufficiently long period for them to receive dividends, or for them to pay calls.

1839 was a depressed year and there was consequently no speculative fever in railway shares. We are unable to tell whether these clergy subscribed in the speculative year of 1835/36 since they all received shares to the value of less than £1,000 in 1839/40 and, assuming that they took them on the *pro rata* basis, they would therefore have held less than £2,000 of the original stock. (The reader is reminded that the 1839 issue was of £50 shares.) We have only the list of those who subscribed £2,000 or more in the earlier year, and it contains none of the clergy mentioned. But if we cannot prove that clergymen-subscribers of a mania year were not mere

---

[100] *Reports & Accounts*, 17 January 1839.
[101] Proceedings of the Finance Committee of the Manchester & Leeds, e.g. 16 August 1838 and 10 July 1840.
[102] *Ibid.*, 5 September 1845.
[103] Cf. B. C. Hunt, *The Development of the Business Corporation in England: 1800–1867* (1936), p. 106.
[104] Proceedings of the Finance Committee, e.g. 23 November 1838, 10 July 1839, and 5 February 1842.

speculators, we can at least emphasise the genuine investment motives that lay behind the acquisition of shares by most of the clergy who supported the Manchester & Leeds. Several of them paid considerable sums in advance of calls, as the Finance Committee minutes show.[105]

There is one other point which may be mentioned in this context of clerks' subscriptions. It must be true that their salaries could not in general have been very large. Morier Evans, speaking of London, said:[106]

> 'Most of the private bankers employ between forty and fifty clerks each, and the fair average of salary they receive is £200 a year.'

If we are to believe the evidence put forward by Grindon, the Manchester banker's clerk, for example, was often far from mediocre or impecunious, and some of them later became successful bankers themselves. According to Grindon, the salary of one of the clerks (William Morton, who died in 1839) of Jones Loyd & Company, was said to be £2,000 per annum.[107] Thomas Barlow Jervis, who subscribed £1,150 to the Manchester & Leeds in 1839, and also subscribed to the Ashton, Stalybridge & Liverpool Junction in 1844, was chief clerk at Jones Loyd at the time. In 1848 he became a partner upon the reorganisation of the bank following the retirement of Edward Loyd.[108] These clerks would have been able to invest in railways. It is possible that Jervis and others like him were merely signing contracts on behalf of clients of their banks, without stating power of attorney, but this is unlikely, because the Manchester & Leeds was against such practices.[109] Whether such people signed contracts on their own or on others' behalf, they still did not constitute a substantial body of subscribers.

Finally, it may be of some interest to consider the part played by the proverbial widow. This is, of course, the pathetic figure brought into so many controversies over railways, from their early history to nationalisation. Joseph Pease, the Quaker and member of the famous Darlington family, wrote to another Company shareholder in 1842

[105] *Ibid.*, 28 December 1838, 21 June 1839, and 25 June 1841.
[106] D. M. Evans, *City Men and City Manners* (1852), p. 8.
[107] Grindon, *Manchester Banks and Bankers*; for this, and similar information, see, especially, pp. 179–82.
[108] *Ibid.*, pp. 159–63. Edward Loyd was the uncle of Samuel Jones Loyd, later Lord Overstone.
[109] Cf. Proceedings of the Directors of the Manchester & Leeds Railway, e.g. 26 January 1836 and 14 April 1836.

on the proposed establishment of the Manchester & Leeds reserve fund:[110]

> 'The widows, the trust-money of orphans .... Should the interests of these be sacrificed to satisfy the rapacious shareholders? If this is the way to support the prosperity of railways, then permit me to say, perish railways, and live justice and truth immutable. ... Allow me, my friend, to guard thee against putting thy money and thy conscience in the same pocket, for gold is in reality so much harder than conscience that it often wears conscience out.'

For Samuel Salt, the 'heaviest, because the most helpless, sufferers' from the railway depression, were the poor widows and orphans.[111] Lardner maintained that 'the fortunes of the widow and orphan, ... are fraudulently transferred to ... directors, ...'[112] These accusations were no doubt to the point after speculative manias such as the 1845 boom, but this, and so many other similar features of railway finance, have been stressed at the expense of a balanced view of railway development. The widows have been included in the gentlewomen category, and in fact the number of gentlewomen and spinsters in a contract was usually larger than that of widows. But the contribution of the whole group was not very significant, as the figures show: 1 and 4 per cent for the Manchester & Leeds in 1835/36 and 1839/40; 5 per cent for the Bolton & Preston in 1837; 2, 3 and 1 per cent in 1844 for the Ashton, Stalybridge & Liverpool Junction, the Blackburn & Preston, and the Manchester, Bury & Rossendale; and 1, 1, 2, 3, 2 and 1 per cent in 1844/45 for the Blackburn, Burnley, Accrington & Colne, the Liverpool, Ormskirk & Preston, the Liverpool & Bury, the Blackburn, Darwen & Bolton, the Wakefield, Pontefract & Goole, and the Huddersfield & Sheffield Junction respectively.

The figures for 1844/45 are particularly low, yet this was a year of rapidly increasing railway activity, in which we might have expected this type of investor, or speculator, to appear in greater relative strength. Since the widows formed only a small section of the group to which the figures relate, their role in the promising of capital was small, and even absolutely their number was insignificant.[113] Many of the female subscribers to the Manchester & Leeds can,

---

[110] By means of a letter to *The Railway Times*, 26 March 1842. See below, p. 183.
[111] *Railway and Commercial Information* (1850), p. iii.
[112] Dionysius Lardner, *Railway Economy* (1850), p. 514.
[113] Women and clergymen were accused of causing 'bubble' subscription lists— see Evans, *British Corporation Finance*, p. 35.

moreover, be shown to have had a more than speculative interest in the Company. There are, it is true, only three names of women to be found in the 1835/36 contract—the reason is no doubt that the average subscription of a female was less than £2,000—but all three subscribed again in 1839/40, and two of them are mentioned more than once in the Finance Committee minutes as payers of calls in advance. The list of 1839/40 is, however, a full one, and of the 51 female subscribers 13 are shown by the Finance minutes to have paid calls in advance between 1839/40 and 1841.[114] As for the rest, failure to pay calls in advance does not, of course, mean that a person's subscription cannot be regarded as a reliable indication of a source of capital.

The results of this functional analysis of share capital sources will be used, along with the conclusions from the geographical analysis, in Chapter 5, which endeavours to show how far these results conform to the accepted view of the early railway capital market. In Chapter 5 the functional analysis is also used to emphasise the significance for the Lancashire & Yorkshire Railway of its location in an overwhelmingly mercantile and industrial community.

[114] Proceedings of the Finance Committee, *passim.*

The Early Railway Capital Market

GENERALISATIONS about the character of the railway capital market have frequently been accepted, yet the validity of the material, such as lists of subscribers and contemporary accounts of flotations, upon which these assertions must have been based, has been questioned. Perhaps the most widely used work on the financing of incorporated companies in the period up to 1850, is that of G. H. Evans, who states:[1]

> 'The local character of the railways seems to have been dominant until about 1844. . . . Local promotion and finance . . . were the mainstays of the transportation industry until the listing of shares on the London Stock Exchange and the entry of London capitalists into this field of enterprise.'

This implies that the London capitalists came on the railway scene in 1844, but Evans gives very little evidence of railway capital sources to support his statement. Sir John Clapham considered 1836 the turning point,[2] while John Francis noted the interest London took in the London & Birmingham Railway in 1832.[3]

The works of contemporaries such as D. M. Evans, John Francis, Arthur Smith and Herbert Spencer, and of more recent writers such as Cyprian Williams and Gayer, Rostow and Schwartz, contain statements which hardly favour the use of subscription contracts for any purposes other than to demonstrate the fever of speculation which gripped the middle-classes in 1845, and the fraudulent activities of directors, engineers, solicitors, contractors and other culpable participants in railway promotion and financing. Spencer's opinion of the validity of subscription contracts is obvious:[4]

---

[1] G. H. Evans, *British Corporation Finance*, p. 10. Evans does recognise, on the same page, that there had been 'a number of departures from local promotion, finance and control'.

[2] When 'Blind capital, seeking its 5 per cent' intervened: *An Economic History of Modern Britain*, I, p. 388.

[3] John Francis, *A History of the English Railway* . . . (1851), I, pp. 180–82.

[4] H. Spencer, 'Railway Morals and Railway Policy', *Edinburgh Review*, October 1854, p. 421.

> 'The general public ... do not forget the doings of stags and
> stock-jobbers and runaway directors; they remember how men
> of straw held shares amounting to £100,000 and even £200,000;
> ... how subscription contracts were made up with the signatures
> bought at 10s. and 4s. each, and porters and errand-boys made
> themselves liable for £30,000 and £40,000 apiece.'

Of the directors of the Manchester & Leeds Arthur Smith asked,
after the fashion of Mark Antony:[5]

> '... still the Directors may *not* have employed a broker to
> manoeuvre the share market, nor have propagated inflated
> reports, and may still hold every share they ever possessed, and
> if they do, are they not honourable men?'

D. M. Evans's vivid description of the frenzy of 1845 is one of the
best, and one of the most entertaining, of the accounts of the mania,
and is too well known to require any quotation.[6] In spite of all this,
there are the statements of G. H. Evans and Clapham to the effect
that the financing of railways was mainly local before the mid-1840s.
Clapham wrote:[7]

> 'Hitherto railway success, such as it was, had been due mainly
> to the resolution of small groups of local business men; to the
> enlistment of local patriotism; ....'

One wonders upon what grounds, upon what evidence, these views
are based. If subscription contracts are to be rejected as sources, then
how is it possible to accept Evans's dictum that railways depended
upon local people for their money? The fact is that writers such as
Evans and Clapham based their accounts on contemporary descriptions of flotations, descriptions which must have made use of
subscription contracts. Obviously there is a serious illogicality in the
conventional view. There is, in fact, as much *contemporary* evidence
of the non-local nature of railway financing as of the contrary.

Contracts and contemporary accounts certainly have to be handled
carefully, especially for the mania periods, but the analyses carried
out in Chapter 4 do show that the material is worth studying. In
addition, the account of the early financing of the Liverpool &
Manchester Railway given by Harold Pollins contains some interesting points. His comparison of the list of subscribers to the Liverpool

---

[5] *Railways As They Really Are ... No. VII. The Lancashire and Yorkshire
Railway* (1847), p. 11. Much of the money signed for by the directors was on
behalf of the Company. This practice was sanctioned by Parliament.
[6] *The Commercial Crisis 1847–48* (1848): 'The Railway Mania and its Effects'.
[7] Clapham, I, p. 386. He is here referring to 1836.

& Manchester in 1825/26 with one of shareholders about 1845 shows that at least 25 per cent of those who subscribed in the former years were still holding shares some twenty years later.[8] And twenty years is no mean test of the reliability of these subscribers, who signed the contract during a time of speculation.

How far does the analysis of the Manchester & Leeds' sources of share capital fit into the general view of the early railway capital market, propounded by G. H. Evans and others? It will be remembered that the relative and absolute weight of the 'interested' areas of Lancashire and Yorkshire declined between 1835/36 and 1839/40, with this decline apparently confirmed by the analysis of shareholdings in 1838. Evans knew of this analysis and briefly referred to the 'great degree of local interest' in the Manchester & Leeds.[9] This is perfectly true, although the local interest had decreased somewhat since 1835/36. But the results of the analysis of the 1844 and early 1845 contracts do not indicate that there was a rapid change towards a more perfect market. The percentages contributed by the interested counties were, in fact, sometimes as high as in the earlier years. Whether one regards the signatories of the contracts as investors or speculators, it is interesting to note that Lancashire supplied 98 per cent of the subscriptions to the Bolton & Preston in 1837, and 96 per cent of those to the Blackburn, Darwen & Bolton in 1845. These results are not quite what one would expect, bearing in mind the traditional view.

It has been said that the market for long-term capital was becoming more perfect in the period after 1840, when the public had 'matriculated in the school of Hudson',[10] and emphasis has been placed upon the growth of the 'impersonal' investor:[11]

'. . . the success of the industrial and commercial revolutions had resulted in London and other commercial centres in the growth of a body of capitalists not directly engaged in trade, who were now seeking an outlet, with profit, for their accumulations.'

It was this growth, it has been contended, which brought about the

[8] 'The Finances of the Liverpool and Manchester Railway', *Economic History Review*, Second Series, V, No. 1, 1952, p. 93. The figure of 25 per cent is, moreover, exclusive of those who probably inherited shares. There were several family names in both lists.

[9] *British Corporation Finance*, p. 31n. This is the only reference to any evidence of the distribution of railway shareholdings.

[10] M. M. Postan, 'Recent Trends in the Accumulation of Capital', *Economic History Review*, October 1935, p. 6: 'Capital very nearly became the perfect . . . factor of production . . . impersonal, divisible and capable of easy movement. . . .'

[11] J. B. Jefferys, 'Trends in Business Organisation in Great Britain since 1856' (unpublished Ph.D. Thesis, London, 1938), p. 9.

enactment of limited liability. It was the pressure of the new class of
investors for an outlet for their savings that obtained the Act of 1856,
and the influence of the railways and their supporters were the
immediate factors:[12]

> '. . . no one seems to have queried the right of railway companies
> to have limited liability. It was taken for granted that where a
> large capital . . . was needed . . . the subscribers should be given
> that privilege. . . . But it was only rarely seen that the same
> argument(s) applied to all registered companies. . . . It was the
> railways that won the acceptance of general limited liability. . . .
> The only safe investment for small passive capitalists had been
> the canals and the railways . . . limited liability would open the
> general field of industry to such investments and further national
> prosperity would result.'

That this question of safe investments for 'small' people was in the
minds of contemporaries is illustrated by the terms of reference given
to the Select Committee on Investments for the Savings of the Middle
and Working Classes, which reported in 1850. Railways, not surprisingly at the time, did not loom large either in the report or in
the evidence.[13]

It cannot be denied that many of the ingredients of a perfect
capital market were emerging in the early 1840s. Knowledge of
railways was certainly widespread: there was an immense increase
in the output of railway literature, which varied in quality from the
prophesy that the canals would outlast the railways,[14] to the sound
advice given by a Successful Operator, who urged investors to be
prepared to pay calls.[15] Expectations of returns from railway investment were good and, other things being equal, if the capital market
had been in any pronounced degree perfect, capital would have
responded to expected differences in yield. But the percentage
contributions of London to some of the railway contracts analysed

[12] H. A. Shannon, 'The Coming of General Limited Liability', *Economic History*,
Vol. II, No. 6, pp. 286–88.
[13] B.P.P. 1850 (508) XIX, *Report of the Select Committee*. . . . The terms of
reference were: '. . . to consider and suggest Means of removing Obstacles
and giving Facilities to safe Investments for the Savings of the Middle and
Working Classes. . . .' Only railway debentures were mentioned—see QQ 236-
40. See also John Saville's illuminating article 'Sleeping Partnership and
Limited Liability, 1850–1856', *Economic History Review*, S.S., Vol. VIII,
No. 3, 1956.
[14] Richard Z. Mudge, *Observations on Railways* (1837).
[15] 'A Successful Operator', *A Short and Sure Guide to Railway Speculation* (1845).
This, the *Sixth* Edition, was dedicated to George Hudson, 'Head of the
Railway World'.

in Chapter 4 were very low indeed, and there were no London subscribers to two of them. They do not therefore seem to reflect the pressure of a great amount of capital seeking investment from that city. If the high concentration of subscriptions from Lancashire and, to a lesser extent, from Yorkshire is to be explained, as it may well be, partly by the difficulties facing the Londoner wishing to subscribe to these railways, then the capital market was just that much less than perfect.[16]

But it is not believed that 'rigidities' are the whole answer. Jeffrey's argument that there was an increasing number of 'impersonal' investors up to the time of the enactment of general limited liability is not disputed. What is not clear in his argument is just who were the 'capitalists not directly engaged in trade'. One feels sympathy with those who saw the ambiguity of such statements—for reference to this type of capitalist, who was supposed to be dominating railway development, is by no means new. In a pamphlet written in 1849, C. Locock Webb was concerned with this question of the non-commercial capitalists of the day. Referring to the Railway Commissioners' statement that railways 'should become legitimate investments for the capital of non-commercial persons' because, they assumed, either the 'commercial' capitalists had already withdrawn from the railways, or they were about to do so, he says:[17]

> '. . . it is unintelligible, why that class of persons to whom we are indebted for the prompt development of Railways, whose spirit, energy, and business habits have overcome all difficulties, should give place to a non-commercial class. . . . A "non-commercial" class, in England at least, requires some translation of its meaning. . . . But supposing such a class existed, is it to be imagined that a capital of such an enormous amount remains idle for investment; . . . Who is the stock-holder, but the trading class?'

Allowing for a certain exaggeration for effect, there is much truth in all this. The clear predominance of the merchants and manufacturers in the contracts which were analysed in Chapter 4 did not decline over a period of ten years or so from 1835 to 1845.[18]

Nor do we need to conclude that Professor Shannon was mistaken in attributing a great influence to the railways in bringing about general limited liability. We need only to conclude that the widening,

[16] For a description of the methods of placing shares, see H. Pollins, 'The Marketing of Railway Shares in the First Half of the Nineteenth Century', *Economic History Review*, S.S., Vol. VII, No. 2, December 1954.
[17] *A Letter . . . on Railways, their Accounts and Dividends*, . . . (1849), pp. 41–42.
[18] See above, Chapter 4, Table 17, p. 139.

broadening, perfecting—what you will—of the capital market from 1835 onwards was less marked than has been believed. It may be objected that the company for which there have been put forward the most convincing tests of the validity of its contracts, namely, the Manchester & Leeds, did experience a widening of its capital market. But the local interest remained high, and there are other factors to be considered when discussing the nature of the capital market in this period. First, there is the dating of the contracts. It would be unwise to generalise and say that reliance may be put upon those contracts which were entered into during times of depression, or of comparative depression, while those drawn up during prosperity phases, or booms, should be dismissed. Since the flotation of most of the country's railway companies took place in the mid-1830s and mid-1840s, not to mention the booms of the mid-1850s and 1860s, dismissal of those companies' contracts would mean the abandonment of all hope of ascertaining railway capital sources. And the Liverpool & Manchester and the Manchester & Leeds were both products of boom conditions.

Many of the subscribers of 1835/36 and 1839/40 to the Manchester & Leeds—*the bona fide* investors—reappear in the 1844/45 contracts. They may have become speculators by 1845, but it is important to remember that the railways which issued contracts in 1844/45 were not the products of the great mania of 1845. With only one exception (the Liverpool, Ormskirk & Preston) these railways were *authorised* in that year, and were therefore projected before the mania really got under way. Authorities differ in charting the course of the mania. All agree that the peak of the madness was reached in the early summer, but there is a difference of opinion as to whether the flotations of the summer of 1844 were speculative (in the more restricted sense of the word) undertakings. It is well known that the increase in the number of projected lines which were to be put before Parliament in the session of 1845 caused the establishment of Lord Dalhousie's Board in August 1844. By the October the editors of the *Morning Chronicle* 'were deeply concerned over the headlong rush of capital into railways', although as recently as the January they had stated:[19]

'For two years our capitalists have been anxiously waiting for a revival. . . . Profitable investment there seems to be none.'

On the other hand, some writers draw a distinction between the projects of 1844 and those of 1845. D. M. Evans would probably

---

[19] Quoted in B. C. Hunt, *The Development of the Business Corporation in England, 1800–1867* (1936), p. 103.

have included the former in what he termed 'the primary and legitimate movement', which later became an 'overwhelming and destructive mania' after about April 1845.[20] Francis agreed with this view, and the index of railway share prices constructed by Gayer, Rostow and Schwartz also appears to confirm it: between July and December 1844 it rose exactly seven points, while between January and June 1845 it rose by 33 points, and was yet to reach its peak.[21]

The Blackburn, Burnley, Accrington & Colne contract was filled up between 30 October 1844 and February 1845; all the subscriptions in the Wakefield, Pontefract & Goole were signed for in December 1844, and January 1845; the indenture of the Blackburn, Darwen & Bolton contract was made on 9 January 1845. Accepting Morier Evans's view, we may be confident that our contracts were pre-mania, especially when we remember that for compliance with Standing Orders, copies of Parliamentary deeds had to be deposited in Parliament Office before the presentation of the petitions for the bills.[22] The petitions for our six 1845 bills were presented in February 1845 (five bills), and April 1845 (one bill).[23] The Committee stages were in April and May.[24]

There are further grounds for believing that it would be unreasonable to reject as sources all subscription contracts because it was possible for them to contain the names of speculators, 'men of straw', and fictitious characters. The contracts used in this study were those of Lancashire and Yorkshire companies whose bills were, with only one exception,[25] successful in the sessions for which they were prepared; of companies which built the lines which were sanctioned. They amalgamated to form a company which soon became one of the greatest provincial networks, second only to the North Eastern; and the Lancashire & Yorkshire was one of the comparatively soundly financed companies. The nucleus of the Lancashire & Yorkshire was the Manchester & Leeds which, as its *Reports* & *Accounts* and Finance Committee minutes show, experienced no difficulty in raising either calls on shares or loans in the unfavourable years between 1837 and 1841, and very little even in 1842. In March 1838, at a relatively depressed time, the directors remarked that the state of the call account was 'so gratifying, as well

---

[20] *Commercial Crisis*, p. 3. But as early as 5 April 1845, *The Economist* expected enormous losses from the new projects, whether they were objects of speculation or of genuine investment.
[21] *Growth and Fluctuation*, I, p. 375.
[22] T. Erskine May, *A Treatise Upon the Law, Privileges, Proceedings and Usage of Parliament* (1844), p. 394.
[23] *The Railway Register . . .*, Volume II (1845), pp. 225–31.
[24] B.P.P. 1845 (659), XXXVI, pp. 113, 116 and 118.
[25] The Liverpool, Ormskirk & Preston, which was successful in 1846.

as unprecedented, at this stage of any similar Company's proceedings. . . .'[26] Less than 2 per cent of the calls remained unpaid, a result which the Board attributed to the character of the proprietary, and to the large holdings in Manchester and other places local to the line, the people of which were able, so the directors said, to judge the merits of the Company. The Board was feeling very confident:[27]

> 'It being the intention of the Directors to prosecute the works with all reasonable rapidity, the calls on the Shareholders will necessarily be corresponding with the progress made.'

It did not attempt to delude the proprietors, at this stage of the Company's history at least, by promising them that only a certain proportion of the shares would ever be called up. On the contrary, nothing could be clearer than the following statement of intentions:[28]

> '. . . the Directors have always considered that they should best promote the real interest of the Proprietors by completing the railway at the earliest practicable period: and with such a proprietary they never doubted that the rapid calls, . . . would be responded to with alacrity, and their expectations have not been disappointed.' These were 'unusual circumstances'.

In two years the capital receipts had exceeded £400,000.

In 1840, however, the deepening depression was reflected in the directors' intention to concentrate on borrowing,[29] and the *Report* for the meeting of September 1841 included an assurance that the Board did not want to make calls, because the market value of the Company's stock was depressed.[30] Nevertheless, although the claim of March 1842 that not a single shareholder was in default was a slight exaggeration, investors in the Manchester & Leeds were seldom unwilling to pay up.[31] Unlike the directors of companies such as the unfortunate Eastern Counties, the Manchester & Leeds Board did not have to take legal action to enforce the payment of calls in the crucial period of the construction of the main line, and, moreover, many calls were paid in advance throughout the same period. Even the Report of 17 September 1840 which announced the virtue of loans contained the warning that acceptance of money in advance

---

[26] *Reports & Accounts*, 15 March 1838.
[27] *Ibid., loc. cit.*
[28] *Ibid.*, 17 September 1838.
[29] See above, Chapter 3, for a discussion of the change in policy. As late as February 1844 the Company was obtaining loans at 3¼ per cent from both individuals and institutional investors.
[30] *Reports & Accounts*, 16 September 1841.
[31] *Ibid.*, 17 March 1842.

of calls could not be guaranteed in the future because a proportion of the unpaid calls had been appropriated as security for bonds. By the end of 1840 the total paid in advance had reached over £185,000.[32]

It is not contended that the Company's finances were as sound as they might have been, or should have been. But capital issues such as the first preference issue in 1841 were not avoided by any company, and were the result of the huge expenditure necessary, coupled with bad conditions of trade and industry. Moreover, the 1841 issue was made to obtain loans on the security of the shares, not in order to raise further share capital.[33] Since, as Evans says, there are 'A number of reasons for believing that . . . [appeals to the public to take up preference issues] were not numerous' before 1850,[34] and since most of the issues would therefore have been taken up by the existing shareholders, the proportion that guaranteed stock bore to the whole of the permanent capital is some indication of the state of a company's finances. In fact, Henry Ayres's study of railway finance shows that, in comparison with many other companies, the Lancashire & Yorkshire continued to display the *comparative* financial soundness of its parent company. Ayres's criterion of financial stability was the ratio of paid-up ordinary share capital to other descriptions of stock:[35]

> 'The Ordinary paid-up Share Capital, which ought to constitute the foundation upon which all the other descriptions should be secured, has been overwhelmed by the united claims of Preferential Shareholders, and the holders of Debenture Bonds, in many of our leading Railway Companies.'

He noted the correlation between the low proportion of ordinary paid-up capital, and the poor financial results of many companies.[36] Of the fourteen largest English and Welsh railway companies, in December 1865, only one, the London & North-Western, had a proportion of ordinary paid-up capital which exceeded that of the Lancashire & Yorkshire.[37] The proportions for these fourteen companies varied from 64·24 per cent for the L. & N.W., and 57·82 per cent for the Lancashire & Yorkshire, down to as low as 30·24 for the Great Western.[38] The proportion of ordinary paid-up

---

[32] *Ibid.*, 3 March 1841. [33] See above, Chapter 3.
[34] Evans, *British Corporation Finance*, p. 105.
[35] Henry Ayres, *The Financial Position of Railways* (1868), p. viii.
[36] *Ibid.*, p. X.
[37] *Ibid.*, Appendix, p. 39. This Appendix was a reprint of a Board of Trade Return. The criterion of size was capitalisation.
[38] *Ibid.*, p. XI. There is a detailed discussion of the capital structure of the Lancashire & Yorkshire in Chapter 2, pp. 70–73. The percentage of ordinary paid-up capital of the L. & Y. in 1865 is put at 59 in Table 9.

capital is not, of course, by any means the sole determinant of the rate of dividend, but the level of dividend on ordinary stock was highest in companies like the London & North-Western and the Lancashire & Yorkshire: of the twelve principal companies in 1866, the L. & Y. paid the second highest dividend.[39]

A third, and most important, factor which is thought to have a bearing on this discussion is the role of Lancashire, and to a less extent, Yorkshire, in the early railway capital market. G. H. Evans's remark that local promotion and finance were the mainstays of railways until about 1844 has already been quoted. We are here concerned with finance only, and it is suggested that it is not local finance that should be stressed for this period, but rather the role of Lancashire in providing the money for the principal railways. The importance of Liverpool in this sphere has often been recognised:[40]

> 'Liverpool business men were particularly active in investing beyond their immediate area. . . . the Liverpool party . . . not only took an important share in creating the central link-lines of England between Mersey, Humber, Thames and Severn but, with Stephenson, had the long through-routes before their minds from the first. Lancashire almost owned the London and Birmingham.'

It is true that Evans allowed that there had been 'a number of departures from local promotion, financing and control'. But the impression gained from the various sources is that these 'departures' were, in fact, most of the principal companies floated in the 1830s, so far as financing and, probably, control were concerned.

According to John Francis it was 'the gentlemen of Lancashire . . . in this as in most other railways . . . personally and pecuniarily interested', who decided, by their support of Stephenson, that the route of the London & Birmingham (sanctioned in 1833) should be via Coventry.[41] Of the London & Birmingham and Grand Junction Railways, Thomas Tooke said: 'It has been computed that the Lancashire proprietors form seven eighths of the whole in amount.'[42] C. E. Stretton, in his book on the Midland, makes many references to the Lancashire interest in the constituent companies of the Midland Railway (the Leicester & Swannington, the Midland Counties and the North Midland) and records that as late as 1850,

[39] *Ibid.*, p. XXXIV. It is, perhaps, only fair to Ayres to point out that he did not mention the Lancashire & Yorkshire in his text. Only his general view of railway finance, and his figures, have been used.
[40] Clapham, I, p. 387.
[41] Francis, *History of the English Railway*, I, pp. 166–67.
[42] T. Tooke, *A History of Prices. . . .* (1838), II, p. 275.

at a meeting of the Midland proprietors, it was stated that there were 1,200 shareholders in the Liverpool district, who held £1,623,000 worth of shares.[43] Southern railways, it appears, needed and received strong Lancashire backing. The London & South-Western, sanctioned as the London & Southampton in 1834, was dependent upon outside support because Southampton, as Francis pointed out, lacked the manufacturers, merchants and capitalists of Manchester, Liverpool and Birmingham.[44] The situation of the L. & S.W. was not unique in the south. According to MacDermot, the Great Western had great difficulty in raising its initial capital, and although he does not specifically mention Lancashire subscribers, a considerable part of his space is at times taken up with the doings of the Liverpool party, whose influence and pressure on the Board is emphasised.[45] And it was said in 1838 that:[46]

'The Stock of the Great Western, held in Liverpool alone, amounts to very nearly £500,000, if it does not exceed that sum.'

In the east of England the Eastern Counties Railway, which was the largest line sanctioned in 1836, is, perhaps, the classic example of the Lancashire, and particularly the Liverpool, interest. Less than a third of the capital subscribed to this railway in 1836 came from local sources,[47] and it seems that most of the rest was supplied by Lancashire and north Cheshire. It was stated at the fifth general meeting of the proprietors of the company that 'Lancashire and Cheshire held . . . nearly two-thirds of the entire number of shares', and that 'taxation and representation' should be brought together. The intention was, evidently, to pack the Board. Only one of the six retiring directors was re-elected, and against considerable opposition the five remaining places were all filled by Liverpool men.[48] Francis was of the opinion that without the help of Manchester, Birmingham and Liverpool the scheme would have failed.[49]

In addition to specific references to the participation of Lan-

---

[43] C. E. Stretton, *The History of the Midland Railway* (1901), pp. 8, 32–34, 47 and 144. C. R. Clinker, *The Leicester and Swannington Railway* (Leicestershire Archaeological Society, The Guildhall, Leicester, 1954), disputes the accuracy of Stretton's classic description of the Liverpool interest in this railway.

[44] Francis, *op. cit.*, I, pp. 228 and 230.

[45] E. T. MacDermot, *History of the Great Western Railway* (1927), Vol. I, 1833–1863, Part I, pp. 59, 72 and 73 for examples.

[46] *Circular to Bankers*, No. 522, 13 July 1838. There is also a reference to the large proportion of L. & S.W. stock held in Lancashire.

[47] E. Doble, 'History of the Eastern Counties Railway . . .' (unpublished Ph.D. Thesis, London, 1939), p. 35.

[48] *Railway Times*, 2 March 1839.

[49] Francis, *op. cit.*, I, p. 260.

M

castrians in the financing of particular railways,[50] there is a wealth of comment from contemporary writers on what was felt to be the paramount position of Lancashire in this sphere. Some of the comment was laudatory, some uneasy. John Lalor was worried indeed about the growth of a society typified by Lancashire.[51] He maintained:[52]

> 'With respect to the railways, the truth was first seen and the lead taken by the sanguine, impetuous, over-mastering energy of Lancashire; ... It will appear in a succeeding page that the relation of Lancashire to all England is becoming more than ever a practical question. The men of Lancashire may not be the wisest ... but they have the most WILL, ...'

Even the old adage 'what Lancashire does today, England does tomorrow', was not sufficient for Lalor. Cotton was king in England as well as in the United States, and England could not do even tomorrow what Lancashire was doing today. Attacking the classical assumption that capital would flow from less to more profitable employments, he asked where was the farmer to go with his capital?[53]

> 'To the cotton mills! To join in that fierce race of competition, in which the keenest man in England, without a Lancashire education or Lancashire blood in him, has not the remotest chance of holding his ground!'

Lalor's 'remarkable population' of Lancashire also impressed Thomas Tooke. In discussing the predominance of Lancashire capital in the London & Birmingham and the Grand Junction Railways, he attributed it to two factors:[54]

> 'The one is, the greater knowledge possessed by [Lancastrians] of the nature of such undertakings. ... The other is, that, in consequence of the great and long-continued prosperity of the cotton trade, and the cotton manufactures, there has been an extraordinary accumulation of capital in that district, greatly exceeding the amount that could be profitably reinvested in the same business, great and increasing as that business has been and is.'

---

[50] The examples are not exhausted. We have not yet mentioned Scottish railways which, apparently, also received help. Cf. W. H. Marwick, *Economic Developments in Victorian Scotland* (1936), p. 138: 'The Edinburgh and Glasgow Railway raised about one million pounds ... over a third [was held] by Lancashire merchants.'

[51] John Lalor, *Money and Morals* (1852), especially Ch. IX: 'The New Gold'.

[52] *Ibid.*, p. 85.   [53] *Ibid.*, p. 115.

[54] T. Tooke, *History of Prices*, II, p. 275 n.

Thus the pioneer position of Lancashire merchants and manufacturers is attested by Tooke, as well as by Lalor and the *Circular to Bankers*.

The *Circular* was a London weekly, and it was by no means uncritical of some of the methods by which railways were floated and financed, and it often gave warnings of the dangers of speculation. As early as the end of 1833 it was counselling caution because of the increase in the number of railway and joint stock banking projects. In November 1835, while the railway boom was rapidly developing, it was convinced that it was preposterous to imagine the country being able to afford railways costing £20 million and more in the next ten years.[55] This kind of remark was very common in the 1830s and 1840s, when estimates of the amount of capital available for all investment were compared with the amounts of capital needed by the railways and were judged to be insufficient. In fact, as we know, by 1844 the best part of £60 million had been spent on railways.[56] But it was no doubt the belief that commitments were too great that led to such remarks as:[57]

'It is probable that no railway, not yet executed, would have obtained one-fourth part of the amount . . . subscribed, if every subscriber had been compelled by law, . . . to retain the shares . . . and to continue to pay up until the work should be completed. . . .'

Very probable. On the other hand, the *Circular* seemed to except the Lancashire population from this statement:[58]

'It may not be difficult for wealthy communities, like the population of Lancashire, to fill up subscriptions for railways requiring millions . . . to complete them. . . .'

On several occasions the journal felt it necessary to deny any particular antipathy towards the new system of communication.[59] Its sustained praise of Lancashire enterprise and wealth is therefore all the more noteworthy:[60]

'The north of England being the cradle of this . . . invention . . . it soon took possession of the confidence of men of property and weight in the same part of the country. . . . It is notorious

---

[55] *Circular to Bankers*, No. 382, 13 November 1835.
[56] B.P.P. 1844 (318) XI, *Fifth Report of the Select Committee on Railways*, Appendix 2, p. 5. The amount raised was larger.
[57] *Circular to Bankers*, No. 309, 20 June 1834.
[58] *Ibid.*, No. 422, 19 August 1836.
[59] *Ibid.*, No. 483, 13 October 1837.
[60] *Ibid.*, No. 509, 13 April 1838.

that the largest proprietors of the Liverpool and Manchester, the Grand Junction, the London and Birmingham, the Southampton, and the Great Western, live in Lancashire and the counties abutting upon it. . . . It is believed that more than two-thirds of some of the most costly lines are held in shares by the people of Lancashire and the manufacturing and commercial inhabitants of the West Riding . . . and the north of Cheshire. . . . There can be no rational doubt that all the railways in which the powerful inhabitants of Lancashire and the North of England are deeply interested will be speedily completed, because among themselves they abound in pecuniary resources and are in constant contact with the reservoirs of floating capital, and they possess, moreover, the unreserved confidence of the great dispensers of money power.'

The author of this long article was, like Lalor, concerned with the tremendous growth in Lancashire's power and, like Lalor, he professed some uneasiness at it. The heart of the commercial system was now in Lancashire, not in London; and it was the antagonism of Stephenson and, therefore, of Lancashire people, which was the cause of some railway companies' difficulties. This concentration of power, the *Circular* warned, could be dangerous.

This evidence does suggest that the emphasis on the local nature of railway financing up to 1844 has been misplaced, and if it is granted that Lancashire was a primary source of capital for non-Lancashire companies, then G. H. Evans and J. B. Jefferys were wrong to stress the 'Remoteness [of transport undertakings] from the large capital centres'.[61] Before the wider development of railways in the 1830s, travelling was difficult, and remoteness from London, Lancashire, and other important industrial areas, may well have led to some of the smaller, local lines being financed by local people. But the history of many of the major lines of that decade shows that this obstacle did not prevent promoters from soliciting help from Lancashire and other places, such as London and Birmingham. Since promoters were always interested in showing local support to the Parliamentary committees which considered their bills, the presence of so many Lancashire subscribers in their contracts is of great significance. On the whole, the statement 'No considerable Railway can be completed that depends upon local money for its outlay'[62] seems to be correct.

[61] G. H. Evans, *British Corporation Finance*, p. 6. It is, however, sometimes rather difficult to decide whether Evans intends his remarks to apply to both canals and railways throughout his period.

[62] *Circular to Bankers*, No. 422, 19 August 1836. The term 'local' is evidently

It is argued, therefore, that the high 'local' concentration of the subscriptions to the constituent companies of the Lancashire & Yorkshire Railway should be regarded in a new perspective. Lancashire, not London, was the main reservoir of capital, the area with the surpluses which, as Tooke said, 'could (not) be profitably reinvested in the same business'. Bearing in mind its extensive participation in the financing of companies in other parts of the country, it is not surprising that Lancashire should figure so prominently in the contracts which we have used, and which, after all, were those of mainly Lancashire companies. Nor is it surprising that an area which was undergoing the most rapid industrialisation, and which supplied the bulk of Britain's exports, should have had large reserves of capital. The rate of industrial growth reached its peak in Britain in the three decades up to 1851,[63] and Schlote has shown that the 'rate of expansion 'of exports in the period 1845 to 1855 was the greatest seen in the nineteenth century.[64] According to Imlah, cottons and woollens alone constituted about 55 per cent of Britain's exports in 1850.[65] The eulogising of Lancashire's position at this time by contemporaries is at least supported by such statistics.

It is this very position of Lancashire in the national economy which seems to be one reason for taking notice of the conclusions based upon lists of subscribers who were among the foremost industrialists and merchants of the country. It is not denied that much of the story of, for instance, the mania of 1845 is so convincing that it would be foolhardy to ignore it. It is not argued that 1845 contracts originating in Lancashire and the West Riding (there was a great mania in Leeds) should be treated with any more credulity than those of other areas. But, for earlier years 'boom' lists were often far from being 'bubble' lists. If any contracts are to be relied upon, those of Lancashire must take first place. Together with north Cheshire and the West Riding it dominated the British economy in the middle decades of the nineteenth century which, more than any other period, have been stressed as the age of thrift, of enterprise, and of investment:[66]

'On the one hand, this [the growth of capital] resulted from the

---

used here in a more restricted sense than I have used it in connection with 'interested' counties.
[63] Cf. P. Deane and W. A. Cole, *British Economic Growth 1688–1959* (1962), p. 297; also Brinley Thomas, *Migration and Economic Growth* (1954), p. 124.
[64] W. Schlote, *British Overseas Trade . . .* (1952), p. 41.
[65] A. H. Imlah, 'The Terms of Trade of the United Kingdom', *Journal of Economic History*, November, 1950, p. 184.
[66] A. K. Cairncross, *Home and Foreign Investment*, pp. 1 and 2.

prodigious thrift of the Victorians. ... In the middle of the
nineteenth century the building of British railways and towns
took nearly the whole of Britain's savings.'

This view of the Victorians is common enough. It is therefore difficult
to understand why the evidence of the direction of the investment
effort of those very classes who dominated the subscription contracts
and who epitomised the Victorian virtues—the merchants and manufacturers—should be suspect because manias occurred in 1836 and
1845.

To reject the thesis put forward in this chapter is surely to deny
the generally accepted explanation of the origins of railway development: that the railways would cut transport costs in an expanding
and industrialising economy, which would then be free from the
bottleneck of the canals and roads. It has in fact been argued that
since passenger traffic receipts exceeded income from freight before
the early 1850s, the major impact of the railways was not in commercial transport but in induced industrial development, and even
more significantly, in the spread of the investment habit.[67] The
importance of the railways in these latter spheres is obvious, but the
rest of the argument is unconvincing. In the first place, we are not
told how quickly a new system of transport, which had its fair share
of teething troubles, should have *triumphed*, and no one has suggested
what level goods traffic receipts should have reached before 1850.
Income from freight was not inconsiderable, and there are examples
of lines earning more from goods than from passengers, or of goods
traffic being more buoyant—the Manchester & Leeds is a case in
point[68]—from time to time. It is not inconsistent to argue that canals
and roads were a bottleneck and yet in the early years could still be
competitive by cutting rates from inflated levels. Income from freight
was subject to many influences, government intervention included,
and one would want to know much more about the *quantities* of
freight carried by canal, road and rail. Secondly, while this argument
does briefly mention the problem of the evolution of a reasonably
coherent, unified network and the emergence of the Clearing House,
it is clear that these aspects deserve much more emphasis. Before
1850 the network was in the process of being developed, and it is no
accident that income from freight exceeded passenger receipts in the
early 1850s on a national scale for the first time. There was obviously
less advantage in transporting by rail in the years of uncoordinated,

[67] B. R. Mitchell, 'The Coming of the Railway and U.K. Economic Growth',
Journal of Economic History, Vol. XXIV, September 1964, p. 3.
[68] See above, Chapter 2, pp. 51–52.

piecemeal development.[69] Finally, income from freight seems to have been affected more than passenger receipts in depressed years, and competition after 1848, both between railway and railway, and railway and canal, exerted additional pressure on goods charges at a time when railway facilities were greatly over-expanded compared with the level of the economy and consequently further diluted receipts, especially between 1850 and 1853.[70]

Since the railways dealt with in Chapter 4 drew by far their greatest support from the mercantile and industrial classes, we do not have to look far for the motives of those who subscribed. It is obvious that in the circumstances of the period 1825–50, these classes would not only have the incentive of improved communications for the transport of their goods, but also the possibilities of profit from investing and speculating in railways. They would also have the means to finance this investment. The direct profit motive would naturally attract other classes, which did not have the business incentive. It was, of course, the state of transport by canals, some of which were making tremendous profits, and the rise in expected yields from investment, as well as the possibility of profitable speculation (which, in itself, was dependent, at least initially, on expected high yields), which was instrumental in bringing about the mania of 1845. The rise in the marginal efficiency of capital, in the Keynesian sense, leads, it is argued by economists with such diverse beliefs as Maurice Dobb and Professor Rostow, to a concentration of investment in a restricted sector of the economy. Mr. Dobb says that:[71]

'In a capitalist economy there would seem to exist a prevailing tendency to under-estimate the effect of capital accumulation. . . . To the extent that this is so, there will be a constant tendency to over-invest in projects of a type which yield the prevailing rate of interest. . . . The result of all this will be a tendency to continue investment in a particular type of capital too long. . . .'

Professor Rostow points out:[72]

'The history of business cycles is the history of a succession of booms in which the capital markets have seized upon certain key types of investment which have been made apparently profitable. . . . The psychological tendency of the market to con-

[69] Cf. C. I. Savage, *An Economic History of Transport* (1966), p. 41.
[70] Passengers receipts were also unsatisfactory on the Lancashire & Yorkshire between 1850 and 1855; see above, p. 34.
[71] M. Dobb, *Political Economy and Capitalism* (1940), pp. 286–87.
[72] W. W. Rostow, *The Process of Economic Growth* (1st edn., 1953), p. 124.

centrate its attention clearly leads to increases in capacity, in particular directions, beyond those justified. . . .'

That the history of railway development conforms to these theoretical pronouncements is seen from the situation in the late 1830s and late 1840s. The booms in the middle of these decades clearly resulted in an over-expansion of railways: the rates of traffic development and capital investment did not match one another, and dividends fell. But the point to be stressed here is the interrelation of the supply of capital, the willingness to invest, and the influence of the capitalists of the Lancashire area. The concentration on the speculative activities of the 1830s and 1840s would be easier to understand if the railways had not been built: it is almost with a feeling of surprise that we discover that by far the greater proportion of the pre-1845 mania railways, and a considerable number of the 1845 and post-1845 lines, were completed by 1850–52.

The distinction between those companies which were sanctioned in or before 1845, and those which were projected in that year and sanctioned in 1846 and 1847, has already been emphasised because the former were all completed, while some of the latter were not. Ignoring for the moment the boom of the 1840s, we find that, in round figures, £66 of the £84 million of share and loan capital of all railways authorised up to the end of 1843, had been raised.[73] A large proportion of this money had been authorised between 1833 and 1837, a period which included the mania of late 1835 and 1836. Some companies sanctioned in those years did experience difficulties in raising money: witness the Eastern Counties and, of our companies, the Bolton & Preston.[74] And the frauds and scandals of the mid-1830s, which resulted in the Parliamentary investigation of railway subscription lists in 1837, have been used to discredit contracts.

In fact, by far the greater proportion of the money authorised in this period was raised, and the briefest study of the investigation will show that almost all the companies the committee considered were of the metropolitan or London–South East and London–South Coast type. This lends support to the view that it was London which dominated the *speculation*. The Stock Exchange really took a hand for the first time in 1835/36.[75] It is true that the sums considered by

[73] B.P.P. 1847–48 (565) VIII, Pt. III, *Report of the Secret Committee of the House of Lords on Commercial Distress*, Appendix D, p. 468. The exact figure is £65,639,347, raised by all companies up to 31 December 1843.

[74] 5 Vict. Sess. 2, c. 15, *An Act to facilitate the raising of Capital for the Completion of the Bolton and Preston Railway*. Preamble states that the company had not been able to raise the whole amount of the original capital authorisation.

[75] *Circular to Bankers*, especially No. 397, 26 February 1836. The issue does

the 1837 Select Committee did amount, in some cases, to considerable proportions of the totals subscribed. But with only one exception all the lists brought to the attention of the committee were connected with London, and the general impression is that the tests of non-validity were stringent. The subscription lists belonged to the following companies: the Deptford & Dover, the Westminster Bridge, Deptford & Greenwich, the City or Southwark Bridge & Hammersmith, the South Midland Counties, the Direct London & Brighton (Rennie's line), the Brighton Railway (Stephenson's line), and the South Eastern, Brighton, Lewes, and Newhaven Railway. There was also a report on the contract of the Bath & Weymouth.[76] Even on the lists of these companies the committee made some encouraging remarks. In its first report it stated that most lists were the result of a 'cautious selection from among the mass of applicants',[77] and this was certainly true of the Manchester & Leeds in 1836. Some of the applications for its shares were rejected outright, some were referred to the Finance Committee for further consideration, and in January 1836 it was resolved that the Company should refuse to recognise any person for the signing of deeds other than the original subscriber. The provisional directors would not allow a purchaser of ten 'shares' to sign the deed in place of the person who had obtained the scrip.[78] The Manchester & Leeds, at least, refused to countenance the speculation in scrip that was so distinctive a feature of the mania.

The second report of the 1837 committee referred to the 'strictness' which the directors 'had before observed in respect of the Subscription List',[79] while in the sixth report the opinion was given that in the case of the South Eastern, Brighton, etc., great care had been taken to allot shares to respectable and solvent people. Practically the only objection to any of the subscriptions was that power of attorney had not been stated.[80] (And this was, for all the lists, a principal ground for invalidating subscriptions.) The number of the shares of the City line 'not of the nature of *bona fide* subscriptions' was £99,550 out of a total of £437,550.[81] Of the £606,200 subscribed

refer to speculation in Lancashire, but the main complaints of fraud at this time related to southern railways.

[76] B.P.P. 1837 (243) XVIII, Pt. II, p. 481, *Report on the Bath & Weymouth Railway Subscription List.*

[77] B.P.P. 1837 (226) XVIII, Pt. I, p. 23, *Select Committee on Railway Subscription Lists, First Report: Deptford & Dover Railway Subscription List.*

[78] Proceedings of the Directors, 26 January 1836.

[79] B.P.P. 1837 (428) XVIII, Pt. I, pp. 410–11 (The Westminster Bridge, etc.). This strictness had been relaxed 'some time in January last, ...'

[80] B.P.P. 1837 (520) XVIII, Pt. II, p. 380. (The South Eastern, Brighton, etc.)

[81] B.P.P. 1837 (429) XVIII, Pt. I, p. 555 (*Third Report*).

to the South Midland Counties, £158,150 were regarded as invalid.[82] The subscribers to Rennie's line (the Direct London & Brighton) were, perhaps, the worst offenders, since of £991,425 subscribed, invalid and forfeited shares totalled over £400,000.[83]

Some of the contracts obviously contained the names of 'men of straw' and of fictitious characters. But it is not reasonable to regard an investigation which centred on London—always notorious for speculation—as disqualifying all attempts to analyse subscription contracts for use as capital sources;[84] and even here the picture is not one of unrelieved gloom. Apart from the statements quoted from the reports of the 1837 committee, Grinling recognised that a contract should not be rejected out of hand merely because it contained some fictitious or worthless characters. Referring to the activities of the London & York Railway in 1845, Grinling wrote:[85]

> 'By these means they [the opponents] in a short time compiled quite a long list of subscribers, responsible altogether for upwards of half a million of the London and York capital, who were alleged to be "needy persons, or paupers wholly unable to meet their respective engagements," or appear on the contract by "fictitious names" . . . .'

These names and allegations were embodied in petitions to Parliament and the unfortunate subscribers were hauled up to be examined. But while some 'afforded examples of that unscrupulous speculation from the taint of which, at this time of mania, it was practically impossible to keep even sound enterprises exempt', there were many whose 'character and means to fulfil their engagements were unimpeachable',[86] and only a fairly small proportion of the subscribers who had been attacked were found by the Lords and Commons committees, which examined the contract, to be untraceable or worthless.[87]

But what of the post-1843 railways in general? Since, in addition to bubbles, a number of the commitments of the railway boom and the mania of 1845 were never fulfilled, and since the failure to build was mainly a result of financial stringency, it follows that many of the subscriptions of the mania period, at least, are not to be relied upon.

---

[82] B.P.P. 1837 (495) XVIII, Pt. II, p. 10 (*Fourth Report*). This company's bill had been withdrawn.

[83] B.P.P. 1837 (519) XVIII, Pt. II, p. 166 (*Fifth Report*).

[84] Cf., for instance, H. Pollins, 'The Jews' Role in the Early British Railways', *Jewish Social Studies*, XV, No. 1.

[85] C. H. Grinling, *The History of the Great Northern Railway, 1845–1902* (1903), p. 42.

[86] *Ibid.*, pp. 43–44.   [87] *Ibid.*, p. 45.

There is sufficient evidence of the financial embarrassment caused by the excessive flotations of 1845. This embarrassment extended to the successful projects of 1844 as well as to those of the mania, because many companies obtained authorisations of schemes in both years, and found it hard to meet the demands on their resources. The Manchester & Leeds, free, as we have seen, from such troubles during the depression of 1839–42, found itself faced with a situation which was confronting all companies in 1847. As early as September 1846 the Finance Committee was presented with a 'List of Defaulters in payment of 1st Call, whose Shares had been declared forfeited'. No details of the defaulters were given, and the forfeiture was not confirmed.[88] But by June 1847 a peak of over £500,000 in arrears of calls was reached,[89] and it was a long time before the amount owed to the Company was reduced to an insignificant sum.[90]

The effects of the flood of calls in 1846 and 1847 have been well summarised by E. V. Morgan and C. N. Ward-Perkins. Professor Morgan emphasises the pressure which was felt by the banks as a result of the liabilities incurred by so many investors in 1844 and 1845,[91] and the experience of the Manchester & Leeds when in 1846 it made calls on its industrial and mercantile shareholders illustrates the situation. But, as Mr. Ward-Perkins has pointed out, there was a very positive and beneficial outcome of 'the genuine railway investment'.[92] That there was 'genuine railway investment' can hardly be doubted. Between 1845 and 1851 over 4,500 miles of line were opened, and it is most unlikely that the building of these lines was financed by a new body of shareholders. So far as we can tell, the investing public in the Victorian era was a comparatively small, wealthy group. In his chapter on 'The Victorian Capital Market', Professor Cairncross remarks that 'The typical investor was always a man of wealth', although the number of shareholders, especially in the railways, was increasing.[93] The Commissioners for Railways, in their report for 1848, in spite of their knowledge of the difficulties of the railways, referred to the 'great number of people' who knew little or nothing of commercial matters, but who were 'only desirous to

---

[88] Proceedings of the Finance Committee, 26 September 1846.
[89] *Ibid.*, 16 June 1847.
[90] *Ibid., passim.* Not until July 1851 did the amount in arrears fall below £100,000.
[91] E. V. Morgan, 'Railway Investment, Bank of England Policy and Interest Rates, 1844–48', *Economic History*, Vol. IV, No. 15, February 1940.
[92] C. N. Ward-Perkins, 'The Commercial Crisis of 1847', in A. H. Hansen and R. V. Clemence, *Readings in Business Cycles and National Income* (1953), p. 13. This is a reprint of Mr. Ward-Perkins's article in *Oxford Economic Papers*, January 1950.
[93] A. K. Cairncross, *Home and Foreign Investment*, pp. 84–85.

obtain a secure and advantageous investment'.[94] The Commissioners evidently believed that many subscribers were innocent of speculative of fraudulent activities, but its estimate of the 'great number of people' subscribing, who were not directly connected with trade and industry, was commented on when Locock Webb's pamphlet of 1849 was discussed.[95] It probably stems, as do many of the statements of both contemporary and present-day writers, from an unsystematic study of the lists in the Parliamentary Papers of 1845 and 1846.[96]

These lists—or, rather, the list of 1846—may illustrate the 'manner in which the middle classes participated *en masse*' in the mania of 1845,[97] but it would probably be wrong to conclude that there was any marked increase in the relative importance of some groups or classes compared with earlier years. The analysis of contracts in the previous chapter did not show any significant increase in the proportion of subscriptions from 'small' people: the widows, spinsters, professional people. The merchants and manufacturers still contributed the greater proportion of the amounts promised to the companies. In fact, the percentages of the contracts subscribed by the category 'gentlewomen', for instance, were even lower in the 1844/45 contracts than they were in some of those of the 1830s.

The fact remains that a number of the railways authorised during and after the mania were not built, and that capital powers were allowed to lapse. How serious was this? The positive results of the boom in terms of mileage built have been indicated: in 1852 a total of just over 5,000 of the 9,000 miles sanctioned since 1845, had been opened for traffic.[98] We are concerned with finance, and it is instructive to compare the amounts authorised and the amounts actually raised. By December 1851 £248 million had been paid up on the £369 millions of authorised share and loan capital of all companies.[99] Since about £66 million of this had already been raised by

[94] B.P.P. 1849 (?) XXVII, p. viii.
[95] See above, p. 155.
[96] These lists are in 1845 (317, 625) XL, and 1846 (473) XXXVIII.
[97] Gayer, Rostow and Schwartz, *Growth and Fluctuation*, I, p. 380. The authors must be referring to the 1845 lists, since they say Paper*s*—there was only one list published in 1846, and it gave the details of only those who subscribed £2,000 or more—and those lists are compilations from the contracts of companies which were *authorised* in 1845 (in addition to those whose bills failed), not those *projected* in that year.
[98] H. G. Lewin, *Railway Mania*, p. 473. These are figures compiled by Lewin himself; there are slight discrepancies between them and those of Galton of the Board of Trade.
[99] B.P.P. 1854 (98) LXII, p. 507. The figure of £369 millions is gross: it differs from the net total of £361 millions in the paper cited, which was corrected with the aid of the *Report of the Railway Department for 1854*, B.P.P. 1854–55 (1965) XLVIII, p. vii.

the end of 1843, the resulting figure of £128 millions raised between 1844 and 1851 inclusive, although massive, appears to compare unfavourably with the total of £285 million authorised in the same period.[100] But there is the natural time-lag between the authorisation and the paying-up of capital to be taken into consideration.[101] By 1858 the total amount raised on the £393 million authorised at that date was over £325 million.[102] The picture presented by this last figure is rather too rosy, since the sum of £393 million represents *net* authorisations. For several years, companies obtained Acts reducing their capital commitments. In 1851, for instance, gross authorisations amount to over £9 million, while there was a slight net reduction in the authorised capital of all railways,[103] and in the period 1851 to 1858 net authorisations amounted to only £33 million, but the total raised was £77 million.[104] So while some of the difference between the total raised by 1858, £325 million, and the total authorised, which was £393 million, can be put down to the time-lag, a considerable portion of it would never be raised by the companies for the simple reason that they had not exercised their powers within the specified periods. Estimates of the extent to which such powers were allowed to lapse, vary, but in 1855 it was assumed that approximately £30 to £40 million of the £368 million authorised by 1854 related to lines the powers for which had expired.[105] When all these qualifications are allowed for, however, the amount of money raised is impressive. Of the £284 million (net) authorised between 1844 and 1854, £220 million had been raised, and by the end of 1858, of the £325 million received, £259 million had been concentrated in the fifteen years since 1843. This is striking testimony to the investment effort in only one sector of the British economy in this short period. There has been too much emphasis on the speculative aspects of railway development

---

[100] £84 million had been authorised up to December 1843.

[101] For example, the calls on the Manchester & Leeds £100 shares of 1836 extended over a period of fifteen years.

[102] B.P.P. 1859 (243) XXV, p. 765.

[103] B.P.P. 1852 (37) XLVIII, pp. 438–39. There are many difficulties in using the statistics in Parliamentary Papers. For instance, the authorisations of capital from 1846 to 1854, inclusive, which are in the *Report of the Railway Department for 1854* (B.P.P. 1854–55 (1965) XLVIII, p. vii) are gross figures, and do not tally with those given in the returns mentioned below. This Report is frequently used by writers who do not seem to appreciate that they are gross figures. However, the minor discrepancies between various papers may be ignored.

[104] These calculations are made from a series of returns: 1852 (37) XLVIII; 1854 (98, 168, and 494) LXII; 1854–55 (54 and 510) XLVIII; 1856 (8 and 316) LIV; 1857 Sess. 2 (164 and 340) XXXVII; 1857–58 (132 and 431) LI; 1859 (231 and 243) XXV.

[105] *Report of the Railway Department for 1854*, B.P.P. *loc. cit.*, p. xii.

in the first half of the nineteenth century. The fascinating accounts of
the mania and of Hudson, of the fraudulent, blind and wasteful
propagation of railways,[106] are all relevant. But they occupy too
much space, and the positive results too little.

Even the story of the large sums in arrears of the calls made on
shareholders, from the latter part of 1846 onwards, is not completely
black. That strenuous attempts to meet calls were made by the
shareholders of the Lancashire & Yorkshire Railway, is evident from
the company's Finance Committee minutes, and it is improbable that
they were exceptional.[107] There were many reasons why the efforts
should have been made, not the least of which was the attitude of the
Board to defaulters and its power to institute legal proceedings.
Dividend warrants were retained, interest was charged on the money
in arrear, and transfers of shares vetoed if there had been default.
But whatever the reason, the efforts were made. During 1847, when
the arrears problem was at its height, the paid-up capital of the
Company nevertheless increased by just over £2½ million,[108] while
the increase from the end of 1845 to the end of 1850 was over
£8 million.[109]

The experience of the Lancashire & Yorkshire must have been that
of the older, well-established companies, and it is with these that we
should, after all, be mainly concerned, rather than with the multitude
of small companies, whether they were successfully floated or not.
Most of the lines of the Lancashire & Yorkshire for which powers
had been obtained were built within the comparatively short time
up to 1850.

In conclusion: while it is unnecessary to swing to the extreme view
of writers such as Chattaway,[110] the concrete results of the railway
activity of the 1830s and 1840s are sufficiently great to warrant
further study of the available material to produce a more accurate
and comprehensive view of the capital market and of railway
development. The story of fraudulent promoters, whose subscription
contracts were populated by fictitious characters, is largely irrelevant

---

[106] Cf. Clapham, I, p. 388.
[107] Cf. Grinling, *Great Northern Railway*, pp. 65–71, for an account of the
remarkably good response of the GN shareholders to calls for part, at least,
of 1847. The Company did, however, pay interest.
[108] *Reports & Accounts*, 1 March 1848.
[109] *Ibid.*, 1845 to 1851.
[110] E. D. Chattaway, *Railways: Their Capital and Dividends* . . . (1855–56), p. 5,
referring to the sum of £300 million spent by railways up to 1855, said: 'This
enormous sum of money has been raised without any serious inconvenience
or difficulty. . . .'

in this context. It is of use in illustrating the periodic bursts of speculation which gripped so many people in the nineteenth century. But if the bubbles are separated from the genuine projects, it is highly probable that the development of this important sector of the British economy will no longer be regarded mainly as, to borrow a famous phrase, 'a by-product of the activities of a casino. . . .'[111]

[111] J. M. Keynes, *The General Theory of Employment Interest and Money* (1936), p. 159.

Appendix

THE severe criticisms of the financial practices of early Victorian railways have a salutary effect on anyone using their published accounts. They prevent an uncritical analysis of the financial results; they focus attention on suspect items; and they sometimes necessitate an independent classification of the figures. In this Appendix, most of the descriptions of the tables, and most of the figures themselves, are not to be found in the accounts. They are products of a re-classification of the items given in the accounts, and they are explained in detail. The reclassification would have been necessary regardless of any question of misallocation between capital and revenue accounts, not only because of the need to obtain figures for an analysis which the compilers of the accounts might not have appreciated, but also because of the changes in and the inconsistencies of the statements, and the belated imposition of a standard form of railway account in 1868.

The series begin in 1842 because although the Manchester & Leeds began working its main line throughout in March 1841, 1842 was the first full calendar year of operation. In any case, the results for 1841 are complicated by the carrying over of various traffic results from the piecemeal opening of the line before March 1841, and of some additional balances. There are ten tables of figures for the period 1842 to 1873:

TABLE I
GROSS TRAFFIC RECEIPTS, 1842 TO 1873[1]

Year	Gross Traffic Receipts £000's	Year	Gross Traffic Receipts £000's	Year	Gross Traffic Receipts £000's
1842	227	1853	966	1864	2,024
1843	242	1854	1,014	1865	2,142
1844	289	1855	1,064	1866	2,386
1845	334	1856	1,178	1867	2,487
1846	338	1857	1,229	1868	2,563
1847	357	1858	1,224	1869	2,549
1848	443	1859	1,753	1870	2,653
1849	553	1860	1,954	1871	2,907
1850	740	1861	1,932	1872	3,164
1851	831	1862	1,719	1873	3,318
1852	885	1863	1,832		

Notes:

1. Reference should be made to the notes to Table IV: Gross Receipts on Revenue Account.

2. 'Rents', an item occurring in receipts on revenue account in the Company's accounts, are not included.

3. 'Hull Docks', an item occurring in receipts on revenue account after 1869, is not included. The Lancashire & Yorkshire *subscribed* to Hull Docks, which were opened in July 1869, and the receipts entered presumably consisted of dividends.[2]

4. From 1851 the item 'Blackburn Working Expenses' appears on both sides of the revenue account. As it was a self-cancelling item it had been omitted from the figures for gross traffic receipts and for working expenses. This item disappeared from the revenue account in 1860.

5. From 1851 the item 'Liverpool & Southport Working Expenses' also appears on both sides of the revenue account. As it was a self-cancelling item until 1855 it has been omitted from the figures for 1851 to 1854 included. But in 1855 the figure given under this heading had to be included as the entries on either side of the revenue account no longer cancelled one another, and, moreover, the Liverpool & Southport became the property of the Lancashire & Yorkshire in that year. In 1858 the item disappeared from the revenue account; presumably it was absorbed into the general figures for the Lancashire & Yorkshire.

[1] In this, and in subsequent tables, all figures are to the nearest £1,000.
[2] Cf. *Reports & Accounts*, 17 February 1869.

N

6. The item 'Liverpool & Southport Toll', which appeared in the years 1851 to 1857, is included in gross traffic receipts.

7. The 'Preston & Wyre' entries are included: the Preston & Wyre was worked by the Lancashire & Yorkshire, which took two-thirds of the receipts and paid two-thirds of the working expenses of this railway.

8. The Manchester, Bolton & Bury Canal receipts and working expenses are also included in gross traffic receipts and in working expenses. Similar items for the Preston & Longridge (which first appeared in the accounts in 1869), and the Blackburn, Chorley & Wigan (which first appeared in 1870), have been included. For all three the figures appear on both sides of the revenue account, and in each case the figures differ.

TABLE II

WORKING EXPENSES, 1842 TO 1873

Year	Working Expenses £000's	Year	Working Expenses £000's	Year	Working Expenses £000's
1842	55	1853	378	1864	775
1843	66	1854	391	1865	833
1844	77	1855	400	1866	920
1845	96	1856	436	1867	997
1846	106	1857	458	1868	1,106
1847	125	1858	492	1869	1,083
1848	159	1859	663	1870	1,153
1849	224	1860	740	1871	1,272
1850	300	1861	785	1872	1,437
1851	307	1862	701	1873	1,724
1852	341	1863	720		

Notes:

1. The notes to Tables I and V should be referred to.

2. The difference between 'Working Expenses' and 'Gross Expenditure on Revenue Account' consists in the omission from the former of interest charges, rates, taxes, government duty, depreciation allowances (when charged), and a few miscellaneous, sometimes non-recurring, charges.

3. The figures given in this table differ from those given in the accounts up to 1868. *Included* in the above totals of working expenses are the expenses for the Preston & Wyre, Preston & Longridge, Blackburn, Chorley & Wigan, and the Manchester, Bolton & Bury Canal. *Excluded* are the expenses for the Blackburn (1851–60), and

the Liverpool & Southport (1851–54). See notes to Table I for explanations of these items.

4. The item 'Working Expenses' was dropped from the railway's accounts after 1867. The Company adopted the new form of accounts prescribed by the Regulation of Railways Act, 1868, although adoption could have been deferred until 1869.

TABLE III
NET TRAFFIC RECEIPTS, 1842 TO 1873

Year	Net Traffic Receipts £000's	Year	Net Traffic Receipts £000's	Year	Net Traffic Receipts £000's
1842	172	1853	588	1864	1,249
1843	176	1854	623	1865	1,309
1844	212	1855	664	1866	1,466
1845	238	1856	742	1867	1,490
1846	232	1857	771	1868	1,457
1847	232	1858	732	1869	1,466
1848	284	1859	1,090	1870	1,500
1849	329	1860	1,214	1871	1,635
1850	440	1861	1,147	1872	1,727
1851	524	1862	1,018	1873	1,594
1852	544	1863	1,112		

Note:

1. Net Traffic Receipts are obtained by subtracting Working Expenses from Gross Traffic Receipts.

TABLE IV
GROSS RECEIPTS ON REVENUE ACCOUNT, 1842 TO 1873

Year	Gross Receipts on Rev. Acc. £000's	Year	Gross Receipts on Rev. Acc. £000's	Year	Gross Receipts on Rev. Acc. £000's
1842	232	1853	1,000	1864	2,039
1843	249	1854	1,048	1865	2,162
1844	291	1855	1,091	1866	2,408
1845	339	1856	1,209	1867	2,499
1846	341	1857	1,255	1868	2,570
1847	360	1858	1,242	1869	2,554
1848	446	1859	1,754	1870	2,675
1849	561	1860	1,956	1871	2,918
1850	752	1861	1,943	1872	3,185
1851	878	1862	1,725	1873	3,333
1852	923	1863	1,839		

Notes:

1. Gross Receipts on Revenue Account include, in addition to Gross Traffic Receipts, the favourable balance of rents, any favourable balances of interest from the bankers, and various items which are not included in Gross Traffic Receipts, and which are dealt with under that heading.

TABLE V

GROSS EXPENDITURE ON REVENUE ACCOUNT,
1842 TO 1873

Year	Gross Expend. on Rev. Acc. £000's	Year	Gross Expend. on Rev. Acc. £000's	Year	Gross Expend. on Rev. Acc. £000's
1842	174	1853	651	1864	1,183
1843	169	1854	645	1865	1,268
1844	189	1855	685	1866	1,392
1845	201	1856	728	1867	1,469
1846	180	1857	770	1868	1,497
1847	183	1858	810	1869	1,462
1848	231	1859	1,078	1870	1,527
1849	345	1860	1,137	1871	1,662
1850	561	1861	1,179	1872	1,823
1851	600	1862	1,122	1873	2,111
1852	635	1863	1,132		

Notes:

1. Reference should be made to Table II.

2. Gross Expenditure on Revenue Account *includes* interest on loans, bonds, and 4 per cent Debenture Stock (the issue of which was authorised in August 1859), bond and stamp charges, depreciation allowances (when charged), charges for leased lines (but see Note 3 below), 'bad debts', and working expenses. It *excludes* all dividends on ordinary, preference and guaranteed shares.

3. In the Company's 'Statement of Nett Revenue' there is entered, from 1850 to 1868, a charge for the Sheffield & Barnsley Railway as a leased line. But the charge was to meet interest on guaranteed Barnsley stock, and when the new Parliamentary form of accounts was adopted in 1868, the Barnsley stock charge was in fact omitted from the 'leased line' charges and included in the dividend and interest (on guaranteed stock) account. The charge for the Sheffield & Barnsley has, therefore, been omitted from the figures given above for the whole period from 1850.

TABLE VI
NET REVENUE, 1842 TO 1873

Year	Net Revenue £000's	Year	Net Revenue £000's	Year	Net Revenue £000's
1842	58	1853	349	1864	856
1843	80	1854	403	1865	894
1844	102	1855	406	1866	1,016
1845	138	1856	481	1867	1,030
1846	161	1857	485	1868	1,073
1847	177	1858	432	1869	1,092
1848	215	1859	676	1870	1,148
1849	216	1860	819	1871	1,256
1850	191	1861	764	1872	1,362
1851	278	1862	603	1873	1,222
1852	288	1863	707		

Notes:

1. Net Revenue is obtained by subtracting Gross Expenditure on Revenue Account from Gross Receipts on Revenue Account. It is the balance applicable to dividends on both ordinary and guaranteed and preference stock, excluding Debenture Stock. Whether the Debenture Stock interest should have been included in the figures for Gross Expenditure on Revenue Account, and therefore excluded from the figures for net revenue is, perhaps, open to question. The Stock was designed to put the loan debt of the Company on a permanent footing, and from 1861 permanent 4 per cent Debenture Stock was issued to replace mortgage debentures. It could be argued, therefore, that the new Stock was in the same category as other guaranteed stock. But, in justification of the decision to exclude the interest on it from net revenue figures, it may be said that the Company regarded the interest as different in kind from guaranteed stock interest or dividends, that when Parliament imposed a standardised form of accounts in 1868, the Debenture Stock charge was put in the same account as the mortgage interest, and, finally, that to omit Debenture Stock interest from the figures in Table X (Interest Paid on Loan Capital), would distort the series. The Stock still represented capital expenditure which was financed by loan capital: the latter was merely made permanent.

2. Table VI presents the *annual* results. Its figures do not contain any surpluses brought forward from previous half-years. For this and other reasons (see Notes to Table VII) these figures do not correspond with those shown in the Company's 'Statement of Nett Revenue' as applicable to dividends and interest.

TABLE VII

BALANCES APPLICABLE TO DIVIDENDS AND
DEPRECIATION, 1842 TO 1873

Year	Balances Applicable to Divis. & Dep. £000's	Year	Balances Applicable to Divis. & Dep. £000's	Year	Balances Applicable to Divis. & Dep. £000's
1842	91	1853	360	1864	930
1843	95	1854	409	1865	977
1844	108	1855	437	1866	1,103
1845	144	1856	504	1867	1,128
1846	191	1857	519	1868	1,086
1847	218	1858	477	1869	1,102
1848	229	1859	735	1870	1,146
1849	235	1860	872	1871	1,281
1850	207	1861	823	1872	1,375
1851	277	1862	692	1873	1,233
1852	319	1863	777		

Notes:

1. These figures are the sums which were annually applicable to dividends on ordinary and guaranteed stock, and to depreciation. The charge for loans and, later, Debenture Stock, was not met from these sums.

2. Table VI presented independent calculations of the net revenue earned each year, money which might be applied to dividends on ordinary and guaranteed and preference stock, excluding Debenture Stock. It represents an attempt to assess the annual profits. Table VII differs from Table VI in that the Company's own statements of balances on net revenue account are accepted at their face value, and are used to extract the amount the Company had available each year to pay dividends and to set aside a sum for depreciation.

3. But, once again, Table VII shows figures which will not be found in the published accounts, although these, as they improved, and especially after the standard form was imposed in 1868, can be used with less adjustment. Even so, there are still several explanations to be made.

4. First of all, the problem of annual surpluses remains, even in this table. In Table VI the figures do not include any surpluses at all, neither straightforward surpluses left after the payment of dividends and interest, nor depreciation allowances. This table was compiled to show the year by year results of working the railway. The present table includes surpluses carried forward from December 31 of one

year into the first half of the next. To avoid double counting, any surpluses carried forward from June 30 into the second half of the year have been deducted from the Company's figures for balances applicable to interest and dividends.

5. Table VII also includes depreciation allowances. This is unsatisfactory, but inclusion seemed the best method in view of the many changes in policy over the question of depreciation allowances. The table is designed to show just how much money the Company had available to meet dividends. When the depreciation allowance was first introduced by the Lancashire & Yorkshire it was regarded as expendable as dividends. It was added to any surplus that might be available and carried over to the following year, when it might well be used to pay a dividend. It is necessary to trace the changes in attitude towards the depreciation allowance in order to have a clear idea of the problem involved.

An allowance for the depreciation of the track was first introduced by the Manchester & Leeds in 1842. In that year a total of £11,977 11s. 2d. was set aside as the beginnings of a depreciation fund. By the end of 1843 the fund amounted to £19,014 and already the directors were experiencing temptation. There was a great deal of controversy over the provision out of profits for the deterioration of the Company's capital assets. The controversy was to continue for a long time and the depreciation allowance must always occupy some space in any account of the financial practices of nineteenth-century railway companies. Added to this controversy was the great difference of opinion over the decision by the Board in 1842 to set aside an additional amount 'to secure the maintenance and gradual increase of the present rate of dividend'.[3]

Immediately there was a sizeable sum in reserve (in relation to the then comparatively small amount paid in dividends; see Table IX) the directors could see in it another function. The depreciation allowance, they said in March 1844, might be regarded as[4]

'partaking in some measure of the character of a surplus fund and applicable occasionally as such, with due regard to its primary object of replacing superannuated working stock.'

The last clause must have been added as a sop to their, or their proprietors' consciences. A depreciation fund does not partake of the character of a surplus fund, and is not applicable, under any logically

[3] *Reports & Accounts*, 17 March 1842. See also *The Railway Times*, 19 March, 26 March, and 2 April 1842, for letters and controversy over this. Joseph Pease's views were quoted above, p. 148–49.
[4] *Reports & Accounts*, 14 March 1844.

worked out financial system, to dividends. In the succeeding 'Statement(s) of Nett Revenue' the Board decided to use its depreciation fund for dividends; but it was completely nonplussed on the point of where in the accounts to put the figure. Should it be deducted from a surplus, or added to it? In 1844 and 1845 the directors did both. And if it were to be added, should each year's allowance only be added, or should the whole surplus be cumulative? They were not sure, and they again did both. One half-year they would state the amount of the full reserve fund (including depreciation allowance) but carried forward only the true surplus. Then in the next half-year the surplus carried forward would be the full one, including the depreciation allowance.[5]

Whatever they did with the accounts, it is certain that in the period 1844 to 1846 they used the surpluses, which included depreciation allowances, to meet dividend payments. This does not mean that in *every* half-year the full amount was paid as dividends, but, in any case, in 1846 it was decided to end the farce (although the directors put it differently) and close the depreciation fund:[6]

'. . . the practice of setting aside out of revenue and maintaining a depreciation fund to provide for the renewal of stock may be dispensed with . . . when the current charges for renewals become constant, as is now the case, and approach in amount to the sum annually set aside to cover such charges, a fund distinct from revenue is no longer required. . . .'

The depreciation account was, therefore, to be closed at the end of the year, and renewal of stock was to be charged to current revenue 'as is the practice of other companies'.

For two years, from March 1847 to March 1849, the accounts were much abbreviated and one can only conclude that obscurity was the aim. A suspicious omission from each of the biannual accounts in those two years was any details of receipts and expenditure on capital account for each half-year. The accounts still contained the total cumulative receipts and expenditures at each date, but it is, for instance, impossible to say how much new money was received on advance call account in each half-year; only balances were given. In March 1849 the accounts for the half-year ending 31 December 1848 were a reversion to the pre-1847 form, and it is probably significant that for the first half of 1849 the 'Depreciation and Replacement Allowance' was restarted.[7]

[5] *Ibid.*, 1846 and 1847.   [6] *Ibid.*, 9 September 1846.
[7] *Ibid.*, 5 September 1849. In their report of January 1849 a Committee of Shareholders, which enquired into the allocation of expenses, pressed for the re-establishment of the allowance.

But even this was not the end of the changes of mind over the allowance. In March 1851 a resolution was passed at the half-yearly general meeting stating that henceforth no depreciation fund was to be set aside for the maintenance of rolling stock. This was to be maintained out of revenue as a normal revenue charge. But £20,000 were to be appropriated each year from the revenue for the renewal of permanent way.[8] From now until the end of our period the treatment of this renewal fund was consistent. The amount put by was flexible: it was decreased to £15,000 in 1853/54,[9] but was increased to £25,000 in 1855, £35,000 in 1858, and was £60,000 in 1859.[10] And it now occupied a permanent place as a deduction from the 'Balance Applicable to Dividends and Interest' in the 'Statement of Nett Revenue' or the 'Net Revenue Account' until 1868. It no longer entered into any surpluses which might be carried forward.

It will now be appreciated that obtaining from the accounts figures that are comparable year by year is sometimes difficult. It was necessary, for consistency, to include the depreciation allowance in the balances applicable to dividends because the Company did apply the allowance in that way in the early years. When it did not, in the 1850s and 1860s, the amount set aside has still been included in the figures in Table VII. The attempt to assess the true annual results is contained in Table VI.

6. We have now arrived at the point where the figures in Table VII are applicable to dividends and depreciation. In their 'Statement of Nett Revenue' the Board began by stating any surplus carried forward from the previous year, less some miscellaneous items such as 'bad debts'. The account then showed a deduction from the balance on revenue account on behalf of the depreciation fund. Then the interest on calls in advance and loans (including, after 1861, the interest on 4 per cent Debenture Stock) was deducted; next were listed, and subtracted from the remainder, the charges for leased lines; and, finally, dividends on guaranteed stock were subtracted from the balance. What remained was applicable to the 'general dividend'. This was the procedure towards which the Company progressed, and which was achieved in the 1850s. In compiling Table VII most of the deductions for the leased lines have been accepted, with, again, the major exception of the Sheffield & Barnsley, and also with the minor exception of the charge for the Blackburn Railway. The former was dealt with in Note 3 to Table V. The Blackburn charge was a once only charge of £2,000, which appeared in the accounts in the first half of 1858, and was really a

[8] *Ibid.*, 5 March 1851.   [9] *Ibid.*, 1 March 1854 and 7 March 1855.
[10] *Ibid.*, 5 March 1856, 16 February 1859, and 15 February 1860.

dividend on the Blackburn shares: the Lancashire & Yorkshire had purchased the railway. The charge has been transferred to guaranteed dividend payments. Another, separate, Blackburn charge appeared in the Net Revenue account for the first half of 1859 as a deduction.

As stated in Note 1 to this table, dividends on guaranteed stock have been included in the Balances.

7. Finally, it must be said that all this juggling with the figures was embarked upon with some trepidation. But justification for the classifications adopted, not only for this, but also for the other tables, seems to be afforded by the accounts for 1868. The new form of accounts prescribed by the Act of 1868 made the calculation of net revenue applicable to dividends and depreciation easier. It was found that the basis on which net revenue applicable to these payments was made, was vindicated by the form of accounts adopted in that year. From 1868 the calculation of the Balances involved the use of only two figures in the accounts for the first half, and only three (deduction of the surplus carried over from 30 June) in the second half, of each year. To take another example, the calculation of gross expenditure on revenue account, while an item with a nomenclature used by neither the Company nor the Act, was nevertheless rendered easier by the reduction of the number of figures involved from about sixteen to six. (The number of different sums involved varied from time to time.)

The basic nature of the changes introduced by the Act of 1868 have been touched upon already. The section of the Act on railway accounts was, of course, designed to effect a proper allocation of receipts and expenditure between capital and revenue account. In effect the Lancashire & Yorkshire for some years had been using the allocation prescribed, but the placing of the various sums was changed in 1868. Most of the leased line charges were then allocated either to expenditure on revenue account or to interest charges or to interest on guaranteed stock. In 1868 the Sheffield & Barnsley charge was transferred to the last category, but in 1867 the Company anticipated the Act by transferring a charge for the Blackburn Railway from leased line charges to interest on guaranteed stock. Before 1868 'Stamps and Commission on Loans' charges were charged to Revenue Account; in 1868 the charges were transferred to Net Revenue Account.[11]

[11] Before 1868 here means between 1845 and 1868. Before 1845 bond and mortgage stamp charges went to Capital Account, although right from the opening of the line in 1841 interest on loans was correctly debited to revenue account, with only one or two lapses.

Practically speaking, the 1868 Act, as far as I can tell, effected only a more logical presentation of the accounts of the Lancashire & Yorkshire Railway, not a different allocation of expenses between capital and revenue. Compared with the 1840s, the accounts of the 1860s, both before 1868, and after the adoption of the new form, were much more detailed, comprehensive, and easy to follow. From 1868, particular attention was paid to presenting, in a more illuminating fashion, detail of the capital structure, capital receipts, and analysis of expenditure on revenue account. This was done by means of abstracts.

TABLE VIII

ANALYSIS OF THE CAPITAL STRUCTURE, 1842 TO 1873

Year	Ordinary £000's	Guaranteed and Pref. £000's	Loan £000's	Total £000's
1842	1,299	37	1,627	2,963
1843	1,300	39	1,761	3,100
1844	1,329	39	1,837	3,205
1845	1,574	39	1,817	3,430
1846	2,752	519	1,677	4,948
1847	4,552	628	2,374	7,554
1848	5,163	1,716	2,393	9,272
1849	6,042	1,990	2,612	10,644
1850	5,823	2,639	3,163	11,625
1851	5,848	2,806	3,116	11,770
1852	7,599	1,326	2,843	11,768
1853	7,927	1,326	2,797	12,050
1854	8,147	1,327	2,799	12,273
1855	8,193	1,313	3,186	12,692
1856	8,464	1,054	3,302	12,820
1857	8,892	1,278	3,376	13,546
1858	9,246	1,107	3,336	13,689
1859	12,065	1,870	4,311	18,246
1860	12,078	2,214	4,524	18,816
1861	12,080	2,651	4,527	19,158
1862	12,081	2,758	4,620	19,459
1863	12,082	3,006	4,575	19,663
1864	12,083	3,171	4,798	20,052
1865	12,085	3,469	4,830	20,384
1866	12,609	4,142	5,336	22,087
1867	12,429	4,422	5,601	22,452
1868	12,694	4,382	5,671	22,747

TABLE VIII—*continued*

ANALYSIS OF THE CAPITAL STRUCTURE, 1842 TO 1873

Year	Ordinary £000's	Guaranteed and Pref. £000's	Loan £000's	Total £000's
1869	12,694	4,675	5,675	23,044
1870	12,694	4,940	5,654	23,288
1871	13,335	4,569	5,998	23,902
1872	13,335	4,948	5,971	24,254
1873	13,335	5,827	6,171	25,333

Notes:

1. The figures in this table are not mere authorisations or nominal amounts. They are the sums actually paid up on the various accounts on the 31 December of each year. They do not include sums received on shares which were forfeited owing to non-payment of calls, nor do they include calls paid in advance.

2. The figures for capital paid up on loan include, when the Stock was issued, sums paid into the Company on Debenture Stock.

3. The figures for paid-up guaranteed stock include, from 1850, the sum of £260,050. Until 1868 the Company did not include the charge on this sum in their guaranteed payments. The sum represents the Sheffield & Barnsley stock on which a guaranteed £13,000 per annum was paid. The figure of £260,050 will not be found in the accounts, and the reasons for ignoring the way in which the Company treated this stock and charge were put forward in Note 3 to Table V: Gross Expenditure on Revenue Account (p. 180).

4. The decrease in paid-up ordinary capital in 1850 and 1867 was caused by the forfeiture of shares on which money had already been paid up.

5. It will be remembered, from the discussion of bonds and mortgages in Chapter 3, that the amount of bonds issued was affected by the provisions of the 1844 Act. The decline in bonds in 1849, 1850 and 1851, is hidden in the figures for paid-up loan capital by the increase in the amount of mortgages issued in those years. Bonds decreased from £502,000 in 1848 to £7,000 in 1851, and £2,000 in 1852.

6. The reader will no doubt realise that it is not necessary to explain every increase in paid-up capital by reference to new Parliamentary authorisations. Money was paid up on shares, and was borrowed on loan, often many years after the passing of the Act which authorised the raising of the capital.

7. In Chapter 2 it was stated that at times the accounts were in a hopeless muddle. The period particularly in mind was between the years 1846 and 1849. Added to the complexity and, at times, near incomprehensibility, of the accounts, was the problem of the Preference Fifths. In 1845 it was decided to issue £20 shares as Preference Fifths, with the ultimate aim of absorbing them into the Consolidated Stock of the Company, to replace the mortgage debt of the Manchester & Leeds. If the accounts in the years 1846 to 1849 were a muddle, the status of the Fifths was an even greater mix-up. Early on there were complaints about them; there was considerable litigation; and there were even two attempts to settle the problem by application to Parliament. The idea had been to allow these shares to participate in dividends immediately, and it was frankly admitted that the Company had paid, in 1845, dividends that were lower than could be afforded, in order to build up a reserve fund with which to meet the increased dividend which had to be paid in 1846. The new shares were to receive the full declared dividend on the nominal amount of the shares, less a deduction of 5 per cent on the unpaid portion. That, at least, was the gist of the statement of September 1845. But the matter was not as simple as that, and evidently a number of shareholders thought so.

In March 1848, when the accounts for the second half of 1847 were published the directors included, for the first time, and for the only time in this particular form, 'No. 5—Statement of Manchester & Leeds Revenue Charge for Interest and Dividends', which, they fondly hoped, according to their report, would make the whole business 'as intelligible as possible'. This was in response to the complaints and agitation about the Fifths. But it is most unlikely that anyone who had not carefully read the long report of 1845 and the resolutions passed at the meeting, would have made much sense of the directors' nice distinctions between 'productive', 'unpro- ductive', and 'non-productive' Fifths share capital. Even if he had, the ordinary shareholder would most probably still have been in the dark.

Between September 1845 and March 1848 the directors appear to have decided to make a distinction between 'productive' and 'un- productive' *paid-up* money, and to call the amount of the Fifths stock, that remained *un-paid*, 'non-productive'. The 'productive' portion of the paid-up Fifths capital was no doubt the directors' estimate of the amount which represented lines already in operation. In accordance with their decision of 1845, the Board paid, in March 1848, 7 per cent on this portion. (A dividend at the rate of 7 per cent per annum was declared on ordinary shares for the second half of 1847.) The 'unproductive' portion of the Fifths capital was to receive 5 per cent, while the 'non-productive' portion was to receive a 2 per cent dividend (7 less 5 per cent on the unpaid portion). This last dividend was therefore paid at the expense of the ordinary dividend, although, to mitigate this, no doubt many proprietors held ordinary as well as this preference stock. The charge for the 'non-productive' capital was, according to the accounts, charged to revenue, and so it is quite possible that here at least the Company was not paying dividends out of capital. But we can be certain that the 'unproductive' as distinct from the 'non-productive' portion was serviced from capital receipts. 'Unproductive' capital amounted to £344,596. The dividend of 5 per cent meant a charge of £8,615 against revenue on the Preference Fifths account, but 'on which', Account No. 5 tells us, 'a corresponding charge for Interest is made to credit of Revenue and Debit of Capital'.

The detailed information given in the accounts for the second half of 1847 was never repeated. It is impossible to be sure what was going on. But while it is probable that not all of these bonus dividends were paid in the years 1848 to 1851, in view of the amount of litigation and controversy over the Fifths, there is a very strong impression that the accounts were varied in form in these years, as much from a desire to obscure issues as from lack of experience. There is also the impression that the directors made fairly honest attempts to be consistent and proper, but that the confusion and the pressure of events in these years made them succumb to financial expediency. They would, naturally, be very dependent upon their Company officials, and it was pointed out on p. 41 that the reaction of the Accountant's staff to the suggestion of the auditors that certain items should be charged to revenue and not to capital, was to warn the Board against such a course, because the margin for dividends was low.

Leaving aside the complications and malpractices of this period, it is interesting to note that throughout the 1840s there was never any intention of making the preferences permanent. The preference given to the 1841 issue expired at the end of 1846. The preference given to the Fifths would inevitably cease when all the nominal amount had been paid up. The result in this case is seen in 1852, when the amount of preference and guaranteed capital dropped from £2,806,000 to £1,326,000. There is an exception: the issue of 6 per cent Guaranteed shares in 1848 was a permanent one, and the charge for it may be traced throughout the period, with no complications. But the real era of guaranteed and preference capital was, for the Lancashire & Yorkshire, the period from 1861.

TABLE IX

DIVIDENDS PAID ON ORDINARY, AND GUARANTEED AND PREFERENCE SHARES, 1842 TO 1873

Year	Ordinary £000's	Guaran. & Pref. £000's	Year	Ordinary £000's	Guaran. &Pref. £000's
1842	71	4	1858	369	71
1843	81	4	1859	570	104
1844	97	4	1860	695	111
1845	111	4	1861	635	130
1846	98	74	1862	469	142
1847	130	74	1863	544	154
1848	143	72	1864	710	162
1849	182	45	1865	710	170
1850	116	67	1866	816	196
1851	188	72	1867	825	209
1852	234	72	1868	857	218
1853	275	72	1869	857	230
1854	315	72	1870	889	245
1855	350	72	1871	1,025	247
1856	409	66	1872	1,117	247
1857	415	68	1873	950	274

Notes:

1. Once more, until 1868, these figures are the result of independent calculations. In the years 1842 to 1845, inclusive, the only guaranteed dividend was that on the 1841 shares. These shares received 10 per cent, but as only £2 per share was paid up until 1846, the burden of the preference was small. The accounts did not separate the guaranteed dividend from the general dividend, and so the former was taken to be 4s. per annum on each of the 19,500 shares.

2. In 1846 the last preference dividends were paid on the 1841 shares and, in addition, an *estimate* had to be made of the amount paid on the Preference Fifths. As £446,000 were paid up on these £20 shares, and the general dividend was 7 per cent, the figure for 1846 is calculated as follows: £4,000 (on the 1841 shares); plus £31,000 (7 per cent of £446,000); plus £39,000 (2 per cent of

£1,950,000). The 2 per cent was the product, it may be remembered, of a dividend of 7 per cent less 5 per cent on the amount unpaid on the shares. Since £1,950,000 was the amount unpaid, it received a bonus dividend of 2 per cent. The total guaranteed dividend for 1846 was, therefore, £74,000.

It has been assumed that the Company did abide by its decisions of 1845 in the matter of paying dividends on the Fifths (although it did make a change in 1847), and also that the number of shares issued as Preference Fifths in 1846 was 119,805. This was the number issued by the end of 1847, according to the accounts published for the second half of that year; these accounts were the first to give the number of Fifths issued. Such an assumption is not very satisfactory, but from the amount paid up in December 1846, the estimate of the number of Fifths issued is unlikely to be very inaccurate, and some estimate had to be made.

3. In 1847 the Company paid a dividend of 6s. 6d. on each of the Fifths, for the first half of the year. Again, the number of such shares has been taken to be 119,805. The accounts for the first half of the year, like those for 1846, give no indication that part of the dividend paid was preference dividend. But the usual resolution authorising the payment of dividends included a payment of 6s. 6d. on the £20 shares. The calculation of the amount of dividend for the *second* half of the year is made easy by the Company's once-only statement, already referred to. In total, £74,000 were paid out as guaranteed dividends in 1847.

4. In 1848 the 6 per cent Preference or Guaranteed Shares (the Company used both descriptions at different times) were issued, and an estimate has been made of the amount paid on them. At the end of the year £313,950 had been paid up, and the amount of dividend has been estimated at £9,419. In addition, the Company paid 6s. on each of the 119,805 Fifths in the first half of 1848, and 4s. 6d. on each of the 119,798 Fifths in the second half. (The reduction was due either to forfeiture or merging of the shares.) The total amount paid out was, therefore, less than in 1847.

5. In 1851 it was decided to equalise dividends on Fifths and on old stock, and in 1852 the Fifths dropped out of the Net Revenue account.

6. From and including 1850 the guaranteed and preference dividend figures include £13,000 per annum for the Sheffield & Barnsley, a charge which the Lancashire & Yorkshire included in leased line charges until 1868. For an explanation of the decision to ignore the Company's treatment of this charge, see Note 3 to Table V, and Note 3 to Table VIII.

Table X
INTEREST PAID ON LOAN CAPITAL, 1842 TO 1873

Year	Interest on all Money on Loan £000's	Deduction for Interest on Calls in Advance £000's	Interest on Loan Capital Proper £000's
1842	80	—	80
1843	88	—	88
1844	92	—	92
1845	78	—	78
1846	56	3	53
1847	41	2	39
1848	38	4	34
1849	63	—	63
1850	134	—	134
1851	144	—	144
1852	133	—	133
1853	123	—	123
1854	117	—	117
1855	129	—	129
1856	138	—	138
1857	146	1	145
1858	150	—	150
1859	199	8	191
1860	192	4	188
1861	195	1	194
1862	198	8	190
1863	195	9	186
1864	198	7	191
1865	213	11	202
1866	226	11	215
1867	237	2	235
1868	245	4	241
1869	243	4	239
1870	239	4	235
1871	246	7	239
1872	256	10	246
1873	250	7	243

Notes:

1. Interest on all money on loan includes interest paid on bonds, mortgage debentures, Debenture Stock, calls paid in advance, bond and mortgage stamp duties and charges, and, at various times, commission on loans. It excludes all dividends on ordinary and guaranteed and preference stock, and charges for leased lines.

2. Up to March 1841 all interest charges were debited to capital.

o

After that date, when the complete line was opened, interest on loans was charged to revenue account, but bond and mortgage stamp charges continued to be debited to capital until 1845, when these items were included in the 'General Charges' schedule and were therefore charged to revenue and included in working expenses. After June 1868 'Stamps and Commission on Loans' charges appear in the net Revenue Account, and not in the Revenue Account, together with other interest charges. Throughout the period, and irrespective of the varying practice in the financial statements, these interest charges have been debited to net revenue, and therefore wherever bond and mortgage stamp charges appeared in working expenses (that, is, between 1845 and 1868), they have been subtracted.

3. The much-varied form of accounts renders interest on calls in advance another problem. Between 1842 and 1852 it appears that the item 'interest on loans chargeable to revenue' was a balance, that is, favourable interest items, such as interest on bank deposits, had been used partially to offset interest payments, and therefore the burden of interest may, at times, be understated. This further complication cannot, however, be very serious.

Interest on calls in advance was separated for the first time in 1862. For the years up to 1862 an estimate has been made of the amount that would have been paid out as interest on such money. It should be remembered that the figures are to the nearest £1,000, and that a dash does not mean that there was no interest paid at all. In most years there were certain sums paid in advance, but not always has it been estimated that they were sufficient to carry a thousand pounds in interest. The estimates are, it is hoped, fairly conservative, and are based on the amount of calls in advance shown by the accounts, and a 4 per cent interest rate. As a check the figure for 1862 was calculated on this basis, and compared with the actual amount separated in the accounts. The estimate was £9,000, the actual figure was £8,000.

4. More important than either interest on calls in advance, or interest on favourable balances at the banks, is the problem of 'productive' loan capital. Just as the distinction between 'productive' and 'unproductive' paid-up share capital gave the Lancashire & Yorkshire, and other companies, great opportunities for financial juggling, so did the similar distinction between 'productive' and 'unproductive' paid-up loan capital afford the Company the chance of an arbitrary allocation of interest to either capital or revenue account. There is a strong suspicion that in 1847 and 1848 this chance was taken. In the accounts for the second half of 1847 it is stated that the total of 'Loans productive' was £1,449,012, yet interest was paid on only £781,390 in the second half of 1848. The

respective totals of paid-up loan capital are £2,374,000 and £2,393,000 (see Table VIII, p. 187), so the decrease cannot be explained by a decrease in the total amount on loan to the Company. It is quite obvious that a considerable amount of interest, an amount in excess of the figures given in Table X, was paid in the period 1846 to 1849 inclusive. Whether the debiting of a proportion of interest to capital was justified, is a matter for debate. If the loan capital which was serviced out of capital was genuinely 'unproductive' in the sense that it was money raised to build lines which were not yet in operation, then the Company was doing nothing more than following the practice, which it had adopted, together with the majority of other companies, in earlier years. It was the accepted thing to pay interest on loans out of capital receipts before the line was opened; if interest had not been paid there would not, of course, have been any loans. In these years, 1846 to 1849, there can be no doubt that part of the loan capital was genuinely 'unproductive'. But the extent of the drop in 1848 of the amount of 'productive' loan capital is unexplained, and, it is believed, inexplicable, except in terms of a deliberate understatement of the interest burden.

As in so many other things, the emergence from the 1840s saw improvement, but it is also worth pointing out that 1850 saw the completion of the greater part of the schemes sanctioned in the 1840s. Certainly a proclamation by the directors that in 1850 all schemes would be completed (all schemes, that is, which were prosecuted) could not be accompanied by further talk of 'unproductive' capital. In December the total loan capital on which interest was paid, at an average rate of £4 11s. 8d. per cent, was over £3¼ million; a contrast to the figures of 1847 and 1848. Thus, much of the paid-up loan capital of 1846–49 must have been 'unproductive', but it is very likely that the figure of 'productive' loan capital for 1848 was deliberately understated.

The tables presented in this Appendix are the raw material for the analysis of the financial results between 1842 and 1873 contained in Chapter 2. The explanations of method have been long and, it is feared, rather involved at times. But to present a series of figures, many of which will not be found in the accounts, without an explanation of their compilation, would be asking too much from the reader. This method of approaching the financial results occasions some repetition of tables, but it also enables us to leave many of the methodological difficulties behind, and to concentrate on their analysis. Further tables are presented in Chapter 2, some of which contain series similar to those already put forward, but they do not require many notes.

Bibliography

A. PRIMARY SOURCES

I. COMPANY REPORTS, ACCOUNTS, AND PROCEEDINGS

Reports and Accounts of the Manchester and Leeds Railway Company, 1836 to 1847.

Reports and Accounts of the Lancashire and Yorkshire Railway Company, 1847 to 1888.

Proceedings of the Board of Directors of the Manchester and Leeds Railway Company, 1835 to 1847.

Proceedings of the Board of Directors of the Lancashire and Yorkshire Railway Company, 1847 to 1873.

Proceedings of the Finance Committee of the Manchester and Leeds Railway Company, 1835 to 1847.

Proceedings of the Finance Committee of the Lancashire and Yorkshire Railway Company, 1847 to 1873.

The above records are to be found at the British Transport Historical Records Office. (Hereafter cited as B.T.H.R.O.)

II. MANUSCRIPT EVIDENCE TAKEN ON RAILWAY BILLS

Manchester and Leeds Railway Company: Minutes of Evidence taken before the Lords Committee to whom was referred the Bill intituled 'An Act for enabling the Manchester and Leeds Railway Company to raise a further Sum of Money', 7 May 1841.

Bolton and Preston Railway Company: Evidence taken before the House of Commons Committee on the Bolton and Preston Railway Bill, 21 April 1842.

Manchester, Bury and Rossendale Railway Company: Evidence taken before the House of Commons Committee, 10 June 1845.

The above MSS. are to be found at the House of Lords Record Office. (Hereafter cited as H. of L. R.O.)

III. SUBSCRIPTION CONTRACTS

Preston and Wyre Railway and Harbour Subscription List, 1835, MS. (H. of L. R.O.).

Preston and Wyre Docks Subscription List, 1837, MS. (H. of L. R.O.).

Preston and Wyre Railway Branches Subscription Contract (Printed Copy), 8 Vict. Sess. 1845 (H. of L. R.O.).

III. Subscription Contracts (continued)

Manchester and Leeds Railway Company Subscription Contract, 1836, in Appendix A to B.P.P. 1836 (House of Lords Paper, 147) XII (H. of L. Library).

Manchester and Leeds Railway Company Subscription Contract, 1839, three original deeds (B.T.H.R.O.).

Manchester and Leeds and Heywood Branch Railway Subscription Contract (Printed Copy), 7 Vict. Sess. 1844 (H. of L. R.O.).

Ashton, Stalybridge, and Liverpool Junction Railway Company Subscription Contract (Printed Copy), 7 Vict. Sess. 1844 (H. of L. R.O.).

Bolton and Preston Railway Company Subscription Contract, 1837, in B.P.P. 1837 (95), XLVIII.

Blackburn and Preston Railway Company Subscription Contract (Printed Copy), 7–8 Vict. Sess. 1844 (H. of L. R.O.).

Manchester, Bury, and Rossendale Railway Company Subscription Contract (Printed Copy) 7–8 Vict. Sess. 1844 (H. of L. R.O.).

Blackburn, Burnley, Accrington and Colne Extension Railway Company Subscription Contract (Printed Copy), 8 Vict. Sess. 1845 (H. of L. R.O.). Also in B.P.P. 1845 (317, 625), XL.

Liverpool, Ormskirk, and Preston Railway Company Subscription Contract, 1845 (Printed Copy), (H. of L. R.O.). Also in B.P.P. 1845, *loc. cit.*

Liverpool and Bury Railway Company, 1845: List of subscribers in B.P.P. 1845, *loc. cit.*

Blackburn, Darwen, and Bolton Railway Company, Subscription Contract (Printed Copy), 8 Vict. Sess. 1845 (H. of L. R.O.). Also in B.P.P., 1845, *loc. cit.*

Wakefield, Pontefract, and Goole Railway Company Subscription Contract (Printed Copy), 8 Vict. Sess. 1845 (H. of L. R.O.). Also in B.P.P., 1845, *loc. cit.*

Huddersfield and Sheffield Junction Railway Company, 1845: List of Subscribers in B.P.P., 1845, *loc. cit.*

Manchester and Leeds Railway Extensions Subscription Contract (Printed Copy), 9 Vict. Sess. 1846 (H. of L. R.O.).

Manchester and Leeds Railway Branches Subscription Contract (Printed Copy), 10 Vict. Sess. 1847 (H. of L. R.O.).

IV. ACTS OF PARLIAMENT

1 W. IV c. 56 (1831). *An Act for making . . . a Railway . . . from . . . Wigan to . . . Preston.*

1 & 2 W. IV c. 60 (1831). *An Act to enable the Manchester, Bolton, and Bury Canal Navigation to make and maintain a Railway from Manchester to Bolton and Bury.*

4 W. IV c. 25 (1834). *An Act for uniting the Wigan Branch Railway Company and the Preston and Wigan Railway Company.*

5 & 6 W. IV c. 58 (1835). *An Act for making a Railway from Preston to Wyre, and for improving the Harbour of Wyre. . . .*

IV. Acts of Parliament (continued)

6 & 7 W. IV c. 107 (1836). *An Act for making a Railway from Leeds to Derby, to be called 'The North Midland Railway'.*

6 & 7 W. IV c. 111 (1836). *An Act for making a Railway from Manchester to Leeds.*

7 W. IV c. 24 (1837). *An Act for enabling the Manchester and Leeds Railway Company to vary the Line of such Railway, . . .*

7 W. IV c. 28 (1837). *An Act to alter the Line of the Preston and Wyre Railway, . . .*

7 W. IV c. 29 (1837). *An Act for making and maintaining a Dock or Docks at Wyre. . . .*

1 Vict. c. 121 (1837). *An Act for making a Railway from Bolton-le-Moors to Preston. . . .*

1 & 2 Vict. c. 56 (1838). *An Act to enable the Bolton and Preston . . . to extend and to alter . . . to make Branches. . . .*

2 Vict. c. 1 (1839). *An Act to amend the several Acts relating to the Preston and Wyre Railway and Harbour Company.*

2 & 3 Vict. c. 54 (1839). *An Act to amend the several Acts relating to the Preston and Wyre Railway and Harbour Company, and the Preston and Wyre Dock Company, and to consolidate the said Companies.*

2 & 3 Vict. c. 55 (1839). *An Act for extending and for altering the Line of the Manchester and Leeds Railway, and for making Branches therefrom, . . .*

4 Vict. c. 25 (1841). *An Act for enabling the Manchester and Leeds Railway Company to raise a further Sum of Money.*

5 Vict. sess. 2, c. 15 (1842). *An Act to facilitate the raising of Capital for the Completion of the Bolton and Preston Railway.*

7 Vict. c. 2 (1844). *An Act to effectuate the Sale by the Bolton and Preston Railway Company of their Railway . . . to the North Union Railway Company.*

7 Vict. c. 16 (1844). *An Act for maintaining a Railway from the Manchester and Leeds Railway to Heywood; . . .*

7 Vict. c. 34 (1844). *An Act for making a Railway from the Town of Blackburn to the North Union Railway in . . . Farrington near Preston, . . .*

7 & 8 Vict. c. 55 (1844). *An Act to amend the several Acts relating to the Preston and Wyre Railway, Harbour, and Dock Company.*

7 & 8 Vict. c. 60 (1844). *An Act for making a Railway from the Manchester and Bolton Railway . . . to be called 'The Manchester, Bury, and Rossendale Railway'.*

7 & 8 Vict. c. 82 (1844). *An Act for making a Railway from the Manchester and Leeds Railway to the Towns of Ashton-under-Lyne and Staly Bridge.*

7 & 8 Vict. c. 85 (1844). *An Act to attach certain Conditions to the Construction of Future Railways . . . . (Railway Regulation Act, 1844).*

8 Vict. c. 16 (1845). *An Act for consolidating in One Act the Provisions usually inserted in Acts with respect to the Constitution of Companies incorporated for carrying on Undertakings of a Public Nature. (Companies Clauses Consolidation Act, 1845.)*

IV. Acts of Parliament (continued)

8 & 9 Vict. c. 35 (1845). *An Act for extending the Manchester, Bury, and Rossendale Railway to . . . Blackburn, Burnley, Accrington, and Colne. (The East Lancashire Railway Act, 1845.)*

8 & 9 Vict. c. 39 (1845). *An Act for making a Railway from Huddersfield . . . to or near Penistone . . . to form a Junction with the Sheffield, Ashton-under-Lyne, and Manchester Railway.*

8 & 9 Vict. c. 44 (1845). *An Act for making a Railway from Blackburn to Bolton . . . to be called 'The Blackburn, Darwen, and Bolton Railway'.*

8 & 9 Vict. c. 54 (1845). *An Act . . . relating to the Manchester and Leeds Railway, and for making a Branch therefrom to Burnley; and for extending the Oldham and Heywood Branches.*

8 & 9 Vict. c. 101 (1845). (Act to rename the Manchester, Bury & Rossendale, the East Lancashire Railway Company.)

8 & 9 Vict. c. 103 (1845). *An Act for altering the Line of the Blackburn and Preston Railway. . . .* (Including a junction with the Blackburn, Burnley, Accrington & Colne.)

8 & 9 Vict. c. 109 (1845). *An Act for amending the Act relating to the Ashton, Staly Bridge, and Liverpool Junction Railway, and for making a Branch therefrom to Ardwick.*

8 & 9 Vict. c. 125 (1845). *An Act . . . to enable* [the Preston & Wyre Railway Harbour & Dock Company] *to make Three several Branch Railways.*

8 & 9 Vict. c. 166 (1845). *An Act for making a Railway from Liverpool to Wigan, Bolton, and Bury, with several Branches therefrom.*

8 & 9 Vict. c. 171 (1845). *An Act to enable the Manchester and Leeds Railway Company to raise an additional Sum of Money; . . .*

8 & 9 Vict. c. 172 (1845). *An Act for making a Railway from the Manchester and Leeds Railway at Wakefield to . . . Pontefract and Goole, with certain Branches therefrom.*

9 & 10 Vict. c. 90 (1846). *An Act for making a Railway . . . 'The Liverpool, Manchester, and Newcastle-upon-Tyne Junction Railway'. . . .*

9 & 10 Vict. c. 231 (1846). *An Act for vesting in the Grand Junction Railway Company and the Manchester and Leeds Railway Company the North Union Railway, . . .*

9 & 10 Vict. c. 241 (1846). *An Act to authorize the Hull and Selby Railway Company to lease or sell their Railway to the York and North Midland Railway Company and the Manchester and Leeds Railway Company, or to one of them.*

9 & 10 Vict. c. 246 (1846). *An Act for making a Railway from Preston . . . to Clitheroe. . . .* (The Fleetwood, Preston, and West Riding Junction Railway Act.)

9 & 10 Vict. c. 265 (1846). *An Act for making a Railway with Branches . . . to be called 'The Blackburn, Clitheroe, and North-western Junction Railway'.*

9 & 10 Vict. c. 276 (1846). *An Act to enable the East Lancashire Railway Company to alter the Line . . . and to make Branches therefrom. . . .*

IV. Acts of Parliament (continued)

9 & 10 Vict. c. 277 (1846). *An Act to incorporate the Huddersfield and Sheffield Junction Railway Company with the Manchester and Leeds Railway Company.*

9 & 10 Vict. c. 282 (1846). *An Act to incorporate the Liverpool and Bury Railway Company with the Manchester and Leeds Railway Company.*

9 & 10 Vict. c. 302 (1846). *An Act to unite and consolidate the Blackburn and Preston Railway Company with the East Lancashire Railway Company.*

9 & 10 Vict. c. 306 (1846). *An Act to enable the Manchester and Leeds Railway Company to make several Branch Railways, and to authorize the Amalgamation of the Preston and Wyre Railway, Harbour, and Dock Company with the Manchester and Leeds Railway Company.*

9 & 10 Vict. c. 354 (1846). *An Act for making certain Lines of Railway . . . to be called 'The Sheffield, Rotherham, Barnsley, Wakefield, Huddersfield, and Goole Railway'.*

9 & 10 Vict. c. 378 (1846). *An Act to incorporate the Manchester, Bolton, and Bury Canal Navigation and Railway Company with the Manchester and Leeds Railway Company.*

9 & 10 Vict. c. 381 (1846). *An Act for making a Railway from the Liverpool and Bury Railway to the North Union and Blackburn and Preston Railways, with Branches therefrom, to be called 'The Liverpool, Ormskirk, and Preston Railway'.*

9 & 10 Vict. c. 390 (1846). *An Act for making certain Lines of Railway . . . to be called 'The West Riding Union Railways'.*

10 & 11 Vict. c. 103 (1847). *An Act to enable the Manchester and Leeds Railway Company to make an Extension of the Holmfirth Branch of the Huddersfield and Sheffield Junction Railway.*

10 & 11 Vict. c. 163 (1847). *An Act to enable the Manchester and Leeds Railway Company to make certain Branches, Extensions, . . . and to alter the Name of the Company.*

10 & 11 Vict. c. 221 (1847). *An Act for making a Railway from Southport through Wigan to Pendleton . . . to be called 'The Manchester and Southport Railway'.*

10 & 11 Vict. c. 232 (1847). *An Act for making certain Lines of Railway . . . to be called 'The Oldham Alliance Railway'.*

10 & 11 Vict. c. 289 (1847). *An Act to enable the East Lancashire Railway Company to extend . . . into Preston; . . .*

12 & 13 Vict. c. 1 (1849). *An Act to alter . . . some Provisions of the Lancashire and Yorkshire Railway Company's several Acts. . . .*

12 & 13 Vict. c. 74 (1849). *An Act for vesting in the Lancashire and Yorkshire Railway Company and the London and North-western Railway Company the Preston and Wyre Railway, Harbour, and Dock. . . .*

13 & 14 Vict. c. 83 (1850). *An Act to enlarge the Powers of the Lancashire and Yorkshire Railway Company, . . .*

IV. Acts of Parliament (continued)

13 & 14 Vict. c. 99 (1850). *An Act to enable the Liverpool, Crosby, and Southport Railway Company to sell or lease their Railway to the Lancashire and Yorkshire Railway Company.*

15 Vict. c. 96 (1852). *An Act to enable the Lancashire and Yorkshire and York and North Midland Railway Companies to enter into Arrangements as to the Working and Management of their Railways.*

15 & 16 Vict. c. 132 (1852). *An Act for abandoning certain Parts of the . . . Lancashire and Yorkshire Railway Company; and for constructing certain new Works. . . .*

17 Vict. c. 58 (1854). *An Act for enabling the Lancashire and Yorkshire Railway Company to construct a Railway from Kirkdale to the Liverpool Docks. . . .*

17 & 18 Vict. c. 117 (1854). *An Act for vesting in the East Lancashire Railway Company, jointly with the Lancashire and Yorkshire Railway Company, certain parts of the Manchester and Southport Railway. . . .*

V. PARLIAMENTARY PAPERS

1836 (H. of L., 147) XII. *Report of the Lords Committee on the Manchester and Leeds Railway Bill.*

1837 (95) XLVIII. *Bolton and Preston Railway Subscription List.*

1837 (243) XVIII, Pt. I. *Report on the Bath and Weymouth Railway Subscription List.*

1837 (226) XVIII, Pt. I. *Select Committee on Railway Subscription Lists, First Report: Deptford and Dover Subscription List.*

1837 (428) —— *Second Report: Westminster Bridge, Deptford and Greenwich Railway Subscription List.*

1837 (429) —— *Third Report: City, or Southwark Bridge and Hammersmith Railway Subscription List.*

1837 (495) XVIII, Pt. II. —— *Fourth Report: South Midland Counties Railway Subscription List.*

1837 (519) —— *Fifth Report: Direct London and Brighton Railway (Rennie's Line) Subscription List.*

1837 (520) —— *Sixth Report: South Eastern, Brighton, Lewes, and Newhaven Railway Subscription List.*

1837 (537) —— *Seventh Report: Brighton Railway (Stephenson's Line) Subscription List.*

1839 (222) X. *Select Committee on Railways, First Report.*

1839 (517) —— *Second Report.*

1839 (242) XIII. *Committee on the London and Birmingham Railway Bill,* Minutes of Evidence, and Appendix No. 32 to Minutes of Evidence.

1843 (496) XXII. *The Population Abstract for 1841.*

1844 (318) XI. *Fifth Report of the Select Committee on Railways,* Appendices.

1844 (588) XXXVIII. *Standing Orders on Second Class Bills.*

P

V. Parliamentary Papers (continued)

1845 (135) XXXVIII. *Second Report of the Select Committee on Railway Bills*, Appendix.

1845 (317) XL. Subscription contracts.

1845 (625) XL. Subscription contracts.

1845 (383) XXXVI. *Estimates of Cost of Construction of certain Railways* (Liverpool & Bury, etc.).

1845 (637) XXXIX. *Railway Bills passed in Session 1845.*

1845 (659) XXXVI. *Committee Stages on Bills* (Liverpool & Bury, etc.).

1846 (275) XIII. *Second Report of the Select Committee on Railways and Canals Amalgamation.*

1847–48 (565) VIII, Pt. III. *Report of the Secret Committee of the House of Lords on Commercial Distress*, Appendix.

1850 (508) XIX. *Report of the Select Committee on Investments for the Savings of the Middle and Working Classes*, Minutes of Evidence.

1852 (37) XLVIII. *Returns of Railway Companies of Capital, . . . for 1851.*

1854 (98, 168, 494) LXII. —— *for 1851, 1857, and 1853.*

1854–55 (54, 510) XLVIII. —— *for 1854.*

1856 (8, 316) LIV. —— *for 1855.*

1857 Sess. 2 (164, 340), XXXVII. —— *for 1856.*

1857–58 (132, 431) LI. —— *for 1857.*

1859 (231, 243) XXV. —— *for 1858.*

1854–55 (1965) XLVIII. *Report of the Railway Department for 1854.*

1867 (3844) XXXVIII, Pt. I. *Report of the Royal Commission on Railways.*

1872 (364) XIII, Pt. II. *Report of the Joint Select Committee on Railway Companies Amalgamation*, Appendices.

B. SECONDARY SOURCES

I. BOOKS AND PAMPHLETS (publication in London unless otherwise stated)

Anon., *Railway Debentures and How to Deal with Them* (1867).

Anon., *A Companion to the Manchester and Leeds Railway, 1841* (Halifax, 1841).

Anon. [W. Galt], *Railway Reform; its Expediency and Practicability Considered* (3rd edn., 1844).

Ashton, T. S., *An Eighteenth Century Industrialist* (Manchester, 1939).

'A Successful Operator', *A Short and Sure Guide to Railway Speculation* (1845).

Ayres, Henry, *The Financial Position of Railways* (1868).

Bagehot, W., *Lombard Street* (14th edn., 1920).

Baines, Thomas, *History of the Commerce and Town of Liverpool. . . .* (1852).

Butterworth, Edwin, *A Descriptive History of the Manchester and Leeds Railway* (Manchester, 1845) (Typescript Copy, B.T.H.R.O.).

Cairncross, A. K., *Home and Foreign Investment, 1870–1913* (Cambridge, 1953).

I. Books and Pamphlets (continued)

Chapman, S. J., *The Lancashire Cotton Industry: A Study in Economic Development* (Manchester, 1904).

Chattaway, E. D., *Railways: Their Capital and Dividends,* . . . (1855–56).

Clapham, J. H., *The Woollen and Worsted Industries* (1907).

—— *An Economic History of Modern Britain* (Cambridge, 1930), Vol. I.

—— *The Bank of England: A History* (Cambridge, 1944), Vol. II.

Clark, G. D., *Provisional Railway Code, with Instructions to Scripholders,* . . . (1846).

Cleveland-Stevens, E., *English Railways: Their Development and Their Relation to the State* (1915).

Clinker, C. R., *The Leicester and Swannington Railway* (Leicester, 1954).

Committee of Consultation, *Report of the Committee of Consultation: Appointed by the Meeting of Shareholders . . . March 6th, 1850* (1850).

Committee of Shareholders, *Concluding Report of the Committee of Shareholders* (Manchester, 1849).

Deane, P., and Cole, W. A., *British Economic Growth, 1688–1959* (Cambridge, 1962).

Dobb, M., *Political Economy and Capitalism* (1940).

'Civil Engineer', *Plan for Lessening the Taxation . . . by the Purchase and Improved Administration of the Railways.* . . . (1860).

Ellison, T., *The Cotton Trade of Great Britain* (1886).

Evans, D. Morier, *The Commercial Crisis of 1847–1848* (1848).

—— *City Men and City Manners.* . . . (1852).

—— *Facts, Failures and Frauds* (1859).

—— *The History of the Commercial Crisis, 1857–58* (1859).

—— *Speculative Notes and Notes on Speculations* (1864)

Evans, G. H., *British Corporation Finance, 1775–1850* (Baltimore, 1936).

Fisher, Irving, *The Theory of Interest* (New York, 1930).

Francis, John, *A History of the English Railway . . . 1820–1845* (1851).

Galt, W., *Railway Reform: Its Importance and Practicability.* . . . (1865).

Gayer, A. D., Rostow, W. W., and Schwartz, A., *The Growth and Fluctuation of the British Economy, 1790–1850* (Oxford, 1953).

Greville, M. D., 'Genealogical Table of the Railways of Lancashire' (August 1952, unpublished).

Grindon, Leo H., *Manchester Banks and Bankers* (Manchester, 1878).

Grinling, C. H., *The History of the Great Northern Railway, 1845–1902* (1903).

Hughes, J., *Liverpool Banks and Bankers, 1760–1837* (Liverpool, 1906).

Hunt, B. C., *The Development of the Business Corporation in England: 1800–1867* (Cambridge, Mass., 1936).

Jackman, W. T., *The Development of Transportation in Modern England* (Cambridge, 1916).

Keynes, J. M., *The General Theory of Employment Interest and Money* (1936).

I. Books and Pamphlets (continued)

Lalor, John, *Money and Morals* (1852).

Lardner, Dionysius, *Railway Economy* (1850).

Lee, C. E., *Passenger Class Distinctions* (1946).

Lewin, H. G., *Early British Railways, 1801–1844* (1925).

—— *The Railway Mania and its Aftermath, 1845–1852* (1936).

Lewis, S., *A Topographical Dictionary of England* (4th edn., 1840).

MacDermot, E. T., *History of the Great Western Railway* (1927), Vol. I.

Macturk, G. G., *A History of the Hull Railways* (Hull, 1879).

Wadsworth, A. P., and Mann, J. De L., *The Cotton Trade and Industrial Lancashire, 1600–1780* (Manchester, 1931).

Martin, R. M., *Railways—Past, Present, and Prospective* (2nd edn., 1849).

Marwick, W. H., *Economic Developments in Victorian Scotland* (1936).

Matthews, R. C. O., *A Study in Trade-Cycle History: Economic Fluctuations in Great Britain, 1833–42* (Cambridge, 1954).

May, T. Erskine, *A Treatise Upon the Law, Privileges, Proceedings and Usage of Parliament* (1844).

Mudge, Richard Z., *Observations on Railways* (1837).

Normington, T., *The Lancashire and Yorkshire Railway* (Manchester, 1898).

Porter, T., *The Progress of the Nation* (1847).

Redford, A., *Manchester Merchants and Foreign Trade, 1794–1858* (Manchester, 1934).

Rostow, W. W., *British Economy of the Nineteenth Century* (Oxford, 1948).

—— *The Process of Economic Growth* (Oxford, 1953).

Salt, Samuel, *Railway and Commercial Information* (1850).

Savage, C. I., *An Economic History of Transport* (1966).

Schlote, W., *British Overseas Trade from 1700 to the 1930's* (Oxford, 1952).

Scrivenor, H., *The Railways of the United Kingdom Statistically considered* (1849).

Sherrington, C. E., *A Hundred Years of Inland Transport* (1934).

Simnett, W. E., *Railway Amalgamation in Great Britain* (1923).

Smith, Arthur, *The Bubble of the Age; . . .* (1848).

—— *Railways as they Really Are. . . . No. VII. The Lancashire and Yorkshire Railway* (1847).

Spencer, R., *A Survey of the History, Commerce, and Manufactures of Lancashire* (1897).

Stretton, C. E., *The History of the Midland Railway* (1901).

Taylor, W. Cooke, *Notes of a Tour in the Manufacturing Districts of Lancashire* (2nd edn., 1842).

Thomas, Brinley, *Migration and Economic Growth* (Cambridge, 1954).

Thomas, Joseph Lee, *A Letter on the Present Position of Railways. . . .* (1867).

Tomlinson, W. W., *The North Eastern Railway: Its Rise and Development* (Newcastle, 1914).

Tooke, Thomas, *A History of Prices* (1838).

I. Books and Pamphlets (continued)

Tooke, Thomas, and Newmarch, W., *A History of Prices* (1857).

Tupling, G. H., *The Economic History of Rossendale* (Manchester, 1927).

Veevers, Harrison, *Index to Provisions of Acts of Parliament . . . relating to the Lancashire and Yorkshire Railway; and a List of Acts of Parliament authorising the Construction of the Various Portions of the Railway* (1921).

Veitch, G. S., *The Struggle for the Liverpool and Manchester Railway* (Liverpool, 1930).

Webb, C. Locock, *A Letter . . . on Railways, their Accounts and Dividends, . . .* (1849).

Wheeler, James, *Manchester: Its Political, Social and Commercial History* (1836).

Whitehead, Jeffery, *Railway Finance* [1867–8?].

Whitehead, John, *Railway and Government Guarantee . . .* (4th edn., 1847).

Williams, O. Cyprian, *The Historical Development of Private Bill Procedure and Standing Orders* (1948), Pt. I.

Wrigley, Thomas, *Railway Reform. A Plan for the Effectual Separation of Capital from Revenue* (1868). Also published in Bury in 1867.

II. UNPUBLISHED THESES

Doble, E., 'History of the Eastern Counties Railway in Relation to Economic Development' (Ph.D. Thesis, London, 1939).

Jefferys, J. B., 'Trends in Business Organisation in Great Britain since 1856, . . .' (Ph.D. Thesis, London, 1938).

Kingsford, P. W., 'Railway Labour 1830–1870' (Ph.D. Thesis, London, 1951).

III. PERIODICALS

Circular to Bankers, July 1829 to March 1839.
Railway Register, 1845–46.
Railway Times, 1838–44.

IV. ARTICLES

Anon., 'The Lancashire and Yorkshire Railway. Its History and Development', *Railway Magazine*, Vol. XXVIII, No. 164, February 1911.

Anon., 'The Lancashire and Yorkshire Railway', *The Railway Year Book*, 1921.

Cannan, Edwin, 'The Growth of Manchester and Liverpool, 1801–91', *Economic Journal*, Vol. 4, 1894.

Daniels, G. W., 'A Turnout of Bolton Machine Makers in 1831', *Economic History*, Vol. I, No. 4, 1929.

Jefferys, J. B., 'The Denomination and Character of Shares, 1855–1885', *Economic History Review*, Vol. XVI, No. 1, 1946.

Kenwood, A. G., 'Railway Investment in Britain 1825–1875', *Economica*, Vol. XXXII, 1965.

IV. Articles (continued)

Mitchell, B. R., 'The Coming of the Railway and United Kingdom Economic Growth', *Journal of Economic History*, Vol. XXIV, No. 3, 1964.

Morgan, E. V., 'Railway Investment, Bank of England Policy and Interest Rates, 1844–48', *Economic History*, Vol. IV, No. 15, February 1940.

Pollins, H., 'The Finances of the Liverpool and Manchester Railway', *Economic History Review*, Second Series, V, No. 1, 1952.

—— 'A Note on Railway Constructional Costs, 1825 to 1850', *Economica*, November 1952.

—— 'The Marketing of Railway Shares in the First Half of the Nineteenth Century', *Economic History Review*, S.S. Vol. VII, No. 2, December 1954.

—— 'Aspects of Railway Accounting before 1868', in Littleton and Yamey (eds.), *Studies in the History of Accounting* (1956).

—— 'Railway Auditing—A Report of 1867', *Accounting Research*, Vol. 8, No. 1, January 1957.

Postan, M. M., 'Recent Trends in the Accumulation of Capital', *Economic History Review*, October 1935.

Saville, J., 'Sleeping Partnership and Limited Liability, 1850–1856', *Economic History Review*, S.S. Vol. VIII, No. 3, 1956.

Shannon, H. A., 'The Coming of General Limited Liability', *Economic History*, Vol. II, 6, 1931.

Spencer, H., 'Railway Morals and Railway Policy', *Edinburgh Review*, October 1854.

Spring, D., 'The English Landed Estate in the Age of Coal and Iron: 1830–1880', *Journal of Economic History*, Vol. IX, No. 1, 1951.

Ward-Perkins, C. N., 'The Commercial Crisis of 1847' in A. H. Hansen and R. V. Clemence, *Readings in Business Cycles and National Income* (1953).

Index

THE MANCHESTER AND LEEDS RAILWAY IN 1841

With other lines built by that date and later absorbed by the Manchester and Leeds or Lancashire and Yorkshire Railway Companies

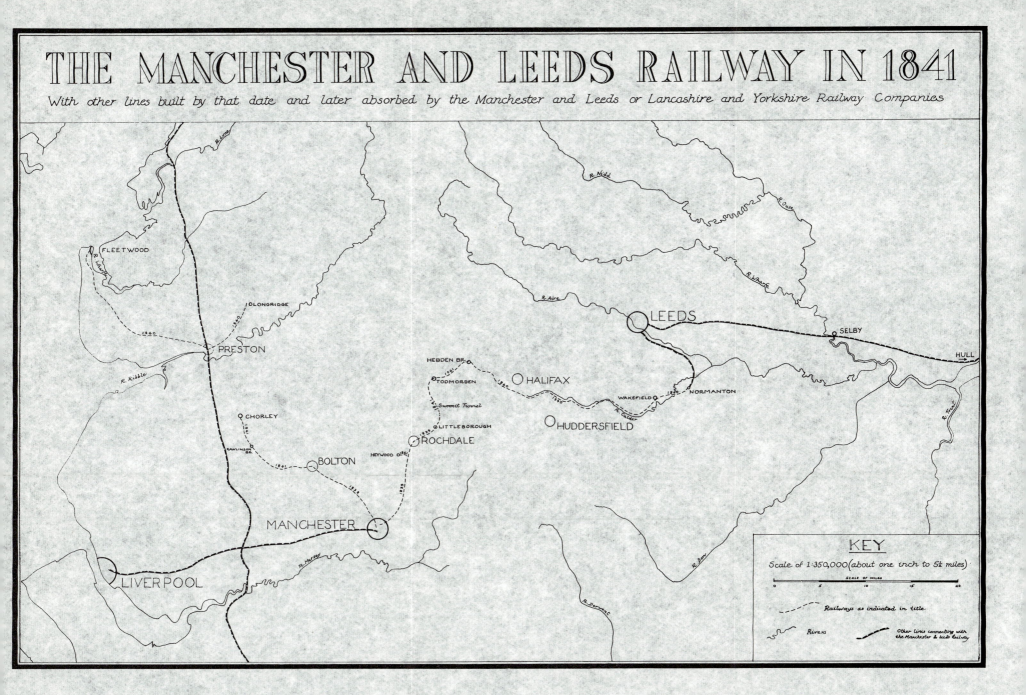

FLEETWOOD

OLONGRIDGE

PRESTON

LEEDS

SELBY

HULL

R. Aire

HEBDEN BR.

HALIFAX

TODMORDEN

CHORLEY

Summit Tunnel

WAKEFIELD

NORMANTON

HUDDERSFIELD

LITTLEBOROUGH

RAWLINSON BR.

ROCHDALE

HEYWOOD

BOLTON

MANCHESTER

LIVERPOOL

R. Mersey

R. Ribble

KEY

Scale of 1:350,000 (about one inch to 5½ miles)

SCALE OF MILES

0   5   10   15   20

- - - - - - Railways as indicated in title

〜〜〜 Rivers

▬▬▬ Other lines connecting with the Manchester & Leeds Railway

THE MANCHESTER AND LEEDS RAILWAY IN 1841

With other lines later absorbed by the Manchester and Leeds or Lancashire and Yorkshire Companies